AMERICAN POLITICAL INSTITUTIONS
IN THE 1970s

AMERICAN POLITICAL INSTITUTIONS IN THE 1970s

edited by

MAX BELOFF
Principal, University College at Buckingham

and

VIVIAN VALE
Lecturer in Politics, University of Southampton

ROWMAN AND LITTLEFIELD
TOTOWA, NEW JERSEY

First published in the United States 1975 by

ROWMAN AND LITTLEFIELD
Totowa, N. J.

ISBN 0 87471 587 3

Printed in Great Britain

Contents

Contributors

Max Beloff *is the first Principal of the new University College at Buckingham*

Peter Fotheringham *is Lecturer in Politics at the University of Glasgow*

Julius Gould *is Professor in Sociology in the University of Nottingham*

John D. Lees *is Senior Lecturer in American Government at Keele University*

Peter Madgwick *is Reader in Political Science at the University College of Wales, Aberystwyth*

H. G. Nicholas *is Rhodes Professor of American History and Institutions in the University of Oxford and Fellow of New College*

R. H. Pear *is Professor of Politics in the University of Nottingham*

Vivian Vale *is Lecturer in Politics at the University of Southampton*

Max Beloff

Introduction

THE CONFERENCE WHICH MET AT MANCHESTER TO DISCUSS THE
papers in this volume* took place shortly after the American presidential election of 1972, with its overwhelming victory for President
Richard Nixon over George McGovern. It also had to take into
account the fact that the margin between the two presidential
candidates was not reflected in the results of the concurrent
elections for the Senate, the House of Representatives or the state
governors. The apparent absence of a 'coat-tails' effect could be put
down by disappointed Republicans to the very restricted and highly
personalized nature of Mr Nixon's own campaign. But the view of
someone less involved might be that though the circumstances of
the presidential contest were remarkable, in that the Democratic
standard-bearer had captured the party machine for a minority
faction which narrowed his ultimate appeal, and though he himself
suffered from being an increasingly implausible candidate for the

*A conference was held on 17–19 November 1972 in Manchester to discuss
American political institutions in the light of the elections of November 1972.
The conference was organized jointly by *Government and Opposition* and the
Government Department of the University of Manchester, and was supported
by a grant from the Nuffield Foundation. The participants were: Prof. G.
Almond (Stanford, California); Prof. Raymond Aron (Sorbonne); Prof. M.
Beloff (All Souls) *chairman*; Mr R. A. Burchell (Manchester); Dr Mary Ellison
(Keele); Prof. S. Feingold (City University, New York); Prof. S. E. Finer
(Manchester); Mr P. Fotheringham (Glasgow); Mr R. A. Garson (Keele);
Prof. J. Gould (Nottingham); Dr J. E. S. Hayward (Keele); Prof. G. Ionescu
(Manchester); Mr D. Kavanagh (Manchester); Prof. Robert E. Lane (Yale);
Dr J. D. Lees (Keele); Dr I. de Madariaga (London); Mr P. J. Madgwick
(University College of Aberystwyth); Mr R. A. Maidment (Manchester); Prof.
P. D. Marshall (Manchester); Dr K. Medhurst (Manchester); Mr D. H. S.
Morris (Manchester); Mr L. Minkin (Manchester); Mr G. Moyser (Manchester);
Prof. H. G. Nicholas (New College); Prof. R. H. Pear (Nottingham); Dr G.
Roberts (Manchester UMIST); Mr J. Schwarzmantal (Leeds); Mr M. Steed
(Manchester); Mr V. Vale (Southampton) *rapporteur*; Dr W. Wallace (Man-
chester); Dr M. J. Walles (Leeds); Mr R. Williams (Manchester); Mr M.
O'Donnell (Keele).

burden of the most powerful elective office in the world, the recent elections showed that American party ties remained almost as binding on most voters as at any previous epoch. If there was some further move towards a 'two-party South' its speed was that of a glacier rather than of a torrent. The American electorate seemed as fixed in its ways as most electorates – less volatile perhaps than the British; and part of this stability translated itself into a high level of non-participation. But this also was traditional.

The impact of this evidence about the conservative and traditionalist behaviour of most sectors of the American electorate was enhanced by the fact that only a few years earlier it had been common form to regard the United States as passing through a crisis as formidable and as far-reaching as those brought about by the great depression or, earlier than that, by the slavery controversy that led to the civil war. In 1968 it could well be asked whether the institutions of the United States had the necessary flexibility to enable the country to cope with the problems of the last third of the 20th century. It is true that even in 1972, the element of violence was not altogether lacking; the removal of Governor Wallace from the list of candidates by the bullet of a would-be assassin may indeed have had an important effect on the outcome at least in statistical terms; but the national and international impact of this event could not be compared with the repercussions of the murders of Robert Kennedy and Martin Luther King. The ability of President Nixon to ride the Vietnam storm despite his failure to announce a settlement was very significant if we reflect on the way in which so powerful and striking a president as Lyndon Johnson was forced to renounce any intention of running again because he had failed to defuse this issue. We had talk of race war; but the cities did not go up in flames one after the other as some had prophesied; we had talk of the generation gap, but nothing happened at the Miami Democratic Convention to compare with the scenes at Chicago, four years before. We had talk of the crisis of the American economy, and ended up with a British government looking anxiously to see whether it could learn any lessons from the way in which the Nixon Administration had handled inflation.

It is also clear that the change in atmosphere which was so obviously reflected in the behaviour of American voters was not the result of any miracles worked by the Nixon Administration itself. There had been no 'new deal'. It is true that the hostility to the Vietnam war had been moderated by the change in the way in which it was being fought which meant that far fewer American lives were at risk, even though the sufferings of the Vietnamese were not thereby much diminished, and a cynic would be tempted to say that the antipathy that American youth showed towards the war and which was buttressed by such high moral language showed a curious diminution of intensity as soon as it became no longer a question of risking their own lives. But on the issues of internal policy other than inflation: race-relations; the state of the cities; the destruction of the environment; crime and violence – if they were alive in 1968, why are they alive no longer? Once again, the cynic might answer by saying that in an advanced industrial society, the state of the economy particularly as it reveals itself in inflation is so over-riding an issue that a government that can cope with that can rest easy on the others.

Or one could put it still more crudely and say that despite all the talk of alienation on the part of youth or other identifiable sections of society, the main core of American society whether 'middle-class' or 'working-class' is still integrated within a structure of action and belief that anchors it to the existing order; what is outside is for one reason or another too weak to affect the course of events and will ordinarily be too conscious of this weakness to try very seriously to do so by such legal means as are available to it or by extra-legal ones. It requires some issue that divides the majority into warring sections – such as Vietnam briefly provided – to give the situation the appearance of fluidity and as soon as the particular issue passes, conservatism reasserts itself.

No society has been so investigated and pondered about as the American; the gathering at Manchester was in the long line of European preoccupations with American society and its fate to which we owe some of the masterpieces of European political literature. The presence of our American guests reminded us that one does not need to be a foreigner in order to be interested in America. American political science has increasingly devoted itself to the domestic scene and its techniques have enabled one to explore with greater precision areas that were previously only the subject of hypothesis and speculation. Yet, of course, such a science is only of limited validity since it has no predictive capacity; it can get from the data nothing but what it puts in. Seismography can tell us where earthquakes are more likely; it cannot predict particular earthquakes – at least not yet. Nothing was further from the confidence of President Kennedy's inaugural address than the sullen and violent self-questioning of 1968; nothing was further removed from that apocalyptic interlude than the calm that prevailed at the time of President Nixon's victory in 1972. Given the situation the political science fraternity will not be at a loss for explanations; but the way forward remains as obscure as ever.

It is perhaps a pity that whereas economic, political and socio-logical studies in the United States all claim increasing numbers of devotees, history as a discipline is out of fashion – particularly that history that deals in relatively long-term perspectives. It is perhaps only by going back to America's beginnings, to the social philo-sophy of the Founding Fathers and to the nature of the govern-mental system they created that one can acquire some idea of what is at stake in the debates over particular American institutions whose most recent years are dealt with in the subsequent papers in this volume. Despite all the daunting effects of more than one techno-logical revolution and of its accompanying economic changes, there is no domestic issue that at present divides Americans that was not in some form or another faced and considered in the generation of Thomas Jefferson.

Most political problems arise from the clash within single societies, and often within the minds and hearts of individuals, of general principles that are in contradiction with each other or with the brute facts of nature. In proclaiming the equality of men, the Founding Fathers pushed aside its relevance to the question of colour – a question which had been with Americans since the first settle-ments. Before Jefferson died the question had caught up with them and it has been with them ever since. Slavery; emancipation; separate but equal; integration; positive discrimination – these are in the main line; repatriation; recognition as a national group – these have been eccentric ideas for most people, most of the time. But the issue is not resolved; and to look only at so recent a phenomenon as the urban 'ghetto' is to make it doubtful that it can be. And is it not at least revealing that the last demonstration in the Washington of 1972 was one by the American Indians? (In a year which has also seen much activity by and on behalf of the Australian aborigines, something should be said about the ghosts of history.)

The Founding Fathers assumed a society in which property would be widely diffused and in which prosperity or the reverse would largely reflect the individual's own efforts. They had therefore no philosophy of poverty other than that which enjoined charity to victims of misfortune. To a very large extent this basic set of social attitudes is still alive; it is true that a much higher proportion of Americans than would then have been thought conceivable are dependent upon earnings rather than ownership; but claims on society's total output, whether as wages or as part of a social security structure, produce an outlook not very far removed from that of the property-owners of an earlier date. What society cannot cope with except outside this framework, if at all, are what appear to be the permanently disadvantaged. What if the odds against success make personal effort unavailing?

'Pollution', the newest and most fashionable 'problem', is also one of the oldest. Indifference to the destruction of the environment and a concentration upon short-term benefits to be extracted from nature's bounty is characteristic of all expanding societies unless there is some system of rigid social control. The exhaustion of the soil through the continuous cropping of tobacco; loss of soil through deforestation or up and down ploughing; none of this differs substantially from the killing of the American lakes or the poisoning of the air of California or the fouling of Pacific beaches of which people have now come to take notice. All conservationist or anti-pollution policies involve expense – that is to say eating into the profits of the present generation for the sake of a wider community interest, or of posterity. Such restraint on current enjoyment is hard to fit in to an individualist creed.

The unsolved problem of the American campuses – how to preserve standards if access is to be total and classification rejected? – was not there when Jefferson produced his frankly elitist plans for the University of Virginia. But once one has admitted the claim of each individual to be given an education at the expense of society at large, the drawing of a line between primary and secondary, or between secondary and higher, becomes difficult to justify in principle – if everyone is to be literate why is everyone not to be a Ph.D.?

One feature of the last few years which might appear novel is the launching into the American arena of competitive ideas of single books which claim to present a general explanation of what is wrong, and some panacea for putting things right, or the emergence of single prophets or of individuals treated as such. But is this not merely a transference to a secular plane of the religious 'awakenings' that punctuate the century of enlightenment? The *Greening of America* is in a good American tradition of Utopia by way of conversion.

Finally and most germane of all to the subjects dealt with in the papers that follow is the legacy of the original American antipathy to strong central government. It is true that both the great American crises of the past – civil war and New Deal – have resulted in an extension of the relative power of the federal government as compared with the states; though with the general growth of government intervention, the states are absolutely speaking more powerful than ever, spend more, employ more people. But the restraints of federalism have replaced those inherent in the separation of powers as the principle has been interpreted in respect of American government. It was the intention of most of the Founding Fathers to make government action difficult and complicated so as to prevent arbitrary action; in that respect their success has been undeniable.

No impression emerges more powerfully from the chapters in this volume, than the enormous difficulty in America of getting things done at municipal and state levels as well as the federal level, even when a policy has been framed by the appropriate authority. The suspicion of government inherent in the Jeffersonian philosophy has the result of making government more complex, not simpler, of multiplying separate institutions rather than eliminating them. Sometimes one feels that the odds against anything coming out of the legislative machine at all, or against a programme proving effective once it has emerged, are so considerable that it is a wonder that the whole system does not break down through sheer over-loading in the way in which one speculates on a traffic jam in Manhattan of such dimensions that the flow of vehicles can never get started again.

In this context it is natural to look for where energizing principles may appear in the political system. The most obvious case in recent decades has been the initiatives that have come from the Supreme Court. It was the Court that gave the lead in the general field of civil liberties, and that has so far prevented the understandable concern with law and order and the growth of crime to allow a whittling down of the rights of the individual accused at the behest of the government. More than this, in the field of race relations it was the Court that set going the process of desegregation with important long-range effects in education, and more direct ones in the sphere of voting rights and consequent minority representation. But in both these fields it has been positive discrimination that has been over-ruled in the name of the constitution, not new rights which have been extended; and in both, the speed of progress has depended upon the willing collaboration of the other branches of government, both at the federal level and in the states. In terms of innovation, the Court's intervention was most extraordinary in the question of apportionment; but here the Court intervened to protect what were after all majorities prevented by an entrenched system of privilege from exercising rights to which the accepted ideology fully entitled them.

In the problems that now face the United States, there is no obviously similar role for an initiative from the Court; what needs to be done is for legislature and executive to decide. For this reason the fact that President Nixon's nominations are intended to create a more 'conservative' Court may not be of great importance; a period of constitutional digestion may be in order; time may be needed to work out what the constitution means today after so many reversals of previously held positions. One would hazard the guess that the general outlook of the Court may only matter if there is a major attempt to encroach on personal liberties in the way in which they are now defined, particularly in respect of freedom of speech, publication and association. Even so this might only be marginally important either in respect of a tougher attitude towards 'permissiveness' or in respect of new measures to deal with crimes of violence. If Congress were to pass a genuine 'gun-law' it is hard to see the Court ruling it unconstitutional on the basis of the Second Amendment. In the same way one would not imagine that the pre-1937 doctrines of freedom of contract would be revived to impede anti-pollution legislation which cannot but affect property rights.

The only serious risk of the Court doing less than it might to uphold one set of American values would be if there were a real or imaginary revival of the totalitarian threat to them all. It has been noted that it was in relation to action taken under cover of protecting society against totalitarian inroads that the Warren Court was at its most cautious, and was most disinclined to go beyond procedural safeguards for the individual. What Americans have found least tolerable in the past is an apparent threat to the national consensus; and when that threat has appeared, they have shown the massive intolerance that Tocqueville feared would be characteristic of all democracies. Both Congress and the state legislatures have shown themselves at different times very hot on the trail of sedition and the courts on the whole reluctant to deny, perhaps rightly, that the extent of the danger and the means to cope with it are matters for the elected representatives of the people, not for the courts.

Is such a period of internal tension likely to recur? The answer to this question depends on developments in two areas neither of which were directly the subject of articles in this collection, though both were alluded to in the subsequent discussion. What degree of homogeneity has the American people actually attained and what degree is thought sufficient for safety? What is likely to be the impact of external events upon America's domestic political life in the near future?

One must again remember the extent to which there is an American ideology inherited from the Founding Fathers and the fact that whereas some of it is explicit, some of it was simply taken for granted and nowhere appears in the constitution. Of the implicit assumptions, the most important is that the United States is a nation with all the elements in common that one usually associates with that idea. While it is not for instance anywhere laid down that the language of the United States shall be English or a derivative therefrom, much of the American pattern of education and other instruments of socialization must be taken as intended primarily to make certain that the implicit assumption about a single national language shall be fact, however polygot the immigrant intake.

It could be argued that the nation was thought of also as white and even as Protestant, in a very loose sense; that the coloured and the Catholic and the Jew were not quite Americans. On all this there has been a degree of flexibility, except on language. And to the evolution of a more flexible attitude the political parties, with their receptivity to new elements in the population, have contributed a great deal. It is natural therefore that quite apart from its effect on party fortunes, attention should be paid to the shift of 'ethnic' votes from the Democratic to the Republican column. If Americans of whatever ethnic origin vote according to socio-economic status or from motives of direct self-interest or ideological preference, then it is felt, the nation-building impetus is retained; when some groups, Blacks or Spanish-speaking elements, resist that tendency or bow to it only to a slight degree, then there is cause for alarm. We have in the world examples of unitary societies and plural societies – the United States is the principal example of a plural society with a unitary ideology – although one could not be quite certain that its great rival, the Soviet Union, will not one day reveal itself as another example of the same thing.

Whether these derogations from national unity are at any time important will however depend on external circumstances; the

Japanese-Americans of the West Coast might have gone on living their useful and harmless lives without hindrance, had it not been for Pearl Harbour. One cannot, as George Washington rightly divined, have an America active in world affairs and not feel the effects at home.

By the exercise of self-discipline the participants in our conference managed to discuss most of these problems without direct reference to the fact that the institutions of the contemporary United States have to deal not merely with America's domestic problems but also with all that results from the burdens she has assumed in the rest of the world as a result of the Hitler war and the 'Cold War'. It was left to Raymond Aron to remind us in the concluding discussion that among the other apparently fixed elements in the constitutional system was the predominant role of the President in foreign affairs and the awe-inspiring responsibilities that this fact imposed upon a single individual. (A few weeks later the full import of this situation was to be brought home to everyone when President Nixon authorized the renewal of the mass bombing of North Vietnam after a breakdown in the Paris peace talks as to whose nature he was able to remain almost wholly uncommunicative.)

But the uniqueness of the American position in relation to world affairs lies in the substance of the issues involved as much as in the peculiarities of the institutions involved in handling them. The presuppositions of the traditional attitude were that if America left the world alone, the world would leave America alone. The degree of self-sufficiency, as compared to the commercial nations of western Europe, attained by the American economy seemed to point towards the belief that America not only should but could ignore what happened anywhere else. 'Fortress America' would not need to go onto siege rations.

None of this now looks the same. America has not been immune to the movement of ideas in the world – some of its minorities are exceptionally alive to anything that happens elsewhere that they can turn to their own use. American public figures assume the right to comment freely on the actions of other governments even in ways that amount to a blatant interference with internal affairs; the American government has been for periods, and in some parts of the world still is, the principal reason why particular regimes remain in power. And material interests – not in any sinister sense only – are also involved in the outcome of conflicts in other continents. The changing pattern of energy consumption, the specialization on exports of sectors of the American economy – notably agriculture – mean an abiding concern with a great many different developments outside America's borders. A country whose currency has become the major medium of international exchange cannot be indifferent to how other people manage their monetary affairs.

America today, like Palmerston's Britain but on a vastly greater scale, feels entitled to interfere wherever in the world she feels she has an interest to defend; and again like Palmerston's Britain but on an even vaster scale, her cultural penetration accompanies each assertion of her material and political influence.

The result has been that throughout the world America is better known than any other country or at least there is no other foreign country of which so many people are aware for so much of the time. In many quarters this knowledge or partial knowledge is tinged with gratitude or affection or at least hope. But it can also result in fear, hatred and incurable suspicion.

The dilemma of Vietnam has thrown all these facts into the fiercest possible glare of publicity. The dilemma has been the most agonizing that any civilized country could face; the Americans have had to admit to being unable to secure a political decision, which corresponds as closely as possible to the notions of self-determination to which they are committed, rather than annihilate a small country by the use of their unparalleled technical superiority. In the long run the element of defeat is likely to bulk large, with consequences of profound importance for themselves and their friends everywhere.

Whichever way the dilemma is resolved or whatever way may be found of avoiding it for the time being, one cannot help feeling that the outcome will profoundly strengthen the hands of all those who call for a return to the wisdom of the Founding Fathers. The Nixon presidency may well come to be seen as a watershed between the internationalist-minded United States of the later Roosevelt years and of the Truman-Eisenhower-Kennedy-Johnson era and a new period of concentration upon unfinished business at home with all foreign policy questions subordinated to the exigencies of the home front. In such an America, the mood would be a very different one from anything that has been seen for over forty years. More than this one cannot say.

The essays on particular topics in this volume suggest that a high degree of institutional conservatism need not of course preclude some innovations or new directions in policy, and that even during recent years, changes can be perceived.

On the constitutional side, as R. H. Pear shows in his essay on the Supreme Court, it is not certain that a definite choice of 'conservative' justices such as President Nixon has made will necessarily bring about a major change in the impact of the Court's decisions, although the areas on which the Court will concentrate its attention may shift with changing personnel. The present Court was expected to give some assistance to the forces of law and order in cases where the police seemed unduly hampered in securing convictions; but not much has been done to cause any serious anxiety about the curtailment of the rights of the accused. The most notable decision of the Court, the ending of the death penalty might be regarded as more a continuation of the previous line, though it was of course put through against the votes of the Nixon appointees. What would seem to emerge from Pear's essay is that the role of the Court as educator may be played in the immediate future in a rather low key.

The question of the executive branch of government is approached in rather different ways by H. G. Nicholas in dealing with the presidency, and by V. Vale in his account of the continued expansion and increasing complexity of the federal bureaucracy. Nicholas is concerned with the presidency as it has existed since President Eisenhower's time when the modern fragmentation of the two parties began to mean in his view that each presidential candidate had to construct his own. The logic of this was carried to its conclusion in the Miami Convention of the Democratic Party when McGovern created a party that almost deliberately excluded from its ranks important sectors of the historic Democratic coalition. One result of the enfeeblement of party to which Nicholas believes recent presidents have all contributed when in office by their neglect of the party in the country, is the increase in the personalization of presidential government and of the methods by which presidents conduct the country's business. The importance of the White House staff as against the departments is not just a measure of the extraordinary ascendancy seemingly acquired by Dr Kissinger in the field of foreign affairs but inherent in the way American government is now conducted. This spells the failure of Eisenhower's attempt to make something of the cabinet and means a very considerable measure of autonomous action except in fields where legislation is required. Congress's control of finance seems a poor weapon against a determined president.

Vale shows that even on the legislative side the mass of what is proposed comes from within the governmental machine, and that even here the White House staff has an important role to play in sift-ing such proposals and in assigning priorities. The other main sub-ject treated in Vale's paper is the administrative side of the new re-lationship between the federal government and the states, and to a lesser but growing extent between the federal government and the localities. The examination of the difficulties that have emerged in the use of federal funds for programmes that can only be effectively de-vised and controlled locally helps to explain, quite apart from any ideological prejudice against increased federal spending for local pur-poses, the greater scepticism that now prevails about the capacities of American government to deal with some of the major social and political problems of the country.

The argument is carried forward in P. Madgwick's essay on the American city, which for many British students of American govern-ment is likely to be the one that breaks most new ground. His argument that while British government has been a force, if not always an effective one, for the equalization of resources and oppor-tunities between areas, the American system tends to defend or even create inequalities and provides a manner of looking at federalism quite a long way from the classical mode. The politicization of the competing agencies of municipal government and the active role of their employee organizations also helps to explain fragmentation, while the difficulties that confront reforming mayors (not altogether dissimilar from those that confront reforming presidents) are set out with some precision. Finally and in a way which differentiates the present from earlier eras of social reform in the cities, there is the greater element of doubt as to whether the actual diagnosis of the reasons why expectations outrun performance is the correct one. Is money the solvent that it was once thought to be or are the problems of poverty more recalcitrant than has been thought?

What is brought out at all levels of government is the importance of party; the views as to the current weaknesses of the parties as ways of focusing policy brought out by both Nicholas and Madgwick from their different angles of approach are supported by the analysis of the parties themselves in P. Fotheringham's paper. The decentra-lization that remains their most distinctive feature has not been eroded by some decline in the importance of sectional issues and some increase in the weight of socio-economic factors in determining party allegiance. The weight of the parties has been a negative rather than a positive factor in promoting consistent policies directed to-wards influencing social development in any clearly thought out way.

The bargaining element in the making of policy remains more important than any ideological drive.

In his essay on Congress, J. D. Lees shows how difficult American observers have found it to agree on the extent to which Congress has sucessfully reorganized itself for the more positive role that the central institutions of the country have come to play. Much ingenuity has gone into reorganizing procedures and in endowing Congress and Congressmen with greater resources for the collection and collation of relevant information. But this surface activity may have less long-term political importance than the gradual erosion of conservative controls over committee chairmanships combined with the effects of redistricting in the House. It is likely that if the country becomes more liberal so too will Congress but, as can be seen from Lees's treatment of Congress's role and claims in the sphere of foreign policy, all these things taken together still cannot ensure for Congress an initiatory role from which the separation of powers continues to debar it.

Although written independently the articles themselves together with the subsequent discussion show a fairly considerable measure of agreement as to the relative weight of the different parts of the system and the extent to which each part responds to change. From the material here presented, the reader may be able to form his own views of how in the history of American institutions the present phase is likely to figure – as a period of consolidation, or as the starting-point for an era of innovation? He will certainly find no lack of material upon which to form a judgement either upon this basic issue, or upon what we set out to look at originally, the viability or credibility of the American system as a whole.

H. G. Nicholas

The Insulation of the Presidency

IN THE CABINET ROOM of RICHARD NIXON'S WHITE HOUSE THERE hang two portraits, one of Woodrow Wilson and one of Dwight D. Eisenhower. Report has it that they are the personal selection of the present incumbent, representing those of his predecessors whom he most admires. If so, they constitute an interesting choice, an unusual combination. Woodrow Wilson, in the type-casting of history, is a typical 'strong' President, the innovative leader who rules as well as reigns, the convinced mandatory of the popular will. Eisenhower, by contrast, represents a unique attempt in our time to recreate the 'weak' or 'strict constructionist' President of an earlier age, a quasi-monarchical head of state who does not seek to rule and does not claim for himself a larger or more authoritative mandate than that of his legislative colleagues. Moreover Wilson, despite his repudiation by the American people, saw himself as an active leader of his party, while Eisenhower, despite his landslide victories, thought it improper (or found it distasteful) to use the presidency as an instrument of party advantage.

In presenting two such strikingly different models for emulation or criticism the presidency is unique amongst the institutions of American government. It is the target, time and time again, of two opposite and frequently simultaneous criticisms – that it is too strong and that it is too weak. Presidents are accused of being dictators, high-handed autocrats riding rough-shod over the constitution, and, often in one and the same breath, of being supine and impotent, of not combating this or that evil in the body politic, of not giving Congress or the country enough 'lead', of not 'doing something about it', whatever the 'it' of the moment may be. By contrast Congress is comparatively immune from the accusation at least of tyranny; an individual committee may be criticized as a 'Star Chamber' or an individual legislator as a 'browbeater', but neither house as a whole is feared for what Senator Fulbright (referring exclusively to the executive branch) calls the 'arrogance of power'. Instead, the fairly consistent fate of Congress is to be blamed for inaction, inadequacy, impotence. The Supreme Court, in recent years especially, has got used to an opposite line of criticism. Its members have even been threatened with impeachment for their sweeping and high-handed rulings. They have repeatedly – and from opposite sides – been accused of reading their own predilections into the constitution. But they have very seldom had to face accusations of inaction, of being too supine vis-à-vis their neighbour branches of government. When this has happened it has mainly been at moments of acute national emergency, when the courts have acted as if they believed that *inter arma silent leges*. Such was the doubtfully admirable acquiescence of the Court in the second world war in the face of the enforced evacuation from the West Coast of the Japanese Nisei. But in general it is what the Court does, and not what it abstains from doing, that excites the interest, approval or indignation of the American electorate.

Why is the poor denizen of the White House thus selected for the unique distinction of being shot at from both sides? Why is he expected to be the embodiment, as presumably Richard Nixon hopes he is, of both Woodrow Wilson and Dwight D. Eisenhower, of the ruler and of the constitutional monarch, of reform and conservatism, of action and acquiescence – and this in one and the same President at one and the same time? In part, of course, the paradox flows directly from the incorporation in one person of the ceremonial head of state and the active political executive. Yet there are other presidents in the world who thus combine the dignified and efficient functions of government and yet do not run, in consequence, into the opposing gales of criticism that are the poor American President's lot. No doubt something is due to that national psychology which historians know to be a fact of life and social scientists believe to be a figment of historians' sloppy imagination: Americans have always been a people of rising expectations who at the same time believe they have already found the philosopher's stone. Providing a satisfactory leadership for a mobile Zion is bound to tax any merely human institution to its limits.

But it is also observable that the burden I refer to has not always weighed so heavily upon the presidency as it does today. The President has always been shot at, but he has not always been shot at from both sides and he has not always been shot at alone. Jefferson, Jackson and Lincoln, 'strong' Presidents of the republic's first century, were all accused of tyrannical aspirations and behaviour and simultaneously of supine inadequacy, but they all rested their power, or their impotence, upon a broad base in Congress and the country and all enjoyed the comfort of sharing their buffets with their colleagues in their party. The post-Civil War Presidents, of whom little was expected and from whom even less was forthcoming, were able almost to abdicate their office and play second fiddle to Congress. The revival of presidential power, as under Theodore Roosevelt, was, for all his talk of personal assertion ('I took Panama') in fact accompanied by much close co-ordination with Congress and his party. Woodrow Wilson, for all his conviction of having a personal mandate, modelled himself, as far as the American system permitted, upon the British Prime Minister and sought in Congress a parliamentary following and endorsement. Franklin Roosevelt's leadership, intensely personal as it was, was always exercised through Congress (even in the Hundred Days) and through the Democratic Party (even when, as in 1938, he tried to purge it). Harry Truman, an activist if ever there was one, was pre-eminently a party man, however much he might find himself frustrated by the behaviour of conservative Democrats in a 'do-nothing' Congress.

But with the coming of Eisenhower to the White House a change begins to come over the presidency. It is a change in the status and the role, one might almost say the location, of the office in the constitutional system and it is a change that persists through the very different incumbencies of John Kennedy, Lyndon Johnson and Richard Nixon. This change can be traced by observing the relations that the President has with his party, his congress and his cabinet, and in the developments that have occurred in the organization of the White House itself and in the President's handling of press and broadcasting.

THE PRESIDENT AND HIS PARTY

At first sight the presidency is still very much a party office. Whatever the constitution may say, the first qualification for the President is that he be the nominee of one of the two great parties and then, under a party banner, defeat his rival party standard-bearer at the polls. When in office he is the undisputed head of his party; he appoints the National Chairman, dominates the National Committee, and shapes the party convention which will re-nominate him for his second term. All this is true, but it is no longer true in the same way as it was true for Jackson or Lincoln or McKinley or Wilson or even Franklin Roosevelt. The American national party is now a shadow organization. It was always fragmented by the facts of federation. It was at the state level alone that it lived from day to day; its national existence was an intermittent, four-year phenomenon. But it is now fragmented into smaller units; with the decline of the boss, of the 'regular' machine organization, it has become a thing of bits and pieces – in this city an emanation of a trade union, in that of a black power grouping, in one suburb an adjunct of the women's clubs, in another an affiliate of the American Medical Association. In general it is a shell, waiting to be filled by anyone with the energy and time and money to take it over.

In this situation the would-be President can no longer emerge by long apprenticeship in the ranks, working his way up the hierarchy, as Lincoln or Cleveland did; nor can he capture the party at one go, as Woodrow Wilson did. He has instead to build his *own* following out of the bits and pieces of the party that are lying around, plus whatever other bits and pieces – of independents, or even of the rival organization – that he can attract. Thus, though the Democratic or Republican label is his to wear, the successful aspirant to the nomination has, in effect, to construct his own national party for his own purposes.

Thus Eisenhower, who significantly could have had either nomination for the asking, floated into office on a broad sea of support which extended from the Republican right (though not the far right) to substantial areas of the Democratic middle ground. He did not need the party: the party needed him. He was not interested in it, he never fully understood it. He made no effort, save when pressed, to act on its behalf.

John Kennedy was, in one sense, a politician of the old school, coming from a state where politics of the classic machine type still persisted. He had a wide acquaintance and, through his family and clan, an unusually wide connection with Democratic politicos across the country. Even so his capture of the White House was made possible not by the support of the 'regular organization' but by the efforts, money and skill of the team which he had himself built across the country. In effect he used the experience and expertise which he had learnt inside the party to build his own organization parallel to that of the formal Democratic Party.

Lyndon Johnson was an even more professional politician by training and experience than John Kennedy, but when the time came, in 1964, for him to re-capture the White House in his own right, he too relied upon his own organization, building indeed in large measure on what he had inherited from his predecessor.

Richard Nixon was so deeply dyed a party man, had spent so much of his life doing, day in day out, the chores of the Republican Party, that he was known by the sobriquet of 'Mr Republican'. Yet not only was this very fact paradoxically held by many Republicans to be a serious disqualification – which tells us something of its own about the relationship of party and presidency – but he himself, like his predecessors, went out to build a personal following in 1968. Once the nomination was secured, the campaign itself was run not from Washington, the headquarters of the Republican National Committee, but from New York, by Nixon's own men, under the direction of his law partner, John Mitchell, subsequently his Attorney-General.

In 1972 McGovern and his supporters went even further. Having broken in disgust with the regular Democratic Party in 1968, they went all out in the ensuing year to take the party away from the professional machine-minders, to reform its composition and re-fashion it around the personality and policies of their candidate. In Miami Beach in 1972 the party acquired not only a new image but also a new structure and membership. It became a party of participa-tion in place of a party of organization. Despite the identity of name the McGovernites had, in effect, invented a new party to sustain their nominee's candidacy.

Elected then in company with rather than in any sense on the back of their parties, the Presidents of the post-Truman era have been increasingly indifferent to the claims of party when in office. Eisenhower designedly sought to transcend party and to present himself as the President, one could almost say the king, of all Americans. He viewed partisanship as a derogation from his proper role and left to his Vice-President, Richard Nixon, the superinten-dence and cosseting of the Republican Party in the country. When pressed, he threw his weight behind Republican candidates at mid-term as well as presidential elections; the results were not encouraging and in 1958 he turned the job over to Richard Nixon. At the end, this most popular of post-war presidents left his party weaker than he found it, both in Congress and in the country.

Kennedy, proceeding from opposite assumptions, had on the whole a surprisingly similar effect. He interested himself deeply and continuously in Democratic Party affairs, interfering in local con-

tests, even 'purging' those Democrats whom he disliked, like De
Sapio and Prendergast in New York; indeed when he was assassina-
ted it was on a party errand – an endeavour to heal the rift among
the Texas Democrats. But the result was to subordinate the party
to the White House. Such incipient, independently rooted party
growths as there were, e.g. the Democratic Advisory Council, were
crushed because they might compete with the directorate at the
White House. Thus the party remained largely an extension of the
Kennedy personal network.

Johnson continued what Kennedy had begun. With his deep-
seated suspiciousness he distrusted a party which, except within
Congress, had persistently turned down his claims – in 1956 for
Stevenson, in 1960 for Kennedy. He transferred effective control
to the White House, not to revitalize the party so much as to smother
it. For a notorious party politician, Johnson underwent a striking
change in the White House; perhaps as a result of his landslide
victory in 1964 he came to regard the Democratic Party organization
as either otiose or menacing. Either way he enfeebled it, as Hubert
Humphrey learnt to his cost in 1968.

Even 'Mr Republican', now that he is President, has shown a
surprising indifference to the party that he heads. Party leaders have
been starved of patronage and audiences. The President's indisputable
right to remove and appoint the National Committee Chairman
was exercised with such ineptitude as to weaken rather than strength-
en the organization. In the four years of Nixon's first term there
have been four Republican Committee chairmen – a rate of turnover
reflecting presidential whims more than party interests. Nixon's
energetic mid-term campaigning in 1970 brought him little or no
reward; though the President claimed 'ideological' gains, his party
certainly lost ground at the polls. Whether by reason of this rebuff
or because of a more deep-seated belief that his presidential prospects
did not jibe with those of his party, Nixon's 1972 strategy was very
different. He did the minimum of explicit campaigning and, with a
very few exceptions, devoted all of his efforts to his own re-election.
The supporting campaign was waged not under the GOP however,
but by a 'Committee to Re-elect the President'. The emphasis
(e.g. in slogans like 'Four More Years') fell always on the President,
never on the party leader. And Republican candidates, for their part,
were equally anxious to stand on their own feet; few sought or
displayed Nixonian endorsements; many went out of their way to
avoid them. And of course the results, with their display of split-

ticket voting and a virtual absence of presidential 'coat-tail' effect confirmed that in thus distinguishing between president and party the candidates were only reflecting the mood of the voters.

A clear reflection of the modern President's desire to cut loose from his party, to rise above and beyond its associations, is provided by the recurrent concern to recruit members of the other party for prominent posts in the President's Administration. When Roosevelt did this, appointing in 1940 the two prominent Republicans, Henry Stimson and Frank Knox, to the Secretaryships of War and Navy, this was merely an 'emergency' move aimed at consolidating national unity in a system where coalition government is impossible. When Eisenhower appointed Martin Durkin, a Chicago Democrat, as Secretary of Labour, this was evidently due to the difficulty of recruiting an adequate spokesman for that particular pressure group, organized labour, from the ranks of a party of the right. But when Kennedy put a Republican, however little partisan, at the Treasury (Douglas Dillon), another, however little publicized, at Defence (McNamara), a third, albeit academic, at the key controls in the White House (McGeorge Bundy), and a fourth one, open and avowed, at the CIA (McCone), this reflected something different – a feeling that the administration should extend its appeal beyond party, that a President with a hairsbreadth majority should broaden his base.

Johnson's pursuit of consensus required no Republican assistance, but that was because he was determined to say, like Walt Whitman, 'In all people I see myself, none more and not one a barleycorn less'.

Nixon, like Kennedy narrowly based, like Johnson consensus-minded, but also, unlike Johnson, nervous of his own capacity to embrace America's diversity, made it his aim from the first to reach out across party lines. He pledged as much in his 1968 campaign and when elected he made no secret of his ardent attempt to recruit for his administration such Democrats as Hubert Humphrey, Sargent Shriver, Clark Clifford, and Senator Jackson. As it turned out he had to be content with Daniel Patrick Moynihan in the White House, as head of his Council for Urban Affairs, a Democrat indeed, but rather a renegade one. However, the determination persisted, and in 1971 Nixon was able to announce a raid across party lines more remarkable than any since the war, when Governor Connally of Texas became Secretary of the Treasury. Its significance as a sign of the down-grading of party attachments was underlined by the widespread if mistaken assumption that this was only a prelude to Connally's nomination as Vice-President on the Republican ticket, in 1972. The fact that such an illusion could be seriously entertained reflected a significant change in the reality of the presidency. It is no longer regarded as predominantly or even necessarily a party office, but as the chief magistracy of the nation. Though the launching pad of party may be necessary to put the President into orbit, once aloft he is free to set his course and maintain it according to his own conception of the national interest; if he chooses to pay attention to ground control it is a ground control manned not by party managers and regulars but by the wizards of the new technology, those trained to read and manipulate the dials of public opinion and public relations. But of those more anon.

THE PRESIDENT AND THE BUREAUCRACY

The President lives in a house – a White House, to be precise – but increasingly his house has become his castle, a castle to which he can retire behind the drawbridge of executive privilege and from which he can dominate the surrounding countryside. In keeping with this, the President's staff has now expanded to over 500 persons from the couple of secretaries who did duty half a century ago. And this, of course, is not all. To accommodate them the White House has not only gone underground; it has also gone next door, to what was once the State Department, and thence it has proceeded across the street. It has in fact expanded into a larger entity, the Executive Office of the President, a huge establishment of more than half a dozen key agencies with a total staff of over four and a half thousand. This office, the creation of Franklin Roosevelt, has a variety of components, many of them not readily distinguishable from ordinary departments of government, but several of them directly serving the President in the task of directing and controlling the sprawling federal bureaucracy. All have their significance for students of public administration. What here most concerns us is the White House staff itself.

Increasing in size and importance with every president, the White House staff in its scale and functions reflects the expanding power and independence of the presidential office. The classic charts of the American executive branch show a series of departments coming to a pyramidical point, through the cabinet, in the person of the President himself. The more sophisticated version is three-dimensional, to show how power and connection also run directly from government departments to Congress via the appropriate congressional committee. But increasingly the President's lines of control run not through the cabinet at all but direct through his personal assistants to the departments and often not to the head of the department but to a bureau chief or lower. Moreover, on closer inspection, it will often become apparent that there have been set up, within the White House itself, miniature replicas of departments paralleling their functions but surpassing their importance, since of course such a replica enjoys the most valuable of all instruments of power, direct access to the President himself. This can be seen at present most strikingly, of course, in the field of foreign relations, where the State Department finds its functions duplicated or overridden by the President's Assistant for National Security Affairs.

How has this come about? It has its origins in the pressures of expanding government and the inadequacy of the cabinet as an instrument of co-ordination and control. The cabinet is the great non-institution of American government, whose label conceals a virtual absence of function. In the days when the President emerged from and rested on a firm party base, his cabinet pretty regularly reflected elements of real political strength in his party. Even then, however, the President was always infinitely more than *primus inter pares*; the mandate, after all, was exclusively his; the cabinet – *his* cabinet, his to appoint, to dismiss, to ignore, to override. Yet down to and partly through the New Deal it retained a certain status and represented a certain assemblage of political power which the President could use in controlling the bureaucracy and which proportionately he was obliged to respect. But as the personal ascendancy of the President has become more pronounced, so the appeal of cabinet membership to other really powerful political figures has declined. Moreover, as the bureaucracy burgeoned, much of its operations fell outside the 'old-line' departments altogether into the Executive Office and so never went through the cabinet at all. As the President's power expanded, that of the cabinet shrank. Already under Franklin Roosevelt important decisions were taken elsewhere and co-ordination became an exclusively White House function.

Under Eisenhower, for all the formal deference paid to cabinet functioning, this process was accelerated. A commander-in-chief in any case prefers hierarchy to committee, and Eisenhower, in organizing his White House staff to report to him over the whole range of government through the single channel of Sherman Adams, was creating a palace guard which, although in theory concerned only with the President's own business, in fact took over more and more of the cabinet's functions. Dulles excepted, all cabinet members found that the way to the President lay through Adams. Significantly, even after the fall of Adams, when Eisenhower was incapacitated by illness, it mattered more what Hagerty, his press secretary and confidant, wanted, than what the cabinet might think desirable or appropriate.

Kennedy was obsessed by the problem of getting on top of the huge bureaucracy that the Eisenhower Administration, for all its outward efficiency, had often signally failed to control. He discarded hierarchy in his White House staff, preferring to be the hub of a many-spoked wheel. But he did not thereby reduce, or seek to reduce, the potency of his palace guard. Indeed he weakened the heads of departments and the cabinet even more. In making appointments, he often, as in the State Department, chose Assistant Secretaries and Under-Secretaries before he appointed Secretaries themselves, to guarantee loyalty at deeper levels than the top. In administration, similarly, he reached out directly to officials low in the hierarchy, to instruct, to threaten or to reward. The aim was always to bring the President's personal power and policy to bear directly on the remotest cog of the administrative machine. The White House staff waxed fat and strong on this, and the cabinet waned. Kennedy frankly proclaimed cabinet meetings to be 'a waste of time', though he never insulated himself from individual cabinet members.

Johnson professed, perhaps genuinely, to hold the cabinet in esteem. Meetings were regularly held with agendas and records of decisions. But in effect the cabinet was being given the bear hug treatment. Johnson's overpowering personality dominated the sessions; there was a minimum of deliberation or indeed of genuine decision-taking. By contrast, Johnson himself was accessible enough, but it was accessibility at a price. Department heads soon learnt to be chary about taking their problems to him, because the interview was swiftly turned inside out, into a presidential monologue followed by a presidential exposition of *his* problems and the imposition of a series of presidential demands or inquisitions.

Richard Nixon inherits from his old chief, Eisenhower, a great belief in the value of organization in the White House. Significantly, he made all his principal appointments to his personal staff before he chose his cabinet or even his Budget Director. Order and hierarchy are the order of the day, but there is no single Sherman Adams; instead there are 'the Germans', also known as 'the Berlin Wall' – H. R. (Bob) Haldeman, the keeper of the President's appointment book; John Ehrlichman, who is given a general oversight of domestic affairs; and of course Henry Kissinger, National Security Adviser. Despite rather more than the usual fanfares accompanying the announcement of cabinet appointments, including a special television presentation of them to the nation, Richard Nixon has had as little use for this institution as any of his predecessors. In his first year, the cabinet met only on twelve occasions. Nixon found it an unsuitable vehicle for decision-making. Instead he set up what were virtually two sub-cabinets centred on the White House. The National Security Council (NSC) was, on paper, already in existence. Created in 1947 to provide the United States with an equivalent, *mutatis mutandis*, of Britain's long-standing Committee of Imperial Defence, it consisted *ex officio* of the principal foreign policy and defence officials, with a staff to organize and operate it. As might be expected, Eisenhower believed in it and elaborated it; Kennedy abolished most of its substructure but used it under *his* Kissinger (McGeorge Bundy) as the main forum for discussion and advice, but practically never for decision; Johnson similarly by-passed it for what he called 'the Tuesday Cabinet', a gathering of five or six dominant figures. Nixon, however, a tidy man, revived the NSC and put Kissinger, also a tidy man, to look after it. A pruned NSC became the only forum for top-level review and policy-making, with Kissinger preparing its agenda and the State and Defence Departments and the CIA limited to one seat each on the key 'Review Group' – a small, tight, executive body on which the White House Assistant is at least the equal of a Secretary of State. (N.B. Though for executive purposes small, it is serviced by a staff of over one hundred.)

Parallel to the NSC for foreign affairs, there is the Domestic Council under Ehrlichman as executive director, to advise the President 'on the whole range of domestic policy' and consisting of the heads of all departments concerned with domestic affairs.[1] Here too a substantial staff, comparable to Kissinger's, underpins the White House role.

Nor does this exhaust the arsenal of White House controls over the bureaucracy. In Franklin Roosevelt's time, the Bureau of the Budget had been brought into being to exercise over other departments some of those supervisory functions which in Britain are entrusted to the Treasury. With time, its power and effectiveness increased; in many areas indeed it discharged some of the co-ordinating role which the cabinet so signally failed to perform. But though *in* the Executive Office of the President, it was *outside* the White House itself. It belonged, so to say, to the presidency as an institution rather than to any particular president in person. But in 1970, at the same time as he set up the Domestic Council, Nixon also created a new Office of Management and Budget (OMB) inside the White House itself, to be headed initially by George Shultz, pre-viously Secretary of Labour. Its function is to superintend and assess the way in which government programmes are executed – an ex-panded version of the role of the old Bureau of the Budget which is now subsumed in the new Office. Exactly what the powers of OMB will be, it is too soon as yet to say. It was reported that its establishment was viewed critically by members of the cabinet who saw in it yet another down-grading of their status. Certainly they had reasons for being suspicious. Impotent collectively, they were frustrated individually. In the case of the Secretary of the Interior, Walter Hickel, this frustration found expression in an indignant resignation. Having succeeded in penetrating 'the Berlin Wall' to see the President on only three occasions in sixteen months, Hickel's resignation was preceded by a letter with the forthright recom-mendation that Nixon 'consider meeting, on an *individual* and conversational basis, with members of his Cabinet'.[2]

That such a development might occur was foreseen when Franklin Roosevelt first instituted that expansion of the White House which was the inescapable consequence of the New Deal's expansion of federal government itself. But Roosevelt himself was emphatic that his administrative assistants were to be 'personal aides to the President and should have no authority over anyone in any depart-ment or agency, including the Executive Office of the President'. The order which set up that office was clear and emphatic: 'In no event shall the administrative assistants be interposed between the President and any one of the divisions of the Executive Office of the President' (Executive Order No. 8248, 8 September 1939). Unfor-tunately, the pressures of administrative convenience and human nature all work the other way. The man who is able to say 'The President wants . . .' is seldom able (and, if able, seldom anxious) to avoid the aura which wraps around the supreme office itself. He becomes an *alter ego* of the President, an extension of his personality

and power. The White House, moreover, is not only an office; it
is also a court. And the first principle of a court is that power is
correlative to physical proximity to the person of the king. And
only if the king himself curbs his minions, resists their flattery and,
when necessary, dispenses with even their assistance, is this tendency
for power to flow around his footstool likely to be contained. Most
presidents are not cast in a mould of such vicarious modesty.

Thus it has come about that as executive activities and responsibilities have expanded – and of course their expansion has been as
inescapable as it has been extensive – so the presidency has become
self-sufficient and self-regulating, maintaining its own controls and
its own nerve centre. More than ever before the President has become
free to run the government with his own men in his own way. Of
course the sprawling bureaucracy has its own momentum and its
own inertia; it is not to be lightly turned from its course or quickened
in its tempo. But where policy making is concerned the President
is more than ever before autonomous, able to get his own information, free to consult, free to ignore, free to annex, as it were, to the
White House, to operate under his personal eye, whatever segment
of the huge administration he desires to honour with his personal
attention. He remains one man, able to do only what one man can do.
But just as the tool increases the capabilities of the craftsman, so the
armoury of administrative instruments which is the modern White
House extends the capabilities of the President to a degree unprecedented in American history.

RELATIONS WITH CONGRESS

In mediaeval Britain when the court grew too powerful, men
looked to the barons and the knights of the shire to redress the
balance. In the American monarchy, the barons are the Senate and
the knights the House of Representatives. Congress, in theory, is
the countervailing force to an over-potent president. The days are
gone for ever, of course (if indeed they ever existed), when the
balance of power between the two was to be found in a strict
separation – Congress passing the laws, the President executing them.
More and more the two have become mixed up together. A big
executive requires lots of legislation; more laws mean a larger
bureaucracy to execute them. Each area needs the other. Eisenhower
was probably the last President to indulge the hope that he and
his Congress could lead independent lives; the hope did not survive

his early days in office. Congress was soon begging the President to resume, like some Tudor monarch, his responsibility for setting its legislative targets – a responsibility which not so long ago it had denounced as executive tyranny. The President very quickly found that he had to take stands on congressional legislation; there were some bills which he had to have and some, equally, like the Bricker Amendment, which he had to defeat.

But in the process of making this discovery, Eisenhower made another, namely that it was not enough for him to rely upon his party in Congress, even when that party enjoyed a majority in both houses. This classic device for uniting executive and legislature could not be relied upon even with an accommodating President. To make good its deficiencies, Eisenhower found himself forging an alliance with that congressional politician extraordinary, the Senate Democratic Leader, Lyndon B. Johnson. The policies of supra-party consensus which Eisenhower had used with such success in his presidential election campaign were now carried over into the relations of White House and Congress. This appealed strongly to Eisenhower's concept of the presidency as a quasi-monarchical office – the President of *all* the people – but it carried the obvious corollary for better or for worse of reducing his dependence on his congressional party base.

Kennedy's three years were largely filled with frustrating relations with Congress. His own Senate apprenticeship turned out to be of little help. Congress knew him as in no sense a 'regular' Senator; he had always been too junior, too liberal, too impatient, too arrogant. Though he was a party President, with few monarchical illusions, the party he believed in was *his* kind of Democratic Party, which was by no means identical with the Democratic Party in Congress. Moreover, he wanted more than Eisenhower from Congress: he sought to exercise congressional leadership in small matters as well as great. In the end he got neither. But equally Congress was unable to do much to cut Camelot down to size. Whatever may have happened to some of Kennedy's longer-term reforms, the power of the Kennedy White House was felt all along the line.

Johnson, oldest and wiliest of congressional hands, boosted his legislative skills when he moved into the White House with the fuel that remorse and concern for the Kennedy assassination provided him. This reduced Congress in his first, partial term to the most pliant agency that the White House had known since Franklin

Roosevelt's Hundred Days. In the wake of his enormous personal victory in 1964 he sought, like Eisenhower, to translate the politics of consensus into a legislative programme. In this he attained remarkable success, displaying a virtuosity and energy in his own right exceeding even what he manifested as Kennedy's legatee. Congress, in a wide range of domestic legislation, showed a willingness to go along where the White House led to a degree which at the time seemed as creditable as it was remarkable – so heavy were the arrears from Eisenhower's second term and Kennedy's unfinished agenda. The same compliance was initially shown on the foreign policy side, as e.g. over the Gulf of Tonkin incident – but it was also in this area that the politics of consensus first began to unravel, when the credibility gap began to develop over Vietnam. Once this happened, it soon spread to home affairs. A presidency which had reached a pinnacle of executive ascendancy ended in executive frustration and impotence. The attempt to link the two branches of government by a bear hug could not be sustained.

Nixon rivalled Johnson for congressional experience, though not for virtuosity or energy. Nor could he claim an electoral triumph which had pulled in his congressional colleagues in his wake. On the contrary; he was the first President since Zachary Taylor to enter office with both Houses controlled by the opposite party. He therefore sought a congressional politics of consensus not out of strength but out of necessity. In the House, despite the Republicans being in a minority, he could count in many fields on a cross-party support. In the Senate he was less successful. But although he recruited to his White House staff as assistant for congressional relations perhaps the ablest practitioner in the business, Bryce Harlow, who had served Eisenhower in the same capacity, communications between President and Congress were seldom easy. The rest of the President's staff, especially his intimates, were unknown to Congress and ignorant of it. His most trusted cabinet colleague, Mitchell, was a bond-market lawyer with minimal empathy for life as it is lived on the Hill. The fact was that the kind of executive team which Nixon had chosen for himself was bound to be a barrier between him and Congress. They were chosen for personal loyalty and for their ability to protect and aggrandize the President's role. This meant that they were suspicious, even contemptuous of Congress, preferring to construct a presidency which could go it alone rather than one which would collaborate with Congress, on whatever terms. Repeatedly, congressmen were denied the consultation which they thought due to them and which could often have been purchased at minimal cost – e.g. when no congressman was given any notification of the Cambodian invasion until within half an hour of the President's broadcast to the nation. The Senate, in particular, was perpetually presented with *faits accomplis*. It retorted, as in its rejection of Nixon's first two nominations for vacancies on the Supreme Court, by imposing humiliating defeats on the President. The President in turn retaliated by campaigning at mid-term for a Congress which would give him an 'ideological majority'. He failed to secure it. When he did get congressional endorsements, as in 1971 for the economic measures which preceded American devaluation, it was because in a striking *volte-face* he aligned himself with the ideological majority in Congress rather than *vice versa*.

Could Congress then under Nixon claim to have recovered its constitutional role, of being a counterbalance to the President? To some degree, yes, as the fate of the Carswell and Haynesworth nominations most strikingly demonstrated. But Congress's long-developing inability to control the executive's power of shaping policy in such areas as foreign affairs and defence was confirmed over and over again. Sometimes it was confirmed, as it were, by contradiction, as when the Senate in 1971 lashed out at the Foreign Aid Bill and simply voted it down. But such gestures of frustration and desperation were self-defeating; the pillars of the temple only had to be re-erected from the ruins by a badly bruised Samson. More typical was the impotence with which the Senate contemplated the Spanish-American bases agreement. Debated in the Spanish Cortes, it was not even presented to the US Senate for consideration, but simply registered as an executive agreement. The Senate was being by-passed and its protests were ignored. The same story was repeated over and over again on the long, long trail of the Vietnam war. Like the Korean war before it, the war remained undeclared and uncontrolled, while being at the same time at the heart of political controversy and the dominating feature of the nation's public life.

Towards the end of Nixon's first term the country was presented with a most explicit and remarkable demonstration of the ascendancy of the White House over Congress in an area peculiarly Congress's own – the budget. In the weeks preceding its pre-election adjournment in October 1972 the House of Representatives, with the chairman of its Ways and Means Committee, Wilbur Mills, actively approving, voted by 221 to 163 to give the President authority to impose a $250 billion ceiling on expenditure in the current fiscal year. What this meant was that the President would have power to cut at will any programmes already approved by Congress which would in his judgement push the budget past this limit. As near as made no difference this would make the federal budget an entirely executive document. In the event the measure did not pass, but only because the Senate, by a stubborn vote, defended the House from the consequences of its own weakness. But the presidential success in breaching this constitutional barrier emboldened the Secretary of the Treasury to affirm that the President would still withhold funds 'under his basic constitutional powers' that would carry expenditure past the $250 billion mark.

No doubt this reflected Congress's own refusal to put its house in order, to correlate, without presidential bullying, income and expenditure. But this only etched more sharply the general picture of an essentially old-fashioned, negatively conceived legislature facing an increasingly streamlined and positively-minded executive. In home affairs sectional pressures might force a president to accede to congressional demands; in particular any presidential programme requiring new legislation remained dependent on congressional endorsement. But wherever the heavy and, pervasive influence of foreign affairs and national defence was felt it was the presidency, as the agency of action, that made the running. And the power of the purse, over and over again, has proved itself a blunt and often a broken instrument for the control of policy. No longer is it the executive which wishes to spend and the legislature which wishes to save the taxpayers' money. With roles reversed, the shaping power of expenditure passes into the executive's hands and Congress is left largely impotent to control what finally happens to its appropriations. It may pass resolutions, but the President can bend or ignore them. And in the battle for the public will, the battle which finally decides the day, the President has overwhelming advantages.

THE 'IMAGE'

In *Courage and Hesitation: Inside the Nixon Administration*, Allen Drury describes a debate among Nixon's public relations advisers about the timing of the President's annual message, to Congress, on the State of the Union. Should it be at the time-hallowed hour of noon, or in the evening when it would reach the largest television audience? The issue was hardly in doubt, but interest attaches to the arguments used for the later hour – that 'the idea was to strengthen the President's image and help him get re-elected' – this less than two months after his first election was concluded. No longer is the prime concern the securing of congressional support for a programme. The object of victory is – another victory. And the instrument of victory is not a record of performance but the image of a performer. This is indeed 'pure' presidential politics, pure form purged of content, purely presidential, with the other branches of government brought in, if at all, in a purely supporting role.

There is now ample testimony to the role played in presidential elections by the new, or at any rate the newly preponderant techniques of public relations, advertising, market research, etc. What has happened is that a number of different factors have come together to produce a total effect greater than the sum of the parts, since each energizes the others. Thus the development of the new technology of television (a) obliges the candidate to think more than ever about the superficialities of appearance; (b) brings in its trail its whole world of market-research which, whatever the disparities between its pretensions and its real dependability, impinges on the planning of campaigning and the making of policies in a tremendously powerful way; (c) adds enormously to the cost of campaigning, just as market research adds to the cost of what one might call pre-campaigning; (d) relieves the candidate of a good deal of dependence upon party, since it enables him to go directly to the voter – this at a time when the party is already being weakened by a number of other factors; and (e) because television is a one-way medium to a degree that not even the most contrived public meeting can ever be, it further insulates the candidate from the structure of 'working politics', from the 'working' politician and administrator and, above all, from the voter.

Owing to Nixon's ineradicable charmlessness, the television camera has as yet been denied a full opportunity to show what it can do, not only in a formal election campaign but also in that continuous campaign which a president wages from his own first inauguration to his successor's. So the peak effect of these factors has yet to be seen. But certain consequences for the working of the presidency are quite evident. In the first place, it is now enormously more expensive than ever before to seek the presidency of the United States. It was estimated in 1968 to have cost 30 million dollars to elect Nixon. Estimates for 1972 run as high as 42 million dollars.

What is perhaps most important here is the money that has to be found in the pre-nomination stages, before a candidate has his party's backing – and the increment incidentally that this adds to the advantages already enjoyed by every incumbent vis-à-vis any challenger. Secondly, there is the extent to which this costly pre-convention contest relieves the candidate of dependence on his party – or, to put it the other way round, obliges him to seek an independent following and constituency of his own. Thirdly there is the new importance which this pursuit of the electronic vote – 'electronic' meaning 'computerized' as well as 'televiewed' – gives to a new kind of political animal, the denizen of the world of commercial television and advertising. With politics as administration, as dealing with actual people and real conflicts of interest, this type of image-monger has nothing to do. The old politics of the boss and the machine might be corrupt, but at least it was corrupt in a real world. In theory of course these image-mongers could be kept in their place as mere technicians. In fact they not only win places next to the throne but use their position and their skills to influence ends as much as means. It is unnecessary to itemize the ex-employees of J. Walter Thompson who man the White House staff of Richard Nixon and whose power extends to every aspect of the presidential operations. Although the trade of public relations is not unrepresented in Congress and in the party organizations, the typical congressman, like the typical party professional, is a different type of public official entirely.

Were the presidential office mainly concerned with domestic affairs, as historically and 'normally' it has been, this new potency of the 'image' and the arts of manipulation and merchandising would still have major consequences. But these consequences are enormously heightened by the fact that ever since 1960, at the very least, foreign affairs have dominated the attention both of presidents and of the electorate. Foreign affairs are an area in which the disposition and sometimes the necessity to 'trust the man at the controls' is much greater. The much-bruited 'loneliness' of the presidency is never so evident as here. Constitutionally it is an area in which the President enjoys exceptional licence. 'The conduct of foreign relations is executive altogether' said Thomas Jefferson, in days far less imperative than ours. The claim does not go undisputed but in the disputes it is the President who generally has the last word. He can always claim that he alone 'knows' what national security requires, that he has an ultimate custody of the *salus populi*. Moreover, the issues are such as cut across the usual party lines, lines which are constructed around domestic issues. Foreign affairs are consequently ideal raw material for the construction of that supra-party consensus of which, as we have seen, most modern presidents aspire to be the architects.

Thus the presidency is coming to detach itself from the rest of the American constitutional system. Its incumbents arrive at the White House by a route totally different from that which the framework of the Constitution conceived or from that which the American party system encouraged. They are neither the 'notables' of early years, the excellent chosen by the wise, nor the tried and tested veterans of party warfare. Modern media of communication enable the candidate – and still more the incumbent-candidate – to by-pass all the party workers and make his appeal direct to the people themselves and derive whatever he claims to be his mandate from the same all-sufficient source.

In office the President has, of course, to cope with the two great power groupings whose existence is largely independent of his favour or frown, Congress and the bureaucracy. But in the strongly-manned White House he has his own palace guard who can gather the lines of bureaucratic control into their own hands and so escape most of those devices of review and investigation that Congress employs against the regular departments. The President becomes, not just the head of the executive, but an executive within the executive, one moreover far better equipped for fast, consistent, well-publicized and irreversible action. As such he is responsible for much of the time to no-one, save God and the electorate – and the latter only once every four years. Congress, it is true, has not yielded any power to him directly. But in a changed America and a changed world, it finds itself most of the time simply by-passed. It no longer effectively controls the vast budget of modern American government, and the new range of governmental action depends much less on legislation than the old. The semi-permanent condition of foreign war and crisis demotes the legislators and up-grades the Commander-in-Chief. So, for all its ostensible independence, Congress counts for less and less while the President, focus of all eyes, permanent steersman of a restless tiller, manipulator of news and image, counts for more and more.

But the President, in winning freedom from these constitutional trammels, has also incurred a new set of risks. The power he does not have to share is also the blame which he cannot evade. More fatally, from the point of view of the public weal, the independence which he enjoys gives him a power which many will find alarming in a system where no well-organized rival party, no HM Opposition, exists to hold him to accountability. Most hazardous of all, however, is the risk that independence won and maintained by such means as I have been describing may insulate its beneficiary from contact with the real world outside the portals of the White House. Since he is a monarch, his critics can rarely meet him as equals; since he lives outside the legislature he does not have to engage in debate; since he is supra-party he does not have to defer to the demands which such a living political organism would make on him; since he is surrounded by a court of his own choosing he cannot guarantee that he will be told unpleasant truths; since he is himself an image and depends on images he is exposed to constant and insidious pressures to confuse appearance and reality. It is bad enough if he deceives the people, but it is far worse if the President deceives himself.

Vivian Vale

The Collaborative Chaos of Federal Administration

> At this moment in our history, most Americans have concluded that government is not performing well. It promises much, but it does not deliver what it promises. The great danger, in my judgement, is that this momentary disillusionment with government will turn into a more profound and lasting loss of faith.

THUS PRESIDENT NIXON TO CONGRESS ON 25 MARCH 1971, IN HIS message on the subject of governmental reorganization. Intended, like all such communications, to reach beyond his official audience, it nevertheless did not fail to have some sympathetic resonance on Capitol Hill itself when the Senate Committee on Government Operations later went to work upon the specific measures Nixon was proposing. Senator McClellan, the committee's chairman, took the opportunity to conduct a brief *tour d'horizon* of the federal bureaucracy. Over the past twenty years, he pointed out, cabinet departments had increased in number from nine to twelve and the major independent agencies from twenty-seven to forty-one. The federal budget had risen from $42b. to above $225b. and there were now over 2·8 m federal employees. 'The executive branch', he observed, 'is now the largest and most complicated enterprise in the world, with more than 1,400 domestic programmes distributed among 150 separate departments, agencies, bureaux and boards.' The moral he drew: 'There is perhaps no time in history when it has been more important to evaluate governmental effectiveness.'

So much we could have learned from any up-to-date primer on United States government. Between its covers the executive is seen spreading out in a series of circles, not all of them concentric, from the chief executive himself through the departments, the executive agencies independent of them, the so-called regulatory agencies seemingly independent of almost everybody except Congress, into a peripheral twilight where public responsibilities shade off into private. The student need hardly consult the US Government

Organization Manual in order to be made aware of a vast managerial universe whereof, if the President be the sun, the farthest bodies at times appear to be rushing away from him with the speed of light. Viewed more prosaically and in terms of domestic function only, a variety of agencies, offices, commissions and administrations, their titles a taxonomic nightmare, offer the consumer a smorgasbord of economic and social services.

As long ago as 1887 Woodrow Wilson remarked that it was becoming harder to run a constitution than to frame one. Yet an administrative system may become huge without becoming *ipso facto* unmanageable, provided only that its more important components do not develop as independent bases of power. General chaos will not ensue merely because, say, the Corregidor-Bataan Memorial Commission or the Alaska Field Committee occasionally decides to go its own sweet way. As John W. Gardner, former Secretary of Health, Education and Welfare (HEW – itself a mammoth among civil departments) put it to the Senate committee aforesaid: 'We are stuck with bigness. The critical question is how we manage bigness, how we devolve authority to lower levels, how we force our big institutions to remain responsive, how we prevent them from smothering individuality and creativity.'

The sentiments are unimpeachable: the difficulties, alas, seem as intractable as ever. The American quest for administrative salvation has always had to take account of a Madisonian system of fragmented power. Monistic problems have to be solved under pluralistic conditions where the actors are powerful and numerous – not simply the President, his cabinet and the committees of Congress, but bureaucratic programme managers, the agencies and their exigent clientèles. In the sight of many, administration will always remain merely adjunctive to the political process whereby benefits are allocated among competing groups and persons. Three present-day circumstances, however, are novel.

One is the widespread conviction that administration can be truly effective only if it operates simultaneously at different heights of the pyramid that slopes from the presidency down to the 92,000 tax-levying units of the USA. Bureaucratic control there has never approximated to the Weberian 'monocratic' model, and devolution of federally defined and funded programmes to subnational levels has indeed been found regularly requisite since the early New Deal. But during the 1960s and 1970s it has become altogether unprecedented in extent and volume.

Secondly, the benefits for which contemporary America – must we not christen it 'the expectant society'? – looks to Washington are not homogeneous but multiple, classified only for convenient brevity under the overarching categories of environmental and human resources. Delivery requires a high degree of collaboration between departments and agencies, and this is not easy to achieve within a power system as fractionalized as the American. Nixon was simply pointing out that expectations are outrunning the existing means to fulfil them.

Thirdly, considerations of administrative technique must nowadays run in harness with the democratic ethic. This again is in itself not new. Earlier this century Herbert Croly and his fellow progressives, rejecting the Wilsonian doctrine of a purely 'neutral' administration, were ready enough to attribute the short-comings of political democracy to the incompetence and depravity of those who implemented it. But today's young Americans proclaim a crisis of values. Administrative parlance is of 'missions' as often as of programmes; 'public choice' is the watchword and 'citizen participation' a moral imperative. There seems at any rate little immediate danger of American government's becoming, in Stephen K. Bailey's metaphor, an iceberg – cold, largely hidden, and impenetrable. Rather, the federal administration is a warm and luxuriant jungle which the foreign non-specialist enters at his peril. A brief expedition such as this can penetrate its fringes at a few points of a few sectors only (domestic affairs, for example, but not foreign), and even so must rely heavily upon native surveyors for maps and guides.

THE EXECUTIVE OFFICE OF THE PRESIDENT

We are given as axiomatic that the forces prevailing within the executive branch are centrifugal. It contains many power centres and loyalties are divided, certain of its units appearing at times like foster-children whose legal custody must be perpetually contested with Congress. We take to be equally self-evident that as a centralizing counterforce the President is unique. He alone has the entire nation for his constituency; and, insofar as the branch of government he heads must provide for national needs, the executive ought in its policy-making to be a microcosmic reflection of the whole society. The Executive Office of the President, it is argued, must therefore be so designed as to afford him a view of the country's prime concerns from above the timberline of administration. It is illogical as it is regrettable that the President cannot obtain from Congress the unrestricted freedom to mould his own Executive Office and to manage its staff so as best to suit his own personal style of operation. No less plenary an authority is deemed essential to the policy-making responsibility he carries.

Pending this freedom to restructure, some changes within the Executive Office have been recommended. It lacks – so its critics complain – any agency charged with the study of emerging public problems, especially in the nowadays all-important fields of social and environmental policy where capacity for general planning is essential. By the time any sense of need for action has percolated through, circumstances have changed. It possesses no organ for the collation and analysis of what might be called social indicators comparable to the economic indicators available through the President's Council of Economic Advisers. A parallel body, to be denominated his Council of Social Advisers, was not long ago proposed by Senator Walter Mondale in a so-called 'Full Opportunity' bill. And when policy has once been determined, the line of command needful for securing execution runs anything but firmly. Lacking the means for adequate surveillance of an executive itself highly federalized, a reforming President may encounter almost as much difficulty in getting what he wants from his own branch of government as from the legislative. Staff competence within the Executive Office (so its critics allege) for studying and recommending structural reform also needs strengthening. Yet the very size of departmental staff is determined not by the President but Congress. Again, the President possesses no policy-tracking station and only a very poor retrieval system. To find out what schemes are gestating in the bureaux and agencies he must grope rather than prod. What weapons of coercion, as distinct from cajolery or bargaining, lie to his hand – such as authority to fire – are at best politically dangerous to wield when the agency head under scrutiny is *persona grata* on Capitol Hill.

For bringing collaboration out of executive chaos, reliance has come to be placed *faute de mieux* upon two main devices. Both have of late been coming in for criticism as having been carried to excess. The first is the interdepartmental committee (statutory or *ad hoc*) with examples of which the Executive Office is seen to abound. A variation or mutation of this is the 'lead agency' device, whereby representatives from other agencies congregate under the head of the department most relevant to the subject in hand. Indispensable though such bodies are found to be, native critics have not spared their alleged defects. They obscure responsibility by diffusing it; they create, by layering, an infinite regress of delegation; and, since their efficacy depends on continuous agreement, they are peculiarly vulnerable to any lapse of consensus among the collaborators.

The second co-ordinating agent whose over-extension is complained of is the presidential adviser or White House assistant. The President's personal entourage, drawn upon when 'task forces' are constituted, has grown in numbers more rapidly than his institutional staff, and not without comment. If powerful and prominent (it is said) the personal assistant may come between his master and essential contacts. If anonymous and weak, a courtier not a privy councillor, he will be got round. If a president institutionalizes such advisers too greatly they become a kind of sub-government and the object of jealousy from the line bureaucrats.[1] If he does not, they may lack the necessary staff to be effective. If he relies on them too heavily and often, he has created a rival or super cabinet and runs the risk of over-centralizing decision taking in the White House, thereby raising conflicts with cabinet secretaries and key legislators. Whatever the contingency, one thing remains certain. A president's relationship to the executive cannot be one of insulation or autonomy, but of unremitting attention and involvement.

OFFICE OF MANAGEMENT AND BUDGET

For the last fifty years the President's chief organ of central planning, co-ordination and financial control has been the Bureau of the Budget, in 1970 reorganized as the Office of Management and Budget (OMB). All money-spending units of the federal executive must clear their legislative proposals with its Director and his division of legislative reference (some dozen specialists). Since 1950, we are told, the Bureau's work has markedly shifted away from orthodox budgetary review towards programme planning and evaluation, and the format of its recommendations from 'object' budgeting to 'performance' budgeting. For tackling the resource problems raised by increasingly complicated external demands, responsibility rests with its newly-created Office of Executive Management. The Bureau can also draw to good effect upon the cognate skills of such bodies as the Council of Economic Advisers and the Office of Science and Technology.

Central legislative clearance in the executive branch has long been recognized as one of the President's most powerful tools for fashioning his general policy and of vital importance to executive leadership in Congress. From the Bureau's output, too, the legislature takes its cue as to its committees' probable workload – what items the President sees as the most important, as well as where Congress may encounter a veto. Budget, indeed, has acquired such institutional momentum that Eisenhower, who in 1953 had not intended to present Congress with any legislative package, found himself willy-nilly the recipient of his Budget Director's.[2] Of late, however, a President's quest for speed in getting his programmes to the starting line has also been producing a perceptible shift of gravity in their initiation. During the 1960s the Bureau of the Budget's virtual monopoly over central clearance of proposals emanating from the executive branch, formalized under Eisenhower, suffered palpable erosion under his two Democratic successors. Neither Kennedy nor Johnson, it seems, found the bureaucracy either apt or swift to supply all the ideas and advice required for the major legislative programmes he had in mind. The Bureau's functions were therefore significantly augmented, and in some degree usurped, by presidential agents charged with direct intervention in the central clearance process. A congressional liaison office was set up in the White House to operate closely with each cabinet secretary in an attempt to expedite the new omnibus programmes by early collaboration at the highest level. Sometimes the development of legislative proposals under Johnson involved direct communication between the White House and agency heads, which in its quest for ever shorter deadlines bypassed the line bureaucrats.

In bulk, the great majority of legislative proposals still come 'welling up' from the agencies. Of the 16,000 or so requests vetted annually by the OMB, possibly 80–90 per cent have run the normal hierarchical gauntlet for clearance. Of the 300 bills which the Department of Housing and Urban Development (HUD) proposed for a single recent legislative session, most had originated in agencies and other bodies lying within its own departmental orbit and responsive to their respective clientèle groups. Yet clearance of that small minority of legislative items singled out to receive the President's personal attention may often be expedited by agents or task forces in the White House, where under Johnson (we are told) Joseph Califano's office became 'the command post for directing the Great Society campaign'.[3] And under Nixon more of the White

House staff appear to be allocated to this work. When John Ehrlichman succeeded Califano as presidential assistant, he received also the title of executive director of a newly-established Domestic Council – functionally, the cabinet minus its state and defence components – whose staff continued the short-circuiting of OMB on behalf of a small number of proposals accorded high priority. If the OMB's Director remains presidentially oriented and officially charged by Nixon with 'evaluating' proposals, some of the latter now escape his net.

At the same time, much-publicized efforts have been and are being made to heighten the Office's technical efficiency. For some years past it has been the favoured centre for experimentation with systems analysis and other 'scientific' management tools. And now the cost-benefit men, too, have entered the game. In August 1965 President Johnson announced that the planning-programming-budgeting system (PPBS) already in use in the Defence Department under McNamara, would be officially extended to all domestic agencies of the federal government. Through this innovation, hailed by some as a fiscal renaissance, it was hoped that the same techniques heretofore applied when allocating $80b. annually for defence purposes could with advantage be employed to achieve a more rational distribution of about half that sum between 'soft' programmes such as health, education, welfare, civil manpower, community development and housing. Coupled to the five-year budgetary projection, PPBS was expected to yield more exact fore-casting of, and tighter control over, programme costs and impacts. And if, argued its advocates, PPBS could lead to better decisions as to what agencies proposed to Congress, would it not correspondingly improve Congress's ability to evaluate such proposals?

Application of the new system has since been proceeding, by means of OMB directives, rather unevenly. Some units of administration have developed quite sophisticated programmes while others give the appearance of still struggling to comply. The consequences have been, and are still being, vigorously debated. PPBS has occupied numerous congressional hearings.[4] Professional societies have devoted much space in their journals, and much time at their annual conventions, to canvassing its alleged merits and demerits. The verdict cannot fail to provide interest for British students if, as has long been rumoured, certain Whitehall departments and a number of our local authorities have been venturing along much the same lines.[5]

It seems clear that gains have not been uniformly great. Many of the Johnson programmes were conceived and applied with dramatic haste, and short-term considerations played havoc with orderly planning. The financial exigencies of Vietnam made a shambles of priorities. The new strategic weapons system is only one reason why between one-third and one-half of the United States budget is annually earmarked for defence. Moreover, PPBS was introduced very abruptly into civilian agencies, with practically no opportunity for controlled experiment, adequate data bases or technical assistance. Prior experience in the Defence Department was not fully exportable. How does one express in civilian terms the benefit expected to accrue from the concentration of a given fire-power upon a specified target? Indeed the difficulties of measuring 'benefit', being conceptual as well as operational, are formidable; and each administrative unit involved in a programme pursues its own subjective evaluation, which may elude the tools of the PPB analyst. The latter has therefore been slow to develop the kinds of output measurement which would show the government what it is getting for its money.

Midway through 1968 the Bureau of the Budget, reviewing the results of PPBS in sixteen federal domestic agencies, concluded that it had not affected their planning efficiency to an equally significant degree. In the following year a management consultant firm, McKinsey & Co. Inc., employed by the Bureau to design an 'integrated system development effort', drew attention to serious defects and shortcomings that PPBS had not removed. The Senate's subcommittee on Government Operations, though chiefly concerned with national security, spoke of 'exaggerated hopes'. The general verdict seems to be that the new techniques have enabled planning proposals to be put forward in a form more readily intelligible to professional administrators but have not led to improvement in the content of what is proposed. Better means of inter-agency planning do not of themselves strengthen the will for co-operation among the planners. For these reasons PPBS has not been as effective a presidential staff tool as was hoped. Nixon, it seems, has quietly deformalized the system. By an OMB circular of June 1971, agencies are no longer required to submit multi-year programmes and financing plans in detail, with concomitant analytical studies, though they must be prepared to furnish forward estimates upon request and should provide supporting memoranda. Under the brand new name of Programme Planning and Evaluation (PPE),

PPB techniques are still used but the PPBS superstructure has apparently been abandoned.

THE DEPARTMENTS

Looking across from his lonely desk, the President sees an inner ring of twelve cabinet secretaries. Of their departments, some are criticized as too sprawling and heterogeneous (HEW, for instance, whose budget is five times the size of any other civilian agency's); some as too small and clientèle-ridden (Agriculture, Commerce, HUD) or too inbred (State); some as too compartmentalized (Labour); and one at least, the Post Office, is confessedly miscast as a department at all. The need for general remodelling is widely accepted. That internal reorganization is feasible and effectual McNamara demonstrated at Defence. But, tinkering apart, is any general therapy for the cabinet system possible?

One of Nixon's first moves was to establish a centre for the continuous long-range study of executive organization. The President's Advisory Council on the Reorganization of the Executive Branch was established in 1969 – the first such body since the second Hoover Commission began work in 1953 – to undertake an organization-and-management study by task forces under the general chairmanship of the president (Roy L. Ash) of a big private industry. The outcome of their labours was seen in January 1971, when Nixon's state-of-the-Union address envisaged reducing the number of cabinet departments from twelve to eight and regrouping them around 'the great purposes of government', so as better to 'focus and concentrate the responsibility for getting problems solved'. Assuming the transfer of the Post Office's functions to a public corporation, as provided for in 1970, and leaving State, Defence, Treasury and Justice as they are, the President was proposing that the functions of the remaining departments should be re-sorted under four new heads: Natural Resources, Human Resources, Economic Development and Community Development. The last-named would embrace all of the present HUD and some functions of the present HEW, Transportation, Commerce, Agriculture, the Office of Economic Opportunity and one or two other agencies.

Politically the White House has much at stake. One incumbent's 'Great Society' may turn out to be his successor's 'welfare mess'. Yet the chief executive's authority (periodically extended) to propose reorganization of his own branch was restricted nearly a

decade ago when Congress reduced the scope of the Reorganization
Act of 1946. To create or abolish departments (as distinct from
agencies, etc.) now requires special legislation, which so far has not
been forthcoming. A more modest presidential request a few years
back for the merging of Labour and Commerce was turned down,
and proposals for hiving-off a Department of Education from the
present massive HEW have not travelled very far. Once again
events emphasize the President's dependence upon Congress for
leave to devise institutional changes of any consequence. If he does
not receive its approval in respect of his own Executive Office, *a
fortiori* he would seem unlikely to be given a free hand to restructure
the departmental system.

Yet such remodelling is the indispensable precondition for coping
with the wide programmatic base of the kind of planning nowadays
expected from Washington, for this alone could ensure the necessary
intra-departmental flexibility and variety of structure. Thus, the
plight of the cities engages HUD with its special concern for urban
housing; but also Commerce because cities vitally affect economic
development; and HEW, of whose titular services they are a
principal focus; and Agriculture, inasmuch as city dwellers are chief
consumers, and the Interior since they are also the most numerous
clientèle for natural resources. Nixon's proposals have been ap-
plauded as splitting up the present ossified demarcations without
sacrificing the benefit of composite planning essential to multiple
programmes. It is also urged that departmental restructuring should
include some apparatus for amplifying the Secretary's voice in
legislative proposals, budgeting aggregates, and the principal
personnel appointments. Yet how, ask the doubters, can his managerial responsibilities and those of the more important agency heads
be enhanced without stifling the initiative and discretion of subordinate bureaux, where so many proposals for reform have their
genesis?

Administrative rigidity, one must add, is no less evident in the
extra-departmental agencies. Many of these are memorials to
problems long dead. Their members none the less display a lively
esprit de corps and apprehension of job security. Mr Justice William O.
Douglas once proposed that this problem of bureaucratic ageing
might be reduced by dissolving every agency after ten years of life.
Yet these creatures, sometimes fiefs, of Congress possess a high
resistance to mortality.

DEVOLUTION AND DECENTRALIZATION

So far our test of institutional performance has applied a kind of spot-checking to the central organs, pure if not simple, of federal administration. It is now time to turn to the scarcely less important, and certainly no less controversial, topic of Washington's inter-action with the states and their subdivisions.

The ground for dispute is a rapidly changing landscape. Gone are the days when progressive states pioneered programmes which would later be emulated nationally. The federal-state sharing ushered in by the Social Security Act of 1935 has so grown that today there is something of Washington in virtually every one of the nation's major public programmes, federal activities overlapping with state and local. The product of these shared and interpenetrating activities is often likened, in culinary metaphor, to a marble or rainbow cake as distinct from a layer cake, baked according to cook-books variously entitled dual federalism, co-operative federalism, creative federalism, and now Nixon's new federalism. Be the recipe what it may, Senator Muskie is not alone in observing that intergovernmental relations constitute nowadays in their totality a veritable fourth branch of United States government.

Can one generalize about these relationships as distinct from merely describing them in action? The one factor common to all multi-level programmes – whether described as New Deal, Fair Deal, New Frontier or Great Society – is obviously the vertical downflow of funds; so obviously that one cynic has been moved to define public planning as 'anything there are federal grants in aid of'.

Yet to almost any goal of social policy there exists a choice of roads. A new programme may be set to run through one or more existing federal bodies (as the latter themselves will probably favour). Or (as the White House often prefers) through a newly-created or reorganized agency. Or (if it is not desired to swell the army of bureaucrats) through the government's sponsoring or treating with a private concern – government by contract, its critics call it – in the expectation that it will be healthily imbued with the profit motive. Along this third course Washington effaces itself by stages, from semi-governmental bodies (COMSAT) through officially sponsored private concerns (the Federal National Mortgage Association) to the independent, non-profit corporation of which RAND is the classic example. Of all research conducted by American private industry nearly two-thirds (we are told) is subsidized from federal funds. Certain goals – 'environmental quality' is one – are of such width as to require a number of departmental avenues to be travelled simultaneously: yet the wider a programme's scope the less it is anyone's particular baby and the harder it is to raise money for. Research follows the dollar. As to implementation, the more decentralized the structure the better the chance of access for its beneficiaries and, hopefully, the more responsive their co-operation. A working party of the American Society for Public Administration not long ago recommended that federal guidelines for certain domestic programmes – model cities and neighbourhood centres were two of them – should include a section 'requiring' the participation of beneficiary groups. The term 'citizen participation', however, has of late acquired overtones of rather unpleasantly militant parochialism. A range of choice, too, is available in funding methods. Federal subsidy may go to the state treasury – as in the postwar federal airport programme – at some risk of distorting the state budget or of becoming cramped within the rigidity of state boundaries and state constitutions. Or it may go direct to the city or locality, at the political risk involved in bypassing the governor and his assembly. The subsidy may be earmarked for a particular class of citizen (federal food stamps) or for a particular geographic region (the Appalachians, for instance). The grant may be categorical or allow for a high degree of local discretion. The theoretically perfect programme selects its methods of planning, funding and implementing from these abundant options so as to ensure that Washington, state and locality work as truly interdependent parts of a system and not as individual competitors in some grand game of grantsmanship.

In practice however – as soon became evident – the patchwork quilt of federal programmes so quickly run up in the 1960s was inadequately planned and very loosely woven. At very few points was the Great Society designed to any sort of template or subjected to rigorous fitting and cutting. Billions of dollars (so its detractors complain) were laid out in a process of trial and error conducted through units of administration which proliferated alarmingly. The government had to hand, indeed, two pertinent reports surviving from the previous decade – of the Kestnbaum Commission on Intergovernmental Relations (1953–55) and from the Joint Federal-State Action Committee (1957–59). But neither of those bodies had accepted as axiomatic the need for genuine sharing of functions between centre and circumference, and both inclined rather towards minimization of activities at the federal level. President Johnson therefore convoked a further Advisory Committee on Intergovernmental Relations which laboured in conjunction with the corresponding subcommittee of Senate over the same area. In November 1966, sternly warning departmental heads that 'more is needed than money alone', the President set in train reforms which were consolidated two years later in the Intergovernmental Co-operation Act of 1968. Briefly, this strives to ensure that federal aid be given to units of general local government rather than to special-purpose units; that such aid be related strictly to the expressed objectives of state, regional and local comprehensive planning; and that the governors and their legislatures be kept fully informed of what aid is coming.

The consolidating tone of this measure was quickly picked up by Nixon. In February 1969 he created by executive order the Office of Intergovernmental Relations (OIR) and placed it within his Executive Office under the general supervision of his Vice-President. To Agnew has in fact been delegated responsibility for quite a number of the present government's domestic functions: but it is too early to predict whether this departure signifies a new and worthwhile role for semi-employed vice-presidents. Meanwhile the role of the OIR is to promote better working relationships among state and local officials (including mayors and county officers) and between them and key federal personnel. To this end the Office provides a 'listening and liaison service', sponsors regular consultations both vertical and horizontal, and serves as a clearing house for recurrent intergovernmental problems.

The OIR itself undertakes no funding. But it upholds the now fashionable principle that the disbursement of federal aid should as far as possible be at the discretion of the recipients. Plans for some kind of block allocation from centre to circumference, first advanced by the then chairman of the Council of Economic Advisers and further shaped during 1964 by a Johnsonian task force, have lately matured under the title of revenue-sharing. As one of the 'six great goals' of domestic policy unveiled by Nixon in his state of the Union address of January 1971, revenue-sharing was proffered as a 'revolutionary' new policy which would infallibly ensure the most appropriate fiscal balance within the federal structure at any given juncture. Turning back federal money among the states with minimal restrictions as to its employment would be, claimed Nixon, the means 'to rescue the states and localities from the brink of financial crisis' and to make government responsive to the people by broadening the locus of financial power downward.

The appropriate measure, in his eyes one of the most important among the 170 pieces of legislation the new President submitted to the first session of the 91st Congress, has recently reached the statute book as the Fiscal Assistance Act of 1972. It proposes to return $30b. of federal revenues over the next five years to states and localities, in the proportions of one- and two-thirds respectively, which will themselves determine within half-a-dozen broad categories how it shall be spent. Particular advantage is expected to accrue to fifteen states and the District of Columbia under an allocation formula devised by the House so as to benefit the most populous areas of the nation. The same measure sets an annual limit of $2·5b. on federal matching grants for specified state and local social service programmes.

It remains to notice one other recent institutional attempt at developing something of the federal presence and powers into the country at large – the new Federal Regional Councils. Here again, a contrivance first tried out in the waning days of the Johnson Administration has been taken further under his successor. By an executive order of March 1969 the latter established ten of these Councils, sited them in large cities, and linked them centrally to the OMB as the body most concerned with programme unification. Thus collaboration is to supersede chaos, as the Federal Regional Councils act as midwives in the smooth delivery to each area of the federal resources that sustain it. Council members – mostly regional directors from the cabinet departments – are at hand not to compete but to co-operate with agency mechanisms already busy in each area with child care, model cities, manpower planning, etc. They are to facilitate mutual discussion or bargaining on the spot, and to preserve contact with Washington headquarters. Some commentators view the regional council contrivance as too weak. But OMB, though deeply committed to the experiment, is rightly cautious about creating a presidentially-controlled, 'supra-programmatic' authority or prefectorial corps in the teeth of the Senator or Congressman's natural jealousy for his own constituency patronage. So the only effective means of federal coercion remains a clumsy one – the threat of withholding funds from unresponsive or 'no-go' localities. Yet here is a new approach to decentralization which may prove to have avoided the worst disadvantages of pluralism.

THE POLITICAL CONTEXT

Organization is never neutral in its effect on policy, and the foreign observer will not presume to contradict American political scientists when they claim that insufficient attention has been paid to the policy role and institutional behaviour of the federal administration, in contrast with that given to Congress. Nevertheless, it is obviously vain to pronounce on the performance of administrative institutions *per se* without regard to the political environment they must operate in, and which Congress so largely determines. True, the executive branch itself does not lack the internal politics observable within any system enveloping many power bases. The relationship between planning and politics, always very uneasy, is the harder to stabilize where, as in the USA, the planning branch of government itself reflects the pluralism of the national scene.

Even so, there is no dodging the conclusion that the biggest threat to good national administration comes from executive-legislative rivalry. This rivalry may be reduced but not eliminated, for it is built into the present American system. One must remember that the surveillance congressional committees exercise is a statutory one. The Legislative Reorganization Act of 1946 specifically laid on them the duty to 'exercise continuous watchfulness of the executive'; and each House has its Committee on Government Operations. Tactically a committee can paralyse an agency through extended investigation and hearings: strategically it may emasculate an agency's administrative vigour by insisting (as in the case of the Interstate Commerce Commission) that its membership be large and that its chairmanship should frequently rotate. The need to make a programme saleable to Congress may seriously detract from the relevance of its content and the usefulness of its scope and design. To what agency a programme is then allocated may be a political decision, as is the level at which it shall be funded. To the administrator, the legislature's budgetary cuts may appear almost arbitrary, sometimes merely a symbolic assertion of Congress's authority. Certainly it is difficult in these circumstances to regard budgeting as a rational analytic process. Rather, the Congress may here seem to act as a kind of vehicular weighing checkpoint, imposing its load maxima from purely partisan considerations. This blemish no amount of technical sophistication on the part of OMB can remove. The legislator is bound to see PPBS, or any other system of cost-benefit analysis, as fraught with peril to his constituency's favourite programmes. Indeed, the more objectively efficient the basis of fiscal scrutiny, the bigger the political threat to him.

Only one generalization can safely be made. Congress will usually be set to defend existing patterns of resource allocation, and in so doing its committees will find allies in the relevant bureaux and their clientèle groups. The existing way of doing business, whatever it may be, will always be the most satisfying to a number of strategically placed legislators, certain agencies and certain lobbies. The impact of congressional scrutiny on federal administration is therefore likely to be highly conservative. As each programme is established it rapidly acquires political self-interest and becomes vulnerable to political manipulation in the quest for survival. And attempts by Washington to have its own agents co-ordinate the administering of it in the field will be resented by the legislator as cutting across his own channels of patronage. Naturally he sees himself as the watchdog for his own area, its constituents and pressure groups. When seeking their electoral support, his influence over the executive is something he is likely to make much of. Without doubt his authority to command information from a federal agency, coupled with his assured access to the media of public communication, gives him a powerful purchase. It is the ubiquitous, yet unsystematic and unpredictable, nature of such interventions that gives Congress, from the executive's viewpoint, its potential for trouble-making.

In fine, congressional oversight of administration may be counter-productive. So, in an attempt to stave off the worst havoc a congressional committee may wreak upon their programmes, administrators will try to safeguard themselves against the chairman's disfavour by going out to meet them. So far as possible, an atmosphere of openness and communicativeness will be encouraged, in which mutual consultation can proceed. Agencies seek to help Congressmen more effectively by establishing special legislative liaison staffs, who may maintain a reference service which will give them speedy information on request. Bureau budgeting officers are in frequent contact with their opposite numbers on the Appropriations Committees of both Houses, and there may be full-scale conferences between bureau chiefs and committee chairmen, with teams from both sides in attendance. It is generally understood that administrators will, however informally, 'pre-clear' their major proposals with the relevant sub-committee or at least its chairman. At its hearings the agency head will be a key witness, whether in public or *in camera*, whether on the President's behalf or his own. And the more he feels compelled to seek a particular *modus vivendi* with his inquisitors, the smaller the room left to him to collaborate in joint policy-making with his fellow bureaucrats. In all these ways the administrator finds himself willy-nilly drawn into playing a political role. The bureau chief must serve at least two masters. The closer he feels his answerability to Congress to be, the weaker the gravitational pull of the President, who in turn is the more often compelled to make trade-offs in order to save the substance of his policies.

One ray of hope the reformers see springs from the evergrowing number of representations which (we are told) Congressmen now receive, from local officials and from disappointed citizens, about the unsatisfactory impact of national welfare programmes. Since these complaints have much in common, it may be that they are beginning to constitute a new and generalized type of pressure which will tend to induce a common response from legislators in place of their former diversity of local attitudes. Or again, the present arbitrariness of legislators' interference in administration would be markedly diminished if the congressional party system were less free-wheeling and more tightly controlled. But that has been for decades part of the liberal's unrealized dream.

The federal executive, we are told,[6] maintains 4500 computers at an annual cost of nearly $2b. Yet technique and cash will not of themselves ensure that the nation's problems do not overwhelm it. All roads for administrative reform lead ultimately to Capitol Hill. Responsibility for supervising the federal administration is a joint one, to be shared reasonably between President and Congress. So long as only the former endeavours to exercise that responsibility in a planned and orderly fashion the administrative process will fail to deliver the goods it is capable of producing. Nixon is at least correct in pointing out the dangerously high correlation between dissatisfaction with federal services and disenchantment with the political system within which they operate. This credibility gap between promise and performance needs narrowing swiftly, and only Congressional reform can accomplish that. The sheer survival of the system today does not guarantee that it will be functional tomorrow.

John D. Lees

Reorganization and Reform in Congress – Legislative Responses to Political and Social Change

ANY ASSESSMENT OF THE PERFORMANCE AND VIABILITY OF THE contemporary Congress presents formidable problems. This is because criticism of Congress has been an almost constant feature of American political discussion, long before current political tensions produced wider comment on the institutional structure as a whole, and also because such an assessment must consider not only the existing capacity and will in Congress to respond to contemporary demands but also the nature of the relationship of Congress to other branches of government, and in particular to the executive. One further difficulty is that there has been, and remains, wide disagreement among observers as to the virtues and defects of Congress.

The roots of contemporary criticism can be traced back to the 1940s, when studies combining normative and descriptive comment[1] expressed serious concern as to whether Congress could discharge its responsibilities adequately. Interest in congressional reform has rarely flagged since, and the frustrations of President Kennedy with the Congresses of the early 1960s produced a rash of reformist writing, including studies by members of Congress,[2] while a study of a rather different kind bore the pessimistic title *Congress in Crisis*.[3] In a real sense Congress may be said to have been 'on trial' or 'in crisis' for a long time. This is not surprising, as David Truman pointed out in an introduction to a valuable collection of essays on Congress published in 1965,[4] since the 20th century has been hard on legislatures in Western democracies. Indeed, Congress has probably suffered less than most in terms of diminished authority, principally because its constitutional separateness has proved to be a considerable asset. While the practical consequences of a system of separate institutions sharing powers may have limited congressional adaptation to mid-20th century realities, the fact of formal separation has been crucial in maintaining Congress as a formidable political force and has permitted its members a high degree of autonomy in determining the role of Congress and the nature of its internal procedures and distribution of influence.

It is only perhaps in the last decade that these internal procedures and patterns of influence have been subject to detailed scrutiny by researchers who have, for the most part, sought to reveal how the Senate and the House of Representatives work rather than prescribe how they ought to work.[5] Consequently, more is now known about the workings of Congress than any other branch of American government, though this does not mean that in the wider sense it has become better understood, or its performance more expertly assessed.

John Saloma has indicated the problems involved in developing standards for evaluating congressional performance.[6] One obvious criterion is public attitudes towards, and evaluation of, Congress, but evidence here suggests that, while significant shifts in public attitudes towards specific political issues or policies can affect congressional behaviour, public evaluation of Congress is general, ambivalent and indirect. If it is at all specific it tends to be one of expecting Congress to co-operate with the President and expedite major features of his legislative programme, reflecting the influence on elite discussion in the early 1960s of the views and writings of the presidential-party responsibility school.[7] Other criteria include assessment of the effectiveness or efficiency of Congress, and its representativeness. Together these criteria provide the broad guidelines which have influenced contemporary analysis of Congress, whether such analysis is based on the presidential-responsible party, the presidential-pluralist, the constitutional balance, or the congressional supremacy models of how Congress should be organized and operate.[8]

Differences of opinion as to the performance of Congress are also related to different views as to what should be its functions. However, any realistic analysis must face two simple facts. Firstly, Congress is neither an arm of the President nor the first branch of government. It is, under the constitution, an equal and co-ordinate branch. Secondly, while suggestions for reform abound, internal changes likely to affect and possibly improve the performance of Congress will be determined by members of Congress themselves. Moreover, it must also be recognized that the basic question at issue is not whether Congress should be stronger than the President or vice-versa, but rather whether Congress can be strengthened to do the pressing work that falls to it to do and to what extent it is equipped to deal with basic problems. Congress remains a law-making body, and, as David Truman has indicated, the crucial test of Congress and of the federal government rests 'in the quality of its policy output in matters of basic consequence for the nation's welfare.'[9]

There is little doubt that important changes have taken place within Congress since the early 1960s, but disagreement exists as to their effect. One respected writer on Congress, Stephen Bailey, states that 'basic political, economic, and sociological change in the American society, and in the world at large, have finally forced a series of adjustments in the structure and role of Congress so profound as to merit the term "revolution"',[10] and that Congress in the 1960s was far more sensitive to the claims of black Americans and the needs of urban populations generally. Yet another equally respected observer affirms that 'Congress fails to address itself to the critical issues of our time. Bogged down by its own venality, it cannot affect the inequitable distribution of income. Bound down by racism, which is sustained by the seniority system, it has little capacity for correcting racial injustice. Distorted by a warped system of representation, it responds to wealth and power, not desperate need. Congress, powerful as it is in some respects, is, alas, nearly irrelevant where the burning issues of our time are concerned.'[11]

Accepting that honest men may differ in interpretation, and over what constitute 'the burning issues of our time', some assessment can be made of the context in which change has taken place in Congress, the general and specific nature of such changes, and of their implications for the capability of Congress to carry out its responsibilities.[12]

BASIC PROBLEMS OF ROLE-DEFINITION

There are both institutional and practical dilemmas in the search to find and maintain a role more or less consistent with public and constituency expectations and tolerable to most members of Congress. One recurring dilemma is the need for co-operation be-

tween the House and the Senate, especially over legislation, in a
practical situation which is often one of tension and rivalry. This is
best reflected in the difference between role-perceptions of most
Senators and most Representatives. The advantages of legislative
autonomy are weakened by the conflicting demands and attitudes
of its members over the respective roles of the House and the
Senate and the internal distribution of influence and authority
within both branches.

A major dilemma also emanated from the increase since 1933 in
executive initiative in formulating legislation, assigning legislative
priorities, and influencing the final content of legislation. What are
the consequences of this for an autonomous legislative body whose
legislative role has declined? One consequence, put starkly, is that
it can defend its autonomy only by refusing to legislate, and can
legislate only by surrendering its autonomy. When Congress holds
up legislation it is criticized, but it also risks criticism when, as in the
89th Congress (1965–66), it appears to acquiesce speedily and
passively with the legislative demands of the President. As Samuel
Huntington remarked; 'If Congress legislates, it subordinates itself
to the President; if it refuses to legislate, it alienates itself from public
opinion.'[13] One way out of such a dilemma is to opt out – to
concede the initiative in originating legislation and expand other
legitimate responsibilities. Such an alternative existed, given the
rapid growth in the size of the federal bureaucracy and the scope of
its activities. Thus an increasing interest has arisen in developing
resources to help facilitate the functions of investigation and information, with particular reference to oversight of administrative
activity. The extension of these responsibilities was not inconsistent
with prevailing public attitudes nor did it involve substantial organizational change, since it coincided with a growing dispersion
of power within Congress as expressed by the increase in the number
of committees, and the weakening of party and other sanctions.
These developments were encouraged, over time, by measures such
as the 1946 Legislative Reorganization Act. One consequence was
the growth and consolidation of the investigative role of Congress
in the 1940s and 1950s, another the increased autonomy within
Congress itself of committees and their chairmen and the institutionalization of the seniority system as the dominant criterion for determining committee chairmen and assigning members to committees.
The early 1960s revealed the real political effect of such developments
for legislative-executive relations, though they were not fully worked

out or necessarily permanent.

PATTERNS OF CHANGE IN THE 1960s

Some general perspective of the nature of change within Congress in the past decade can be seen by reference to the basic impression of Congress presented by many observers, partisan or otherwise, in the early 1960s. Though not necessarily a view which provoked intense public reaction, it was nevertheless influential and damning. It was broadly one of a highly unrepresentative Congress, both in its membership and internal power structure. Party leadership and cohesion was weak, and major decisions were heavily influenced by committees dominated by a group of senile, conservative Southern Democrats with safe seats who used a combination of the seniority system, their leadership positions in the committee structure, a shrewd knowledge of the rules and procedures and an ability to turn a complex and cumbersome legislative process to their advantage, to thwart the efforts of a liberal Democratic President to deal with the major problems facing the nation. In the Senate, decision-making was felt to be dominated by a senior establishment or inner club, largely controlled again by Southern Democrats. In committee decisions and in floor votes in the House and in the Senate, a bipartisan conservative coalition of many Republicans and Southern Democrats too often gained significant successes.

While this was never a wholly accurate description of the situation in Congress, its very simplicity, and the tacit support given to it by many liberal Democrats in Congress, made it a useful conventional wisdom for both partisan and reform argument. Indeed there was a core element of accuracy in the view, which intensive empirical research has partially supported as well as qualified.[14]

At the beginning of the 1970s the internal distribution of influence in the House and the Senate was undergoing considerable change. In a persuasive study of the Senate, Randall Ripley asserts that 'between 1945 and 1968 the Senate has transformed itself from a body in which principal legislative power resided in the chairmen and, to a lesser extent, the ranking minority members of the full standing committees, into a body in which significant legislative power is spread among virtually all Senators of both parties. This also means that the Senate has changed from a body in which most important legislative decisions were dominated by conservative Southern Democrats into a body in which many important decisions are not

dominated by conservative Southern Democrats.'[15] Ripley dis-
tinguishes between institutional and personal power, arguing that
in the 1950s Southern Democrats tended to dominate both areas,
but that gradually in the 1960s, especially after the 89th Congress,
liberal non-Southern Senators of both parties began to develop
personal power that allowed them to neutralize and even overcome
much of the institutional advantage conservative Southerners might
still possess. This process has continued, with party leadership
continuing to play a limited role as the distribution of power has
become increasingly decentralized and dispersed, with influence
remaining individualistic but with greater emphasis on specialized
knowledge rather than formal position. The legislative process
in the Senate is now characterized by the lack of any single dominating force, and a segmented and sporadic flow of legislative business,
many issues being determined by the construction and competition
of relatively firm and visible coalitions. Most junior Senators seem
more satisfied with this situation than did many of their counterparts
with the situation a decade ago. It allows for the thorough consideration of issues and does not preclude coherent action in response to
public concerns, as has been reflected in Senate challenges over
particular aspects of foreign policy, and the votes on the ABM and
SST issues. Pressures for coherent legislative initiatives are likely to
be initiated externally through public or group demands, but could
come from stronger issue-oriented party leadership. New Senators
have more opportunities in committee and elsewhere to exercise
influence, if supported by evidence of extensive external support.

This interpretation is generally supported by Nelson Polsby, who
sees the Senate in the process of change from an 'intensely private
and conservative body to a very public and progressive one; from
one focused on the virtues of age and experience to one devoted
to the young, the vigorous and the ambitious.'[16] He also suggests
that efforts to make the Senate more structured, such as the reduction of the number of committee and sub-committee assignments
for each Senator or requiring strict germaneness in debate, mis-
understand its virtue which is 'to incubate policy innovations, to
advocate, to respond, to launch its great debates, in short, to pursue
the continuous renovation of American public policy through the
hidden hand of the self-promotion of its members'.[17]

The general pattern in the House is also very different. The dominance of committee chairmen and the autonomy of committees has
begun to be eroded. So too has the dominance of Southern Demo-

crats within the House Democratic Party. Writing in 1971 Polsby and Wildavsky report: 'At the start of the decade southerners held eleven committee chairmanships; today they hold eight, which is roughly proportional to the percentage of southerners in the House Democratic party.'[18] Legislative redistricting has also made the House a less unrepresentative body. The actions of the 89th Congress, and the existence of a 'temporary' liberal Democratic majority in the House, reminded observers that Congress can move swiftly in accepting legislative recommendations, indeed perhaps too swiftly.

It was also an indicator to some Representatives that a modest shift towards improved party leadership and group cohesion, especially through the actions of the party caucuses, might alleviate some of the worst effects of existing roadblocks to legislative initiatives. Personal interviews also indicate that congressional elections since 1966 have seen the entry into the House of a considerable number of freshmen in both parties less committed to established norms of deference, apprenticeship and committee specialization, and prepared to challenge these norms.[19] The increased strength of the Democratic Study Group, the improved voting cohesion of liberal Democrats, the emergence of new organizations of legislators such as the Black Caucus, or the Members of Congress for Peace Through Law, even the increased activity at House elections of groups such as the National Committee for a More Effective Congress and the Movement for a New Congress, are all significant developments. The voting records of many House freshmen suggest less preoccupation with parochial matters and a more coherent response to national issues, perhaps reflecting changing constituency demands.

The precise consequences of these tendencies are difficult to assess, especially in a period in which Congress is controlled by one party and the presidency by another, but the basic pattern of change is evident.

PARTICULAR PATTERNS OF CHANGE

Consideration will be given to responses to external and internal demands for change affecting both the functions of Congress and the capacity of its members to improve the quality of their performance.

Change through Legislation – the Legislative Reorganization Act of 1970

Passage of this legislation marked the culmination of a fluctuating but continuous period of pressure for internal reforms from significant groups within both parties in Congress, beginning formally with the creation of the Joint Committee on the Organization of Congress in 1965, continuing with attempts to enact into law several sets of formal recommendations of the Committee, and ending in 1970 with a compromise reform package. Before considering distinctive features of the Act it is worth noting that other procedural changes had been effected during the 1960s.

As early as 1956 the Democratic Study Group had been formed in the House, and in 1963 Senator Joseph Clark commenced his personal challenge to the so-called Senate Establishment, and invigorated the biennial attempts to change the Senate closure rule. In 1961, the House Rules Committee membership was expanded to 15, a reform which, together with the temporary enactment of a modified 21-day rule in the 89th Congress (weakening the ability of standing committees to 'hold up' pending bills in committee), and the acceptance in 1967 of new rules limiting its activities by its new chairman, William Colmer of Mississippi, has resulted in considerable changes in the actions of that committee.[20] In 1973 its new chairman is no longer a Southerner, but the current chairman of the House Democratic Steering Committee and former co-chairman of the Joint Committee on the Organization of Congress, Ray Madden of Indiana. In 1965 and 1969 several Southern Democrats who did not support the Democratic presidential candidates of 1964 and 1968 were 'purged' of their committee and party seniority by the House Democratic caucus. In 1962 and 1971 the selections of new Speakers in the House were both followed by procedural concessions designed to weaken the influences of seniority and the autonomy of committee chairmen. After 1964 several groups of House Republicans worked within their party for changes in party practices and also sought major changes through formal legislation.[21] In the Senate, though Clark and others failed to change the closure rule to make filibusters easier to break, closure was in fact invoked three times in the early 1960s, the most famous examples being the successes in defeating Southern attempts to prevent passage of the 1964 Civil Rights Act and the 1965 Voting Rights Act. Clark also succeeded in effecting significant changes in the size and composition of the Senate Democratic Steering Committee (which is responsible for assigning

Senate Democrats to committees), and Stephen Bailey reports: 'As the decade of the '70's opens, the Democratic Steering Committee in the Senate consists of eight liberals, five moderates, and only four die-hard conservatives.'[22]

If these and other changes seem at best incremental, what of the 1970 Legislative Reorganization Act itself? While it is premature (given the lessons of the 1946 Act) to try to assess the likely full consequences on congressional organization and decision-making, it is possible to consider certain specific formal changes made by the Act, and some immediate consequences.

Pressures for reform legislation came from a wide range of sources, especially in the House; from groups seeking to increase party responsibility in committee organization and decision-making and anxious to dilute the autonomy and secrecy of committee activities, to those seeking to strengthen the oversight role of Congress and the influence of the minority party in committee work, and an improvement in the information resources available to Congress as a whole and to its committees. Those seeking to challenge and weaken the impact of the seniority system had to use alternative methods (and have done so with modest success through the party caucuses in the 92nd Congress), as the terms of reference of the Joint Committee on the Organization of Congress excluded this area, the application of the seniority system with regard to committee assignments and committee leaders being a party device rather than a formal procedure of Congress.

The 1970 Act consisted of four principal sections, relating to the committee system and floor procedures, fiscal controls, sources of congressional information, and general housekeeping. The first section consisted of a set of proposals intended to weaken existing standing committee autonomy, the independent authority of committee chairmen and the strong element of secrecy attached to committee proceedings, and the advantages accruing to senior committee members in terms of information, staff aides and subcommittee chairmanships. The formulation of a committee 'bill of rights' was intended to increase committee accountability and establish a common set of rules applying to all committees, though the Appropriations Committees were exempt from some of the provisions. An attempt to meet some of the major criticisms of standing committee behaviour, the new rules required committees to fix regular dates for meetings, set out procedures to allow for committee meetings to be held if necessary without the committee chairman, required all committee meetings to be open unless a majority vote of the committee deemed otherwise, and committee reports to include all committee votes, including individual votes. All committees were to file, within seven days, reports on decisions taken, including all minority or dissenting reports, and all committee hearings must be made available to other members at least three days before floor consideration of committee recommendations. Other requirements included the denial of proxy voting if demanded by a majority on a committee, more thorough consideration of requests by committees for funds to conduct investigations, and all committee hearings to be open to radio and television coverage.

Important general provisions included procedures allowing for recorded teller votes on amendments to legislative recommendations in the House, speeding up of the process through the use of electronic roll-call and quorum-call voting in the House, and the formal establishment of rules limiting the number of committee and sub-committee chairmanships held by individual Senators (similar limitations were imposed on House Democrats in 1971 by the House Democratic party caucus). A number of minor procedural changes were set out to speed up House consideration of pending bills.

Not all of these requirements have taken immediate effect, but, together with other changes such as increased two-party competition in the South, the death or retirement of many senior Democrats and continued attacks on the seniority system, their full implementation could eliminate some of the undemocratic and anomalous features of the committee system. Reforms, however, do not always have the precise effects intended, and it would be unwise to suggest that fundamental changes will take place. Certainly few of the Congressmen interviewed believed that this will be so, though a large number approved of the tenor of the changes. Brief consideration of the new recorded teller vote procedure and the requirement to open up committee hearings illustrates these general points.

The intention behind the former procedure was to increase participation in voting, forcing House members to provide a clear record of their voting attitudes at all stages of the consideration of legislation, thus preventing the common practice of legislators voting for amendments intended to weaken a bill if such votes were not recorded, but voting for the bill at the formal recorded roll-call vote on final passage, and reporting the latter fact to constituents. The effects of this controversial reform have been mixed. Voting participation on major bills has doubled, and the change crucially affected the fate of the SST bill in 1971 and its rejection by the House. Contrary to the expectations of some Congressmen and others, it has not given the House a 'liberal' voting majority, and has led to the sporadic revival of the 'conservative coalition', confirming the view of some Congressmen that in the past 'liberal' legislation had been protected by persuading some conservatives *not* to support certain amendments where no roll-call vote was taken but merely to vote against final passage. The change has, however, made accessible to the public (and to electoral opponents) a more accurate picture of voting divisions in the House and the voting records of individual legislators. Some opposition has developed in the House to the extensive use of the procedure, one argument being that it worked against the reform goal of speeding up floor consideration of legislation, because recorded teller votes were being demanded on minor and often trivial amendments. Study of such votes indicates that this view is probably exaggerated, and will in any event no longer be relevant when the House begins to use electronic voting.[23]

Regarding the requirement to open up committee meetings, it should be said that some committees already held most of their meetings in open rather than executive session, especially in the Senate. The immediate response has been a modest increase in open committee meetings, the most noteworthy developments being the opening of certain House Appropriations Committee hearings (including those on the budget) and more open sessions of the House Ways and Means Committee. The House Education and Labour Committee meets almost entirely in open session, including important 'mark-up' sessions where final committee recommendations are decided, a lead followed by other committees, notably those with relatively new chairmen. Initial developments have not been dramatic but the evidence does suggest that through the 1970s committee activities will be more open, chairmen will have less independent control, and committees will become both more representative of, and more responsible to, their present bodies. However, this is still a far cry from a major reorganization of committee jurisdictions and the extensive use of joint hearings sought by some reformers.

Another important feature of the Act was the specific mandate to standing committees to extend their administrative oversight activities, reflecting a continued desire to consolidate this aspect of congressional activity in the future. However, the existence of consensus in Congress for the extension of these activities does not mean that they are performed continuously, efficiently or responsibly. The standing committees, as major vehicles for exercising oversight, are likely to respond in an enthusiastic manner but also act in ways consistent with their own group or particular interests. They are the main collectors of information through their staffs or at hearings, but most committees are reluctant to share such information. Study also indicates that many committees have developed a range of non-statutory controls designed to require administrators to be accountable to them or their chairman alone for changes in authorizing or appropriations authority.[24]

In order to improve the performance of the oversight and informing responsibilities, a basic requirement is information. At the risk of oversimplification it can be said that, despite the provision of large personal and committee staff and information adjuncts such as the Legislative Reference Service and the General Accounting Office, Congress lacks a sufficient range of 'independent' information and the tools and expertise fully to utilize such information. Legislators and committees rely heavily on information provided, often reluctantly, by the administrative departments or the executive. The 1970 Act included specific measures to remedy such deficiencies, especially concerning fiscal oversight and budgetary information, but they were not far-reaching. They included the redesignation of the Legislative Reference Service as the Congressional Research Service, with increased staff and responsibilities, and a strengthening of the General Accounting Office, along with increases in the professional staff of standing committees, authorization of the hiring of special consultants by committees, and assistance to professional staff to obtain specialized training.

Some of these changes reflect the resistance of many senior members of key committees to attempts to reduce the relative autonomy of their oversight duties or improve the quality of information readily available to all legislators. Any weakening of standing committee influence over pending legislation may therefore have been gained at the expense of strengthening committee dominance of oversight activities. Change in the future will depend on the strength of demands for further improvement in information-gathering resources controlled by Congress and used in ways consistent with the broad priorities defined by Congress as a whole. This will be difficult to achieve, requiring Congressmen to acquire special expertise and subsume special or individual interests in, for example, looking critically at defence budget requests, a task probaby still beyond the inclination or capacity of many. Interview evidence, however, indicated that a growing number of Representatives are prepared to use computer facilities and data processing techniques to help them in their work on many legislative matters. John Saloma has predicted the existence of computer facilities and analyst staff for use by Congress by 1975, but with access controlled by party leaders or individual committees.[25] The effects on oversight activities could be considerable, though more information does not in itself mean more responsible decisions nor does oversight for its own sake necessarily produce a more responsible bureaucracy. Most observers, however, argue that Congress needs more specialized staff assistance and independent sources of information-gathering to help in both oversight and legislative activities.

Change through Legal Requirement – Congressional Redistricting

An important factor in assessing the representativeness of Congress has been the effect of Supreme Court decisions regarding congressional redistricting. A major criticism of Congress in the early 1960s was that the House in particular under-represented urban and suburban voters, and rural-based legislators held most of the key positions of influence. The effects of congressional redistricting in the late 1960s, and the changes in the apportionment of House seats following the 1970 census, have gone some way to redress this imbalance, despite continued opportunities for gerrymandering. If the number of uncontested or 'safe' seats has not yet markedly diminished, more seats have become more competitive. The increased number of defeated incumbents in primary and general elections to Congress since 1966 is a possible indicator that redrawn districts can stimulate greater party competition. A combination of growing voter volatility and district instability, together with the increase in two-party and primary competition in several states and the extension of the franchise in national elections, will exert a considerable influence on decision-making in Congress in the 1970s. Comment from a recent study of congressional redistricting in North Carolina is illuminating: 'on the congressional level, North Carolina's experience has shown already that redistricting promotes a more competitive two-party system . . . A concomitant decline may take place in the accumulation of seniority within North Carolina's congressional delegation, a likelihood faced also by other Southern states, but this is the price for fair representation and more vigorous party competition relevant to the fundamental changes taking place within the state – new industry, urbanisation and the birth of power in the Negro electorate.'[26]

Turnover of House membership is increasing, as is turnover on key committees such as Appropriations, and the latter may further weaken the internal cohesion that has made such committees powerful in the past. The overall effects of redistricting have not been dramatic, but they have made the House less patently unrepresentative, and may have helped to produce a more favourable environment for the growth of influence of Representatives from urban and suburban areas and the complex demands of their constituents.

Congress and Foreign Policy – The Reassertion of Responsibilities

Since at least 1965 there has been a re-examination by Congress not only of the substance of American foreign policy but also of the procedures by which foreign policy is made, and in particular the appropriate congressional role in these procedures. This latter goal has ultimately united individuals holding very different views as to the merits of particular policies but united by a scepticism about executive and administrative decision-making.

The general dimensions of the current conflict are familiar ones to students of legislative-executive relations and foreign affairs in the United States, but there are important underlying factors which merit consideration. One consequence has been extended discussion about the precise relationship between the constitutional power of Congress to declare war and the constitutional power of the President as Commander-in-Chief to use the armed forces in military activities abroad; other practical consequences include intense conflict over the detail of foreign aid programmes, more critical appraisal of defence budgets, and serious attempts to use the power of the purse and even legislative authority to challenge presidential policies. These raise basic questions as to the nature of the role Congress is likely to play in the future and the resources and capabilities available to Congress to perform such a role.

The change in the situation is reflected in several recent studies, most of which seem to accept the notion of increased congressional involvement but differ as to its extent and nature. Roger Hilsman deems it unlikely that a Democratically-controlled Congress in the future will allow Democratic Presidents the benefit of an unchallenged foreign policy; he accepts Congress's obvious function as critic, does not accept that Congress lacks general information or expertise, but implicitly hopes that Congress will not demand too important a role in day-to-day foreign policy decisions.[27] Francis Wilcox is sympathetic to the current anxieties of Congress, yet sees Congress as the junior partner in the future, with neither the time, the patience, the machinery nor the capacity to take an active part in the day-to-day conduct of foreign policy, but with the facilities 'to serve as a forum, a national sounding board, where the major issues of foreign policy can be thrashed out and where the nature and purposes of American policy can be critically examined.'[28] He sees Congress's role as being one of bringing to bear on foreign policy questions an informed and more or less independent judge-ment of its own, coming to this judgement in public through open debate and discussion, and thereby contributing to the develop-ment of as broad a national consensus as possible in support of the policies eventually arrived at. The achievement of these responsibili-ties would require action by both Congress and the executive. For the latter this means that it should take Congress into its confi-dence more frequently and seek explicit approval for more of its major foreign policy decisions. Wilcox outlines the arguments for a Joint Executive-Legislative Committee on National Security Affairs,[29] and for restricting somewhat the use of executive agree-ments as instruments of foreign policy, and also developing a clear understanding between Congress and the executive about the President's use of American forces abroad.

Arthur Schlesinger has argued that common sense requires congressional participation as well as presidential responsibility in the great decisions of war and peace, and supports congressional checks on presidential actions which might involve the commitment of combat units or where military intervention might ultimately require congressional action, through appropriations, before it is ended. He also suggests the institutionalization of a commission of eight drawn from Congress and the executive which would exchange information and views on critical questions of foreign policy, but with Congress dealing with basic generalities rather than the detail.[30]

Other observers seem prepared to grant Congress a more aggressive and dominant role without serious concern as to whether sufficient of its members have the will to perform such a role and are anxious to do this in the long-term.[31] Some commentators feel that Congress may in fact be better equipped to deal with specific short-term policies than with broad foreign policy decisions.[32] H. B. Westerfield argues that in foreign policy matters Congress can still exercise all its major legislative responsibilities of deliberation, legislation, funding, oversight and legitimation, but if it is to avoid the return to executive supremacy and limited legislative influence there must be sufficient members concerned enough to assert themselves, whether or not constituency demands exist, and to play an activist role in considering the detail of foreign affairs and defence in the future.[33]

In the end it will be such individuals, events and the actions of the President rather than academic analysis that will determine the scope and nature of future congressional involvement in all aspects of foreign affairs. While Congress may have played a responsible role in demonstrating the absence of a national consensus for executive conduct of policy towards Vietnam, any contribution towards the development of a new national consensus and towards laying the basis for a new foreign policy requires both the proper organization of Congress's own facilities and more harmonious formal co-operation with the executive.

Party and Congressional Change

Studies of Congress in the 1950s generally agree that, despite weak party leadership and cohesion, party was the most important indicator and perhaps the dominant determinant of congressional voting. However, if measured in terms of the famous 1950 report of the American Political Science Association entitled *Toward a More Responsible Two-Party System*, which made specific suggestions for change in Congress, and was used by some observers as a yardstick for judging Congress in the early 1960s, the impact of party on change in Congress in the last decade has been modest. The pattern of change in the 1960s, even given the 89th Congress, has been affected far more by the efforts of intra-party and bipartisan groups in Congress to erode prevailing norms and attitudes and oligarchic patterns of decision-making. This has often been achieved in spite of the party leaders, though the results may ultimately serve to strengthen their potential to exercise leadership.

In formal roll calls the 'conservative coalition' can still gain victories, but its overall strength has diminished, cohesive opposition is stronger, and its group and individual impact has been undermined. There has been little evidence of consistent leadership action to maintain party cohesion or discipline, attempts at the latter tending to come from the actions of groups within the parties. Edward

Schneier, in updating the original work of Julius Turner, illustrates this paradoxical point with reference to House voting in the 1960s: 'the data ... suggest that we are on the verge of a break point in our political history; the incidence of party voting has never been lower, yet there are factions within each party that are as cohesive as the parties of any parliamentary regime.'[34] He points to the increased voting unity of northern Democrats and the Republicans, though the latter have also shown that control of the presidency by their party does not necessarily increase their preparedness to allow the President to determine how they should vote. Even in the 89th Congress the relationship between the Democratic President and the northern liberal wing of his party in Congress was one of partnership rather than subordination in many important areas of legislation.

Congress is becoming more amenable to the realization of some of the goals of those seeking increased party responsibility, yet there has been no weakening of its traditional position of independence and co-ordinate status. There has developed a general climate which is more receptive to positive leads in party or programme terms. This might develop further if, for example, party leaders paid greater attention to the assignment of members to committees with an eye to improving party unity on key committees, and stronger efforts were made to encourage the election of individuals from liberal strongholds in the cities who are prepared to make a career of service in the House of Representatives.

CONCLUSION

Change in Congress has come in response to public pressures and in ways which reflect the wider conflicts of contemporary American politics. These changes are not wholly consistent and have taken different forms in the House and the Senate. They include the consolidation of responsibilities such as administrative oversight and review as well as the reassertion of constitutional prerogatives. If the major functions of the contemporary Congress are policy clarification and legitimation, administrative oversight, representation and constituency service, and consensus-building,[35] such changes seem likely to improve the performance of these functions. Whether improved facilities for conducting oversight will be used to challenge rather than strengthen unholy alliances between particular administrative departments or agencies, congressional committees, and interest groups, depends ultimately on members of Congress. Interview evidence indicates an increasing desire among legislators to improve the overall performance of Congress in these areas as well as in the passage of legislation.

The general pattern of developments is unlikely to be affected by the 1972 elections, despite the landslide victory of Richard Nixon in the presidential contest. Republican gains in the House of Representatives were small and seem unlikely to alter the pattern of internal developments indicated earlier. Though few incumbents were defeated in the general elections, the turnover of House members remained high, largely because of retirements and primary defeats. At the beginning of the 93rd Congress half the House membership had begun their service since 1967. Increased turnover had a noticeable effect upon the top positions on several important House standing committees, with six new committee chairmen and a large number of new ranking minority members. Turnover of general standing committee membership continued to increase, even within the more stable Democratic majority, where only about one hundred members on the majority side now possess over a decade of seniority. New Representatives and Senators are also in the main younger, age appearing to have been a factor contributing to the defeat of several incumbents in primaries and at the general election, perhaps indicating the influence of the new young voters enfranchised by the Twenty Sixth Amendment.

There is some evidence therefore of a generational change taking place within Congress which could be very significant in the future. Both bodies are becoming on average younger, and in policy terms an increasing number of their members played little or no part in, and have little concern about, the legislative battles of the 1930s and 1940s, or even the Great Society programmes of the mid-1960s. Many of them are products of the political tensions created by the continuation of American intervention in the war in Vietnam rather than parties to the initial involvement. The effects of this generational influence is likely to be especially significant in the House, and current trends confirm impressions gained from extensive interviews – that the basic orientation of many Representatives is changing both towards the House as an institution and towards particular matters of policy. As groups like the Democratic Study Group and the Black Caucus grow in numerical strength and continue to challenge existing procedures and the use of the seniority system by the parties, so a new set of internal norms may be established. Old bipartisan alliances at the head of major House standing committees such as those on Appropriations, Rules, Judiciary, and Ways and Means, have been broken with the defeat or retirement of senior members of both parties, and their successors will find it difficult to establish similar patterns. The House is likely therefore to continue to become more open, less predictable, but also more representative of the public as a whole, than it was a decade ago.

Similar patterns are discernible in the Senate at the beginning of the 93rd Congress. Turnover of members was the highest since 1958, with the Democrats making modest overall gains. Almost half of the Senators are new since 1967 and only about a quarter have been in the Senate continuously for over fifteen years. The Democratic class of 1958 is beginning to acquire senior positions while the old traditions of the Senate flouted by newcomers such as Robert Kennedy in the 1960s are likely to continue to decline. At the beginning of the 93rd Congress the size of the Senate Democratic Steering Committee was expanded and two young freshman Senators appointed to the committee. In both the House and the Senate there were further efforts in the party caucuses to change existing practices for choosing committee leaders and assigning members to committees. For the first time for many years liberal Senators did not seek to challenge the continuation of the existing closure rule.

In many respects, however, power remains dispersed and scattered unequally throughout Congress as a whole, and the process of considering bills still allows for unnecessary delays and the disproportionate influence of particular individuals or committees. Old norms, procedures and practices are nevertheless under serious challenge, and the committee system is likely in the future to operate in ways more consistent with the wishes of the majority of legislators in a more open environment. Congressional consideration of complex economic, fiscal, and budgetary matters continues to be deficient, but, with some notable exceptions, may be becoming more responsible.[36] Other defects may be more difficult to eradicate. Despite recent efforts, ethical standards in Congress leave much to be desired. It remains difficult if not impossible for the President to obtain approval for any major reorganization of administrative departments he may feel to be necessary.

Decentralized authority in Congress still poses a major obstacle to the possible mobilization and maintenance of a majority coalition behind a programme to alleviate domestic problems, and to pass legislation that is unambiguous in its intents and application. Yet there is a growing potential and inclination among members of both the House and the Senate to define for themselves what are important policy issues even if they lack the necessary group or party cohesion, technical expertise, and information required to put together and pass a coherent set of legislative recommendations. Congress remains better equipped to deal with detail, and to increase specific oversight activities rather than broad legislative initiatives, and therefore in the final analysis the nature of its legislative output in the future may continue to be heavily influenced by the priorities and predispositions of the President. However, the increased constitutional challenge to the authority of Congress implicit in certain actions of President Nixon at the end of his first Administration in resuming American bombing of North Vietnam without consulting Congress, in impounding appropriated funds, in taking advantage of a brief recess of Congress to 'pocket veto' bills, and using executive privilege to protect executive officials from having to testify before committees of Congress, presages a period of tense legislative-executive relations. The situation provides also a further test of the will of members of Congress to assert their constitutional powers and to continue the internal process of reorganization and reform.

Peter Fotheringham

Changes in the American Party System, 1948–72[1]

THE AMERICAN PARTY SYSTEM, LONG CONSIDERED TO BE DOMINATED by two decentralized, non-programmatic and non-governing parties, is once again at the heart of empirical and normative arguments about the adequacy of government in the United States. Political developments since 1948 have revitalized the longstanding debate about the causal links between the constitutional and social bases of American politics, the definitive features of the party system and the attributes and outcomes of the governmental process. Prominent among such developments have been the pronounced volatility of the electorate in national and state elections; realignments in the distribution of electoral support for the parties in several regions; the nomination of 'minority' and 'ideological' candidates by the Republicans in 1964 and the Democrats in 1972; the loss of control over the presidential nomination process, perhaps temporary, by Roosevelt's old coalition of labour leaders, state and city bosses, congressional Democrats and Southern Democrats; reform of the electoral system occasioned by civil rights legislation, the apportionment revolution, the lowering of the voting age and the relaxation of residence qualifications; and the increase in political violence and mass protest which has accompanied the civil rights movement and the attempt to secure the withdrawal of American forces from Vietnam. Consequently, there has been considerable speculation about the potential for changes in the state of party competition, in the structure of the major parties, especially the Democratic Party, and in the functions of party in the political system. Such speculation occurs at a time when many commentators believe that there is a contemporary decline in the significance of party politics, to be added to an earlier decline at the turn of the century, and that there is a crisis in American political life, broadly defined as the failure or the incapacity of government to deal effectively with pressing socio-political problems.[2] What is offered here is an interim evaluation of the implications for the party system of post-1948 developments in party reform and in electoral politics. First, it is useful to give a brief description of the party system as seen by contemporary American political scientists.

THE AMERICAN PARTY SYSTEM

American political scientists have reacted in various ways to the developments enumerated above. There is a marked contrast between those who feel that there is no safe alternative to the limited but vital activities and functions achieved by parties throughout much of American political history and those who believe in the urgent need for or even in the possible emergence of responsible parties to deal with the perceived crisis. Others have discerned a gradual decline in the significance of party in the political system. The cry for responsible parties, once uttered by Woodrow Wilson and E. E. Schattschneider, has been taken up most forcefully by J. M. Burns who defines the party-system as 'a four-party system that compels government by consensus and coalition rather than a two-party system that allows the winning party to govern and the losers to oppose'.[3] The idea of responsible parties is viewed critically by those historians and political scientists who, in stressing that the parties are the product of a particular American environment, adhere to the belief that party characteristics, whatever the implications for government, are still the necessary 'price of union' in a dangerously heterogeneous society. Indeed a leading contemporary exponent of this view considers that 'any serious attempt to reform the parties toward policy responsibility would do violence to history and to modern political institutions'.[4] However one commentator has pointed to the development of conditions favourable to the potential growth of responsible parties, in particular, the decline of sectionalism and an increase in popular awareness of policy differences between the parties.[5] The possibility of a move towards the development of responsible parties is implicitly denied by W. D. Burnham who, in a study of critical realignments in American political history, voices the suspicion that 'the New Deal might come to be regarded one day as a temporary if massive deviation from a secular trend toward the gradual disappearance of the political party in the United States'.[6] A less drastic view of the role of political parties is contained in F. Sorauf's comparative comment that 'politically sophisticated electorates in heterogeneous and pluralistic political systems have come to depend less and less on the organising medium of the political party'.[7] The notion of a major realignment nationally has become a popular academic and journalistic sport. Opposing views as to what is happening to the relative standings of the parties in the electorate have been offered by K. Phillips,[8] who believes in an emerging Republican majority, and by R. F. Hamilton who foresees the development of a 'one-and-a-half-party system' as Republican identifiers are slowly removed from the electorate by the passage of time.[9] The present condition of the parties and the nature of change in the party system can be conveniently discussed with reference to four main headings which amount to a general definition of the American party system.

First, the party system includes a competitive electoral structure whose outlines are influenced by the electoral system, including its sheer magnitude and the frequency of elections; by the separation of governmental institutions and in particular the direct election of the President and fifty state governors; by the statutory regulation of party activities, especially the widespread requirement that party primary elections be held to elect party candidates for political office; and by trends in voting behaviour which, along with the results of surveys of party identification, indicate the relative sizes of the 'parties in the electorate'. The party system is defined by the number of major parties, their records of electoral performance, the significance of minor parties and historical patterns of continuity and change in the preceding indicators. The American party system is thus noted for the persistence of the two-party form at the national level, for the variety of state party systems, for the periodic but not exclusive tendency for a predominant or majority party to win all or almost all federal elections for a period of up to twenty years, and for the occasional significant electoral intervention of genuine third parties or breakaway movements from one of the major parties. The Democrats have been regarded as the normal majority party since 1932, winning nineteen of the twenty-one congressional elections and seven of the eleven presidential elections up to 1972. There is broad agreement that the two-party form is encouraged by constitutional arrangements and by a broad consensus concerning the rules of the American political game. However the various demands for reform and the notion of a contemporary crisis have been the consequence of a challenge to the rules of that game on the part of various sections in the population who have not hitherto been able to participate fully or who have disagreed intensely with the outcomes of the national decision-making process. It must be emphasized that the two-party form has been qualified historically by the loosely structured parties and by the freedom available to Southern Democrats to protect the Southern white position within the existing party system. The two-party form is likely to survive the current mood of dissatisfaction. But there may be significant changes in the state of electoral competition between the parties and in the character of the parties themselves.

Second, the party system is also defined in part by the structure of the principal parties, i.e., by the formal party organizations required by party rules and by state legislation, by patterns of participation in party activities which describe the relationship of party to citizen in American political life, and by the distribution of effective decision-making powers which focuses attention on informal structures. American parties are usually described as loose federations of state and local parties which are heavily decentralized, i.e., the national parties do not control the state parties and the state parties do not always control the local parties in counties and in cities. Decentralization commences with party membership because there is no need to be a paid-up, card-carrying party member; rather, party membership is defined formally in state legislation on participation in party primaries and informally by various degrees of participation in party life, ranging from merely voting regularly for the party to holding party office in the organizational structure required by state legislation. American parties are therefore, given the absence of enrolled mass-membership, classified as 'cadre' parties[10] and distinguished historically by the frequent appearance of 'machines' and 'machine politics'. However party structure has been changing in response to criticisms of the effects of decentralization on the performance of national party activities and there is now a debate about the 'withering-away' of 'machine politics'.[11] The introduction of membership defined by the payment of a fee has become a matter of debate among Democrats wishing to reform the party nationally.[12] Decentralization is most apparent and most critical at the national level where at least three party elements are distinguishable. The national committee and the national convention, which is the top nominating and policy-pronouncing organization, are both federal institutions in terms of composition. It is possible that recent reforms, particularly the increase in the number of states holding presidential primaries and the restructuring of the Democratic National Committee, will change the pattern of internal party politics by taking power away from state and local bosses and dispersing it among primary voters and state and local party officials owing their position to a much wider popular participation in party activities. The third national party component is the congressional party. Each congressional party does possess a formal, elected hierarchy and acts cohesively when the organization of Congress is established at the commencement of each new Congress. However the parties are not responsible in the sense of constantly demonstrating almost perfect cohesion on policy issues. Indeed it is now fairly common to distinguish two wings to each congressional party defined by the manner of their respective constituencies and by their attitudes to the scope and content of proposed governmental action, namely presidential and congressional wings. The presidential (liberal) wing shares the presidential constituency composed of an urban, industrialized electorate while the congressional (conservative) wing is responsive to a more rural and localized electorate. There is still a 'conservative coalition' able to frustrate an active president when he turns his attention to particular national issues such as a minimum wage and medicare.[13] Occasionally the electorate returns a president prepared to act and a congressional majority prepared to support him as from 1932 to 1936 and in 1964. But the evidence available so far supports the notion of decentralized parties where it matters most from a governmental standpoint, i.e., in Congress and in the relationship between a congressional party and an Administration sharing the same party label. Indeed it is difficult to over-emphasize the importance of Southern Democrats as an obstacle to effective action by a Democratic president. Recent studies of legislative behaviour have revealed that the parties have become less cohesive in recent years.[14] In particular the conservative coalition of Southern Democrats and most Republicans increased its influence in the 1960s. Schneier found that 'Southern Democratic insurgency has grown to embrace a widening circle of issues and to include a growing number of congressmen'.[15] However the number of Southern Democrats in the House has been declining in recent years.

Third, a party system is also defined by the activities carried out by the component parties. American parties concentrate on electioneering, i.e., on the recruitment of party candidates and on getting out the vote to secure their election to public office. Further, electioneering is pursued vigorously at the expense of evolving comprehensive party policies or even detailed individual policies to be implemented when the party, at whatever level of government, wins control of all necessary governmental agencies. The concentration on electioneering is the product of several interrelated conditions. The sheer size of the electoral system and the frequency of elections make electioneering a time-consuming activity. Decentralization of government, i.e., federal system and separation of institutions, makes for a wide dispersal of power among party organizations which places obstacles in the way of getting agreement on party policy. The looseness of party membership, the lack of an organized mass base, means that demands for specific policies are weak. In turn, the weakness of social class as a source of comprehensive policy differences (though social class does influence American politics) accounts for the looseness of party membership and the absence of a demand for party programmes. Hence American parties are said to be non-programmatic or non-ideological and non-governing. Even electioneering can be weakly controlled by local party organizations because of the widespread party primary and the increase in political advertising as a campaign technique which makes personal wealth more important at the local level. Democratic celebrities, John Glenn (Ohio) and Ted Sorensen (New York), were defeated in 1970 Senate primaries by relatively unknown but very wealthy opponents who were subsequently defeated by Republican opponents. Finally, the party system can be defined by the contributions it makes to the nature of government, by the consequences of the activities performed, and the manner of performing them. Parties make contributions to political socialization, recruitment, representation, management of conflicts based on various types of political cleavage, national and social integration, the provision of government and peaceful transitions between governments, and so on. The description of the American party system in terms of party structure and party activities has led to a useful distinction between American and most West European, including British, parties. T. Lowi has described American parties as 'unifunctional' because their contributions to the political system are usually 'constituent', i.e., the party system is more concerned with maintaining American constitutional and governmental arrangements than with formulating and implementing policies. In Lowi's own words, the parties 'have managed to keep legitimacy and politics apart' and hence the parties have contributed to 'an extraordinary stability relative to the extreme stress and strain of our heterogeneous and dynamic society'. European parties may be 'bifunctional' or responsible; many perform both constituent and policy activities but Lowi makes it plain that he believes that American parties have performed satisfactorily by most comparative standards.[16] An examination of the attempted reform of the Democratic Party between 1968 and 1972 and of developments in electoral politics since 1948 will indicate how the party system as described above has reacted to the problems emerging from American society.

PARTY REFORM

The turmoil in American political life since the second world war occasioned primarily by conflicts over the integration of black Americans into the society and over America's role in world politics has been accompanied by significant changes in voting behaviour since 1948 and by some reform of the electoral system and of the parties. The 1972 presidential and congressional elections are significant as further indications of where the voting trends are leading and of the achievements of the reform movements in the Democratic Party. In view of the impact of the Democratic reforms upon the results of the 1972 elections it is necessary to analyse party reform before tackling the more difficult problem of electoral politics.

The contribution of the political parties to American political life is partly determined by the electorate's reaction to party candidates and their policies on major campaign issues. The electorate's verdict is particularly important when a new majority party is established as in 1896 and 1932 or when an apparently reformed party is offered as in 1972. The Democratic Party's internal conflicts from the announcement of Eugene McCarthy's presidential candidacy in December 1967 through to the 1972 campaign, in which 'Democrats for Nixon' worked against the election of a Democratic candidate and the top AFL-CIO leadership professed neutrality, are evidence of an attempt to present to the electorate a different Democratic Party and a new type of American party. The different Democratic Party can be defined by McGovern's stand on important issues, his policy proposals, and the composition and the activities of his supporters from precinct to national convention. The new type of American party was intended to be defined in structural terms by an infusion of responsibility – by a disciplined allegiance on the part of national, state and local party organizations to a national leadership located initially in the White House and supported at the grassroots by the beginnings of a mass party membership consisting of the amateur activists who had accomplished so much in presidential primaries for Eugene McCarthy, Robert Kennedy and George McGovern. A McGovern victory in 1972 would not have created such a party immediately but it would have given the reformers an opportunity to set about the task. Even a McGovern victory might have accomplished little in terms of restructuring the Democratic Party if it was accompanied by anything other than a Democratic congressional landslide. As it is the McGovern defeat raises questions about the significance of changes which have occurred in party structure, in party rules and in participation in party activities.

Advocates of responsible parties and advocates of major changes in the direction and scope of governmental policies can attempt to achieve their aims by following three complementary strategies. They can run reform candidates in the hope that the voters will support the candidates, i.e., they can attempt to bring about a realignment in the electorate favourable to their own policy goals. They can attempt to gain control of party organizations at all levels by getting their supporters to participate in party meetings and party activities. And they can attempt to reform national and state party rules and the state regulation of party activities. The three strategies were present in the move to reform the Democratic Party which started at the 1968 Chicago Convention. The first step was the abolition of the unit rule which could be used, mainly by small state delegations, to bind all members of the delegation to the particular candidate preferred by a majority (the unit rule did not operate in states holding presidential primaries). This step, which was proposed by McCarthy's supporters, was taken because Humphrey decided to go along with the move in order to demonstrate his liberal credentials. The convention also voted to guarantee that the selection of delegates in 1972 would be an open process held during 1972 and not earlier. The sitting Democratic National Chairman, Senator Fred Harris of Oklahoma, appointed two commissions to make recommendations on how to implement the reforms. The Commission on Party Structure and Delegate Selection was chaired by Senator McGovern until he resigned in view of his presidential ambitions. The Commission issued its report in April 1970 and its recommendations were accepted by the Democratic National Committee in February 1971. The most important recommendation was derived from the Chicago Convention's commitment to open selection; state parties were to permit all party members to participate in all public party meetings and, to this end, to publicize meetings;

in addition written rules on delegate selection were to be adopted. The aim was to reduce the influence over delegate selection of professional party officials. The number of delegates elected or selected at congressional district level was to be increased at the expense of statewide selection or election. The celebrated quota recommendation was contained in a vague exhortation to state parties to encourage a full representation of minority views in state delegations to the national convention. Quotas were established for the minority groups which were considered to have been discriminated against in the past, such as blacks, women and American youth defined as 18–29 year-olds. The quota principle led to challenges to many delegations being brought before the Credentials Committee and subsequently before the entire convention. Mayor Daley's Chicago delegation, whose members were uncommitted to any candidate but directly elected in the Illinois delegate primary, was rejected because the quotas had not been respected satisfactorily. Subsequently there were charges that many minority groups, e.g., ethnic or religious groups, were not given quotas. The Commission on Rules reported in September 1971 and its recommendations that speechmaking be curtailed, that convention committees meet in public and restrictions be placed on favourite-son candidacies were also adopted.

The reform movement influenced the decisions of six states to introduce or to re-introduce presidential primary legislation bringing the number of states holding such primaries to twenty-two. Nearly two-thirds of 1972 Democratic delegates were elected in primaries or committed by primary results compared to 40 per cent in 1968. However not all such delegates were bound; some states do not permit formal commitment (e.g. New York); others hold advisory preference polls which the delegates can ignore unless they are run as pledged to a particular candidate. The increase in the number of delegates to be won in the primaries will probably make it difficult for serious candidates to avoid the primary route in future, though, if the number of primaries remains constant, it is unlikely that a candidate will win a majority of delegate votes in the primaries unless there are no other serious and successful candidates. However primaries have not only increased their numerical importance in the commitment of delegates to candidates; they also retain their speculative importance as indicators of which candidates can win votes and which cannot.

What were the consequences of the reform of party rules and

procedures and the increase in presidential primaries in the Democratic nomination process? First, the reforms contributed to the nomination of a so-called radical candidate, described as a prairie populist, from an unfashionable state, who was not widely regarded as a major candidate before the primaries commenced.[17] McGovern's radicalism was based on his anti-Vietnam war stand and his promises to reduce drastically the United States' foreward position in international politics and on his domestic proposals regarding welfare, taxation and minimum incomes. His success in winning the nomination was due partly to this radical appeal; in particular, it brought him an enthusiastic, volunteer organization which was particularly effective in delegate primaries.

Even more important was his personal success in several of the binding preference polls which brought him 537 bound delegates compared to 303 delegates for Wallace and 102 delegates for Humphrey. McGovern came to the Miami Convention with about one thousand delegates either formally or informally committed to him by preference polls and by the results of delegate primaries; more than five hundred McGovern delegates came from California and New York. McGovern also fared better than other candidates in states choosing convention delegates in party meetings rather than in primaries. Many such delegates (438) were uncommitted when selected but McGovern won a majority (288) of those who were committed. The reform of delegate selection procedures therefore contributed to McGovern's nomination by facilitating his victory in the first ballot.

Second, the composition of the 1972 convention was markedly different from its predecessors as can be seen in Table 1. The representation of particular groups – youths, women and non-whites (blacks, Chicanos, Indians) – increased spectacularly at the 1972 Democratic convention. It has been estimated that 80 per cent of the delegates in Miami were attending a national convention for the first time. In contrast the number of Senators and Representatives included in state delegations fell considerably. The Republicans also increased representation for these groups, especially the youth group, though women were represented in much greater strength in 1968 and in 1972 than the two other 'minority groups'. The changes at the Republican convention were necessitated by the Democratic reform movement which was appealing to these specific groups; they were also encouraged by the possibility that members of these groups might be won over to the Republican

Party at a time when voting behaviour was generally flexible.

TABLE I

Representation at the Major Party Conventions, 1968 and 1972

Group	Democratic Convention		Republican Convention	
	1968	1972	1968	1972
Youth (18–29)	4%	21·4%	1%	8·7%
Blacks	5·5%	25·2%	1·9%	4%
Women	13%	39·9%	17%	30·1%
Senators	40	15	—	—
Representatives	85	49	—	—

Third, McGovern's nomination and the composition of the Democratic Convention were symbols of and contributions to an internal conflict which led to the withdrawal of national AFL-CIO support for the Democratic presidential candidate, to the formal or informal disassociation of their own congressional campaigns from the presidential campaign by several Congressional Democrats, and to the launching of a 'Democrats for Nixon' campaign effort spearheaded by John Connally, former Governor of Texas and Secretary of the Treasury in the first Nixon Administration. There was much speculation about a battle for control of the Democratic Party between the coalition established by Roosevelt in the 1930s and a new coalition of minority groups and hitherto disaffected sections of the community variously described as suburban liberals, Kennedy-McCarthy remnants, students, peace people, blacks and feminists. Indeed the reform of the party was heralded as the defeat of the old coalition, which would break up, and the creation of the 'first truly democratic national party organisation in the nation's history'.[18] McGovern's nomination was subsequently cited as further evidence of the old guard's defeat. However it is not difficult to envisage Senator Kennedy, if he accepts the risks involved, reuniting many elements in the old and the new Democratic Party in 1976. Organized labour's rejection of McGovern was not at all universal among union officials. The national leaders, who professed to detest Nixon, acted out of real or imagined personal slights suffered at Miami. The main blow to the Democratic campaign came from the loss of the organizational and fund-raising capacities of the Committee on Political Education which, in 1968, had reduced the impact of George Wallace among Northern blue-collar workers. A major preoccupation of Democratic national leaders will be to bring back the unions into the party before the 1976 elections. It is likely that the impact of the racial issue on blue-collar voters will be critical.

There can be little doubt that increased opportunities for participating in Democratic Party politics have been made available. The use made of these opportunities depends ultimately on the identity of the activists who attend party meetings recruiting party officials and party candidates. Some indication of the impact of the reform of the party and of the chances of further reforms will come from the special party conference on reform to be held in 1974. It is premature to suggest that a new type of American party is emerging. But the Democratic Party has been opened up. The party may be contributing to resolving some aspects of the political crisis which split the party not long after the brief appearance in 1965–66 of a responsible, governing party. However that appearance emerged, not from internal party reforms, but from the 1964 Democratic landslide in both presidential and congressional elections.

ELECTORAL POLITICS

American electoral politics in the quarter-century since 1948 have been characterized by significant reforms of the electoral system and by several distinct trends in voting behaviour. Supreme Court decisions, federal and state legislation, and constitutional amendments have enforced uniformity in the size of national and state legislative districts, made it easier for all citizens, but especially black Americans, to participate in the electoral and governmental processes, and lowered the minimum voting age in state and national elections to eighteen. Supreme Court decisions in such cases as Baker v Carr (1962) and Wesberry v Sanders (1964) forced the states into an 'apportionment revolution' by requiring that congressional districts and state legislative districts each be as near equal in population size as practicable within each state. The political effects of reapportionment were increased by the redistribution of House seats among states as a consequence of the results of the 1970 Census. Both forms of reapportionment were thought to favour the Republicans more than the Democrats. The equal size requirement reduced the power of rural areas within states, particularly in the South, and gave more representation to suburban areas. Demographic trends leading to a redistribution of House seats, increasing the representation of

California, Florida, Texas, Arizona and Colorado and decreasing the representation of New York, Pennsylvania and seven other states, were also thought to favour the Republican Party. However reapportionment, i.e., the redrawing of legislative boundaries, remains a political exercise in the hands of the party or parties in control of individual state governments. Democratic gains in the 1970 state elections offset the advantages accruing to the Republicans from the increase in suburban representation. It was estimated that, as of July 1972, the Republicans were likely to make 'a net gain of only five seats' following reapportionment by the states.[19] The Republicans, in November 1972, enjoyed a net gain of one seat in the states gaining or losing districts following the 1970 Census.

Another significant reform, notably the removal of discriminatory practices preventing black Americans from registering and voting, has been introduced by federal legislation and by constitutional amendment. The Twenty-fourth Amendment (1964) prohibits the denial of the right to vote in national elections 'by reason of failure to pay a poll tax or other tax'. The 1965 Voting Rights Act gave the Justice Department the right to supervise voting procedures including registration in states and in counties where registration or voting was less than 50 per cent of the eligible population in the 1964 presidential election. Some of the results have been spectacular, e.g., black registration in Mississippi rose from 5·2 per cent in 1960 to 71 per cent in 1969. The number of blacks registered in the eleven Southern states rose by more than 1·89 million between 1960 and 1970, i.e., from 29·1 per cent to 62 per cent of the black voting-age population; however an 8 per cent rise in the number of whites registered in the South brought in more than 4·7 million white voters. The turnout of blacks in presidential elections did rise in the 1960s from 23 per cent in 1956 to 31 per cent in 1960 and 51 per cent in 1968. The size of the black vote in the Democratic coalition rose from 7 per cent in 1960 to 19 per cent in 1968.[20] The most immediate result of the increasing registration of black voters has been a steep numerical rise in the number of elected black officials. There were fewer than 100 black officials in the South before the passing of the 1965 Voting Rights Act; the total had risen to 684 by December 1970. The number rose nationally from 1126 in June 1969 to 1860 in February 1971 when 0·3 per cent of the more than half-million elected officials in the United States were black, compared to 10 per cent blacks in the voting population. There has been very little sign yet of a populist alliance between blacks and poor whites in the South. Blacks tend to get elected in constituencies where 40 per cent or more of the voting population is black. Of the twelve black Representatives in the 92nd Congress, 1971–72, an increase of five over the previous Congress, ten were elected from the thirteen congressional districts where the electorate was 45 per cent or more black. Only one of these districts was located in the South, Mississippi's fifth district, which did not return a black. One was elected from the 6th district in Illinois which is 35–45 per cent black and one from the 7th district in California which is 25–35 per cent black. Three more blacks were elected in 1972, including one from Texas (Houston) and one from Georgia (Atlanta). The 1970 extension of the Voting Rights Act relaxed residence qualifications which had restricted the number of Americans eligible to vote and contributed therefore to comparatively low turn-out rates. Finally, the Twenty-Sixth Amendment (1971) reduced the minimum voting age in national and state elections to eighteen; as a consequence 11·2 million 18–20 year olds were eligible to register and to vote in 1972, joining the 13·9 million 21–25 year olds who were not old enough to vote in 1968. It has been estimated that 65 per cent of the 25 million new voters would register and that 42 per cent would vote.[21] The potential behaviour of the new voters was the subject of much speculation, giving the Democrats some grounds for optimism when other indications of how the electorate would behave were not favourable. However McGovern enjoyed a narrow 2 per cent over Nixon among 18–24 year olds in November.

The reform of the electoral system can be attributed to various political forces including the growing influence of the civil rights movement in the decade prior to Johnson's landslide victory in 1964, which in turn was crucial to the subsequent passing of the 1965 Voting Rights Act; the decisions of the Warren Court; and the need to appease sections of the community, particularly the blacks and college students, who were violently demonstrating their discontent with the political system. The fear that George Wallace might force the 1968 presidential election into the House of Representatives also gave the reform movement a general impetus. So far attempts to reform or to abolish the electoral college have not been successful. Reform of the electoral system can best be described as an attempt to extend the boundaries of the political system by bringing into the political process Americans whose participation had been actively discouraged. The state of electoral politics has been more immediately affected by the electorate's reaction to the issues and the candidates in recent presidential elections.

There has been mounting speculation since 1968, in the light of presidential election results from 1952 onwards, as to whether a major realignment in the state of party competition has been taking place or is about to take place. Such a realignment could end with a change in the identity of the normal majority party or in the disappearance, perhaps temporary, of a majority party from American electoral politics. The critical realignment of 1932, which was subsequently maintained in presidential and congressional elections until 1952, with the single exception of the 1946 mid-term elections, established the Democratic Party as the majority party. However two features of election results during this period are worth noting. Firstly, Republican candidates received an increased share of electoral college votes in every presidential election from 1940 through 1956; in addition the Republican Party won a majority of House seats outside the Southern and Border states from 1938 onwards.[22] Secondly, Thurmond's victory in four Deep South states (the exception was Georgia) broke up the Solid (Democratic) South and reintroduced the racial issue as an important electoral force though its impact in 1948 was confined to the Deep South. Subsequently the conflict over how much should be done and how quickly to improve the situation of non-white Americans has contributed to the political violence and general unrest associated with the 1960s. The racial issue seems to have been particularly important electorally in 1968 and 1972, contributing to Nixon's two victories.

The question of realignment can be considered after describing four major features of the collective vote since 1952. Firstly, Eisenhower's first victory inaugurated a trend towards repeated volatility in presidential elections as the electorate reacted to the candidates and to the major issues in the campaigns. Neither party has since won more than two successive presidential elections though the second victories of Eisenhower and Nixon may point to the advantages of incumbency; more likely these victories point to the continuing relevance of the forces, candidate-appeal or particular issues, which established them in the White House. There have been wide fluctuations in the size of the winning margin in the popular vote, ranging from 0·2 per cent in 1960 and 0·7 per cent in 1968 to 15·4 per cent in 1956, 22·6 per cent in 1964 and 23 per cent in 1972. Further evidence of volatility in voting behaviour is apparent in the upsurge in ticket splitting – voting for candidates from different parties to different political offices on the same day. The number of split outcomes in gubernatorial and Senate elections did not rise above 27 per cent per annum in the 1950s nor fall below 44 per cent from 1962 onwards.[23] In 1968 the voters of Arkansas supported the candidacies of George Wallace (American Independent Party), J. William Fulbright (Democrat) and Winthrop Rockefeller (Republican). A Republican presidential landslide in 1972 was accompanied by a Democratic gain of two seats in the Senate and a narrow Republican gain of twelve seats in the House. The citizens of the state of Washington gave President Nixon 57 per cent of their votes but elected seven Democrats and no Republicans to the House. The Deep South in its allegiance to Thurmond, Goldwater, Wallace and Nixon (1972) has demonstrated that it remains a section in presidential elections at least.[24] It now seems clear that the Deep South states will support the presidential candidate who is regarded as the least hostile to the political and social views of Southern whites. It remains to be seen if such a candidate will in future be a Republican or George Wallace (or someone like Wallace). Secondly, sectionalism outside the Deep South has continued the decline which began in 1928 and 1932 as electoral politics became increasingly nationalized. Some of the evidence of this nationalization lies in a reduction in the standard deviation in the popular vote by states for the major parties in presidential elections since 1952.[25] Volatility has been nationalized as states demonstrated a willingness to change allegiance. Only one state, Arizona, the home state of the 1964 candidate, has voted for the same party in the six elections from 1952 to 1972 compared to twenty-four states doing so from 1932 to 1948.

Thirdly, there are still distinct regional patterns in presidential and in congressional election results though, fourthly, there have also been significant realignments in the party preferences of several regions. Regionalism, now based mainly on socio-economic distinctions, is illustrated by the list of twenty-one states which voted for every Republican candidate except Goldwater from 1952 to 1972. Most of these states can be counted as Republican strongholds in presidential elections though the 1964 result emphasizes that the Democratic Party can win on occasion. The twenty-one states, which will occupy 37 per cent of the electoral college until 1980, include three of the five Mid-Western states (Illinois and Michigan are the exceptions), five of the six Farm Belt states (Minnesota is the exception) and six of the eight Mountain states (Nevada and New Mexico are the exceptions). Only New Hampshire and Vermont are included from the former Republican stronghold in the North-East and only two, California and Oregon, from the Pacific region. The most interesting set of states subscribing to presidential Republicanism are four states from the Outer South and Border regions, Florida, Oklahoma, Tennessee and Virginia. There is not such an impressive list of states opting regularly for Democratic candidates because of the huge Republican electoral college victories in 1952, 1956 and 1972. Eleven states did vote for the Democratic candidate in 1960 and in 1968 as well as in 1964. Six are located in the North-East while the remainder are scattered throughout the other regions. However these eleven states comprise 31 per cent of the electoral college because several of the largest states are included, i.e. Massachusetts, Michigan, New York and Pennsylvania. The North-East appears crucial to Democratic hopes; Kennedy received 43·8 per cent and Humphrey 58·6 per cent of their electoral college votes from the North-East states.

Similar regional preferences are visible in congressional election results though the electorate has not acted in such a volatile fashion; rather the electorate has tended to distinguish between presidential and congressional contests. Nevertheless there have been regional realignments of major significance for the Congress. The Democrats have controlled Congress after all but two elections since 1932; the exceptions were 1946 and 1952. However there was a marked decline in Democratic representation outside the South and Border states from 1938 which meant that the Democrats had to rely on huge majorities in the South to offset smaller but comfortable Republican majorities elsewhere. From 1946 to 1970 the Democrats won a majority of congressional districts beyond the South and Border states in only three elections, in the Democratic landslides of 1958 and 1964, and in 1970, when the Republican Party in Congress suffered the usual loss of seats on the part of the presidential party in mid-term elections. The trends in changes in party strength in Congress by region are illustrated in Tables 2 to 4. A marked decline in Democratic strength in Southern and Border states in 1952 and from 1962 to 1966 is more than offset by Democratic gains elsewhere, particularly in 1958 and 1964 though the Republicans made a limited recovery in the elections following these two Democratic landslides. Nevertheless the overall Democratic majority has been higher since 1958 than it was from 1950 to 1956. The parties are now fairly evenly matched outside the Southern and Border states.

The Democrats still rely on winning over 75 per cent of the 135 congressional districts in the fifteen Southern and Border states

TABLE 2

Composition of Democratic Majority in House of Representatives, 1946–72[26]

Area	1946	1948	1950	1952	1954	1956	1958	1960	1962	1964	1966	1968	1970	1972
South/ Border	+101	131	123	109	113	111	115	113	100	92	72	70	70	59
Outside South/ Border	−159	−39	−87	−117	−84	−78	+15	−26	−17	+63	−11	−19	+5	−6
Democratic Majority	−58	92	36	−8	29	33	130	87	83	155	61	51	75	53

for the persistence of their majority in the House. The number of southern Democratic congressmen in the House has declined from 103 in 1950 to seventy-four in 1972; Southern Democrats have declined from 44 per cent of Democrats in the House in 1950 to 30 per cent in 1972. A more detailed picture of regional realignments is available in Table 3. In 1950 the Democrats won almost 94 per cent of the 141 Southern and Border districts; the Republicans could win only two seats in the South, both in Tennessee. But the only other region to return a majority of Democratic congressmen was the sparsely populated Mountain area. The Republican share of House seats in the remaining regions varied between 87 per cent in the Farm Belt (only Minnesota returned Democrats to the House) and 55·6 per cent in the Mid-Atlantic states. The five Mid-Western states were particularly important to the Republican Party in the House because of their size; the Republicans enjoyed a net advantage of thirty-nine seats in the Mid-West compared to twenty-three in the Farm Belt and twenty in the North-East.

By 1970 the distribution of House seats is almost exactly reversed in the New England, Mid-Atlantic and Pacific regions which have been consistently returning modest Democratic majorities to the House since 1958 or 1960. The Democrats have also improved their position in the Mid-West and the Farm Belt though these regions are still crucial to the Republican Party in the House. There are variations within regions; in New England, New Hampshire and Vermont have remained steadfastly in the Republican camp while Maine, Connecticut and Massachusetts have joined Rhode Island in each returning a House delegation in which the Democrats

TABLE 3

Distribution of House Seats by Party and Region, 1950, 1970 and 1972

Region No. of States	No. of Seats			Democratic % of Seats		Republican % of Seats	
	1950	1970	1972	1950	1970	1950	1970
New England 6	32	25	25	35·7	64	64·3	36
Mid-Atlantic 5	95	92	88	44·4	56·5	55·6	43·5
Mid-West 5	87	88	86	29·9	40·9	70·1	59·1
Farm Belt 6	31	27	25	12·9	37	87·1	63
Mountain 8	16	17	19	62·5	47	37·7	53
Pacific 5	33	52	57	36·3	59·6	63·7	40·4
Border 4	36	28	27	80·5	82·2	19·5	17·8
Outer South 6	65	69	72	97	69·6	3	30·4
Deep South 5	40	37	36	100	83·8	0	16·2
U.S.A.	435	435	435	53·8	58·6	45·7	41·3

enjoy a majority. In the Mid-West, the improvement in the Democratic position is due mainly to an almost even distribution of Illinois' twenty-four districts and to smaller numerical gains in Indiana and Wisconsin; the large delegations of Michigan and Ohio remain almost two-thirds Republican in composition.

The Republicans were compensated for these losses by gains in the South and in the Mountain states though the Border states remained faithful to the Democrats. In the Deep South the Republicans did not win any seats until they picked up seven in 1964 on Senator Goldwater's coat-tails. They held on to six districts from 1966 to 1970 and then enjoyed another advance in 1972 when gains in Louisiana and Mississippi gave the Republicans at least one Representative in each Deep South state. Georgia (9 Dem., 1 Rep.) and Louisiana (7 Dem., 1 Rep.) remain strongly Democratic while Alabama (4 Dem., 3 Rep.), Mississippi (3 Dem., 2 Rep.) and South Carolina (4 Dem., 2 Rep.) are now more evenly balanced. The Republicans have made more substantial gains in the Outer South as the number of Republican Representatives has risen from two in 1950 to twenty-five in 1972; the gains were first made in 1952 and 1954 (when each state had at least one Republican district) and again in 1962. But the Republicans have enjoyed an increase in representation in every House election since 1966. The two large states, Florida (11 Dem., 4 Rep.) and Texas (20 Dem., 3 Rep.) are still mainly Democratic but Virginia (3 Dem., 7 Rep.) and Tennessee (3 Dem., 5 Rep.) now elect more Republicans than Democrats. Arkansas (3 Dem., 1 Rep.) which has suffered most from re-apportionment losing three seats between 1950 and 1972, has elected one Republican since 1966 while North Carolina (7 Dem., 4 Rep.) has also been moving away from its previously monolithic commitment to the Democratic Party.

The pattern of election results since 1948 therefore reveals an increasingly complex party system as defined by its electoral structure. Any discussion of realignment requires emphasizing the volatility of the electorate in presidential elections and the distinctions between congressional elections and presidential elections and between the North and the South. Congressional elections in the North point to the maintenance of the 1932 realignment and to its reinforcement since 1958. This development is in accord with W. W. Shannon's conclusion that 'the congressional parties . . . reflect the disparate socio-economic characteristics of the constituencies from which their members emerge'.[27] Thus the Democrats have been more successful in highly urbanized districts with large concentrations of blue-collar workers and/or non-whites while the Republicans tend to win less urbanized districts where income-levels are relatively high and where few blue-collar workers and non-whites live. Since 1958 the 300 Northern districts have been returning a net Republican majority of between twenty-six (1960) and six (1972) except when there has been a Democratic landslide (1958 and 1964) or even a slight Republican loss (nine seats in 1970). However the Republicans have been compensated by periodic gains in the South. The regional variations since 1966 are illustrated in Table 4. The Democrats have made small but consistent increases in their net advantage in the Border and Pacific states and in 1972 held on to net 1970 gains in the Farm Belt. The Republicans have increased their representation in the South and in the Mid-Atlantic states and regained in 1972 some of their net losses in the Great Lakes and Mountain regions.

Future control of the House depends upon the interaction of these various trends. If the Republicans continue to improve their representation in the South and in the Mid-Atlantic states and then enjoy a national swing in their favour, then a Republican House majority could emerge in the 1970s. Such a development could be delayed by the usual loss of House seats suffered by the President's party in mid-term elections and by a Democratic presidential victory

TABLE 4
Changes in Composition of Democratic House Majority by Region, 1966–72

Region	1966	1968	1970	1972	Net Change 1966–72
New England	+ 7	+ 5	+ 7	+ 5	− 2
Mid-Atlantic	+16	+14	+12	+ 6	−10
Pacific	+ 8	+ 8	+10	+13	+ 5
Mountain	− 1	− 5	− 1	− 3	− 2
Farm Belt	−17	−17	− 7	− 7	+10
Great Lakes	−24	−24	−16	−20	+ 4
Border	+12	+16	+18	+19	+ 7
Outer South	+35	+29	+27	+22	−13
Deep South	+25	+25	+25	+18	− 7
USA	+61	+51	+75	+53	− 8

in 1976.

The above developments in electoral politics suggest that it is necessary to reconsider the description of the Democratic Party as the normal majority party. This is not to argue that therefore the Republican Party is the new majority party or is going to become the new majority party despite the success of the Republican candidate in four of the six presidential elections from 1952 to 1972. Before taking this argument further it is essential to consider the distribution of voters identifying with the parties as described in the surveys of the University of Michigan's Survey Research Centre. One of the assumptions behind the notion of a majority party is the belief that such a party consistently enjoys the support of a majority or a strong plurality among voters. A much larger Democratic 'party in the electorate' has been consistently evident since 1952; its size has ranged from 43 per cent (strong *and* weak Democrats) in 1970 to 51 per cent in 1964; the proportion of Republican partisans has ranged from 29 per cent in 1956 when Eisenhower was at the height of his personal popularity to 25 per cent in 1970 when another Republican President was in the White House. The gap between Democratic and Republican partisans varies greatly between the South and the non-South and the proportion of 'independents' has increased to overtake both that gap and the proportion of Republican identifiers. Movements in party identification have not been large despite the volatility in voting behaviour.[28] The proportions of both Democrats and Republicans have been decreasing slightly in the 1960s while the proportion of independents showed the greatest change, from 23 per cent in 1964 to 31 per cent in 1970.

It is suggested that party identification is not likely to be an accurate guide to the behaviour of the electorate when many individual voters do not determine their electoral choice according to their views on the issues on which party identification is based. It is reasonable to stress the importance of socio-economic factors with respect to both the distribution of party identification and the virtual Democratic monopoly of national elections between 1932 and 1952 when economic issues were frequently important electoral issues.[29] But economic issues have not been the vital issues since 1952; rather several foreign policy problems including the Korean and Vietnam wars, the racial issue and various aspects of the 'social issue' have dominated presidential election outcomes. Presidential elections would appear to be becoming detached from the party system as defined by the distribution of party identification. Many voters, e.g., 40 per cent of Democratic identifiers in 1972, have been ignoring their partisan commitment when voting for President. The reasons for such behaviour vary. Southern whites are dissatisfied with the liberalism of Northern Democrats, congressional and presidential, on the racial issue. Northern Democratic identifiers were influenced in 1968 by the belief that the Johnson Administration had failed in Vietnam and in the city streets of the United States. There has been considerable speculation about the electoral impact of issues concerning race and urban unrest in 1968 and in 1972. One American political scientist, in a study of 'issue voting', has concluded that 'it is quite possible that the present Democratic party ... cannot withstand the impact of these issues (race and urban unrest) on its blue-collar members'.[30] Senator McGovern's failure suggests that the image of particular candidates, in terms of perceptions of personal competence and policy preferences, can be important also. Yet the debate as to whether McGovern lost so heavily because he was a bad candidate (e.g., his handling of the Eagleton affair), or an unlucky candidate (e.g., the consequences of selecting Eagleton) or a perceived ideological candidate hides the question of whether any Democratic candidate would have beaten President Nixon in 1972. Given the volatility of the electorate in presidential elections, which could still benefit the Democratic Party, the widespread strength of presidential Republicanism beyond the North-East (John Kennedy won fewer states (twenty-three) than

Nixon (twenty-five) in 1960), and the probability that future Demo-cratic candidates will not win many Southern states, then it is now inappropriate to describe the Democratic Party as the majority party in relation to presidential elections. However the volatility in presidential elections and the trends in congressional election results also suggest that a critical realignment, i.e., 'a short, sharp, reorganisation of the mass coalitional bases of the major parties which occur(s) at periodic intervals at the national level'[31] (and which extends to congressional as well as to presidential elections), is not yet clearly in the offing.

Julius Gould

Interests and Pressures

ALL POLITIES ARE PRESSURE COOKERS. THEY DIFFER IN ALL SORTS OF ways – and many of the differences between them reflect the differences in the pressures they contain, in the way the 'cooker' has been designed or has found a durable shape, and in how they respond to the changing force and direction of the pressures. It is no longer fashionable to look with disdain at the special historical importance of such pressures within the American polity: we know all too well that comparable processes exist elsewhere. It remains true, however, that, within a changing context of society and culture, interest groups both public and private, are peculiarly alive and well within the American system. Various social critics, at markedly different levels of insight and proof, have argued that America has become a 'post-industrial', 'technetronic' society or that it has become a 'global village' or that it has been 'greened' via a mysterious change of 'consciousness' or that its fortunes can be gauged through the study of an as yet incomplete realignment of ethnic attachments both among whites and blacks. The social and cultural strains which these and other arguments explore are, none the less, exerted within a political order that, despite the *Sturm und Drang* of the 1960s, has not been subject to any fundamental renovation and innovation. Even if we do not entirely accept the analogy drawn by Huntington between American political institutions and 'the Tudor polity of the sixteenth century', we can endorse his view that 'this static quality of the political system contrasts with the prevalence of change elsewhere within the American system'.[1] That system is the legacy of the Madisonian model of government – of the 'constitution of divided powers' that in the earliest days of the American republic was set up as a barricade against 'the great beast' of majority rule – a system that was tailor-made for a crisscrossing diversity in the relations between political, governmental and extra-governmental interests. It is true again, as for example Huntington and Lipset among others have pointed out, that America pioneered new forms of 'mass participation' through the wide spread of suffrage and the parallel emergence of political parties. But it is also true that neither these modes nor indeed more contemporary modes of 'community participation' have permitted 'the great beast' to enter the citadel. The chanelling and compromise of group interests, never totally crystallized along class cleavages, the changing structure and sophistication of bureaucracy and organization, and not least the recurrent exercise of presidential will – all this has maintained a quite remarkable degree of political continuity. This is not to deny that the Madisonian thinking has played the role of a political myth or a self-fulfilling prophecy: or to deny that it has foreshortened or foreclosed desirable political options or that its acceptance can lead, and has led, to striking irrationalities and inefficiencies. Political scientists have condemned the absence of coherent national parties, the survival, though in a modified and changing form, of 'one party regions' and the perverse workings within Congress of the seniority rule with its conservative and regional bias. They have seen that the new America – in its cities and suburbs – is undergoing many realignments of political loyalties and that in their course the party structures with their rural bases are bound to change. Yet the reformers, even at their most sensitive, do not really know how the inertia of the existing constellation of interests can be overcome. I would myself argue that the barriers are stronger than they are generally prepared to concede. It is likely, for example, that only a presidential initiative could break through the constitutional and social barriers to reform. Yet is it clear that most presidents would prefer a strong, non-confused party system to the present confused situation with its bipartisan options and so very open to pressure from a diversity of extra-Congressional interests? Such an initiative would require Herculean expenditure of energy and time: and even a Kennedy finds more pressing matters that appear to have a greater claim both upon his attention and his ambitions.

THE 'BALANCE OF GROUPS' THEORY

In his *Politics in the USA* M.J.C. Vile notes that 'group pluralism is perhaps *the* American theory of politics'[2] and goes on to claim that for such a politics of group interaction to work successfully there must be 'a broad consensus of agreement about the basis and aims of the society so that no group will attempt to enforce its views upon the rest to the point where civil war might ensue'. It also requires, as he puts it, 'political mechanisms' which can ensure equilibrium without stagnation. Now the doctrines of consensus and equilibrium have, as Vile would agree, not gone unchallenged in recent years – over a period of heightened aspirations, war-induced cleavages, conservative backlash and revolutionary 'radical chic'. There is, so to say, less consensus about consensus than the Madisonian, or the later sociological, doctrines on the subject have presupposed. Yet, to an extent that will surprise only those who seek apocalyptic solutions to 'crisis', many of those reformers who distrust a consensual philosophy, and the imbalances which it has fostered, have sought to work within the 'group interest' structure – and this has been so not least in the areas of current difficulty and concern, such as environmental control or the reform of the welfare benefits system. Of course such an image of group politics underplays – as Vile again recognizes – the positive role which can be played by the presidency in the field of policy determination or resolution. New and significant changes in the direction of policy do not always emerge from group interaction or the *Zeitgeist* alone. As a recent comment on Nixon's welfare package reminds us 'once his support was achieved sceptics became scarce. Once sceptics became scarce policy change became possible.'[3] Whether it is *actually* translated into Congressional action, however, as the history of the welfare proposals since 1965 itself has shown, depends upon a long battle with established interests (and political manoeuvring) both inside and outside Capitol Hill.

The 'balance of groups' theory cannot be a useless guide to the intricacies of American politics – especially when the notion of group pressures is widened to take in the pressures which are exercised from within the executive departments and bureaux of the Administration itself. How do these groups work? Any attempt to list the standard operating procedures of interest group activity is likely to fall upon the distinction, always rather an arbitrary one, between what constitutes 'conventionally accepted' forms of pressure and what does not. Attempts to formalize this so far as concerns the relations between 'lobbies' and Congress have, of course, been made. But it is all too obvious that the legislation and the conventions on the subject have left untouched a grey area which shades from the dubious to the near-corrupt. In the wider area of persuasion and grass roots mobilization there is, at one extreme, recourse to violence, as American as cherry pie – just as at another extreme there is – perhaps equally American – an element of thinly concealed bribery and corruption shading off from the 'conventional' deployment of various inducements and deterrents to legislative action. Vile, writ-

ing in 1970, noted that there was 'a sizeable part of the population
that is potentially ready to step outside the framework of compromise politics to further its "interest" by violent means if
necessary'[4] – such groups being found on the right as well as on the
left. He does not however (and he is not alone in this) raise the
possibility that the use of threats to be violent or reference to acts
of previous violence (especially committed by others) has become –
and not only in the USA – a fairly common recourse among the
non-violent advocates of moderate reform. Such moderates can,
without themselves condoning or committing violence, argue that
'if you don't yield to us you will have to face those violent fellows
over there!': and this argument has often been deployed with
subtlety and ambivalence. It is of course arguable that such a tactic
has its uses as well as its limitations in loosening a real or perceived
situation of conservative stagnation. Its success must depend upon
its credibility – a credibility that can break upon its repeated use,
upon the realization by threatened 'counter interests' that concessions
to moderation, rather than still immoderate ideas, may precipitate
new demands and concessions, and upon the development of a
revived, less nervous conservatism through a heightened general
perception that an existing distribution of wealth, status and power
is under threat.

The study of interest groups has, of course, been much involved
with matters of definition and classification. Existing classifications,
though often and inevitably somewhat general in character, retain
their usefulness – even when they have been drawn from a study of
earlier phases of American social and political history. I do not want
to pursue these questions here. Classification of itself, in any case,
does not seek to offer insight into the 'dynamics' of pressure group
activity – or into the stylized or improvised relationships between
pressure groups and their political points of contact – still less into
the 'pressures' which pressure groups must encounter in return.
Several decades now separate us from the Anti-Saloon League – and
new areas of 'interested' activity have developed: despite the
attention which some of them have received they cannot yet be said
to have been absorbed even into the most valuable recent attempts
at classification. In the contemporary scene the formal political
system co-exists with challenges, for example, from the so-called
military-industrial complex, from new forms of citizen pressure
(not least those associated with environmental and ecological causes)
and from movements for reform and innovation – often of a funda-

mental kind – which have been sponsored, directly or indirectly, by the great foundations – themselves an American social invention of considerable interest.

Rather than attempt a new classification, disguised inadequately as a 'theory' of interest or pressure groups, I have chosen to set out some cases which illustrate the forms and context of some of the contemporary pressures, both of the older and the newer forms and to indicate how they 'live with', exploit or are contained by, the 'given' framework of political institutions.

The range of possible illustrations is, as will be obvious, very large indeed. Some of them are very contemporary and luxuriant – arising not only from the recurrent electoral battles but out of the cleavages (over the Vietnam war, over student rebellions, over women's rights) which have become so obvious in recent years. Many of these cleavages have been very fully publicized (and – almost as fully – documented). I do not, of course, underrate their importance – or their capacity to generate political heat. The examples I have chosen touch upon different, and equally important, areas of social and political controversy: and those who make decisions in these fields face a bewildering variety of concrete pressures. I hope that the cases which I cite, including the more mundane cases, will illuminate as well as illustrate.

'NO-FAULT' INSURANCE: ELEMENTS OF A PROFILE

A not untypical interplay of interests and gambits may be seen in the 'no-fault insurance' debates of the past two years. In the spring of 1971 both the Senate and the House of Representatives held hearings on the proposal from Senators Hart and Magnuson to enact no-fault insurance for those suffering personal injuries in automobile accidents. Stripped of its technicalities the Hart bill sought to ensure that claims would be paid without the prior consideration of who was 'at fault' or had 'caused' the accident. Other provisions related to income loss, medical and other expenses or benefits, and rules to prevent insurance companies from deciding to cancel insurance policies except, for example, for non-payment of premia or driver disqualification. Hart was frank about his intent – it was simply 'to change the present system so that monies paid in go to victims instead of being consumed by the present extremely inefficient system itself'. What is here involved will become clear if we observe that in 1969 it was estimated that over half of each dollar paid in for bodily-injury insurance went not to defray accident claims but to meet company expenses, lawyers' fees and court costs; lawyers' fees in this class of work are now believed to total $1 billion per annum. The Administration's position was favourable to the proposal but, consistently and characteristically, it urged that it be left to the several states to enact their own laws via the elaboration of a model statute. Automobile manufacturers, the big auto-rental companies, Consumers Union, labour interests and the ubiquitous Common Cause[5] all favoured the plan – even though in some cases they thought it was not strong enough. On the other hand, and predictably, it met 'unalterable' opposition from the National Association of Mutual Insurance Agents – whose spokesman saw in it an invitation to chaos: understandably he preferred his own plan for milder and, of course, optional 'adjustments to the reparation system'. The insurance industry was however divided. The American Insurance Association favoured both the principle of 'no-fault' and the scheme itself – having despaired of state initiatives (or, rather, the absence of state initiatives) in this field. Important though this group of companies is, there is another group, the National Association of Independent Insurers, containing five times as many companies (520 in all) and doing considerably more automobile insurance business – and this group opposed the Hart-Magnuson initiative. Also aligned with the opposition was the American Trial Lawyers Association (ATLA). A former senior official of ATLA testified to the Senate Commerce Committee that ATLA members worked on key men in state legislatures in order to foil insurance law reform. (This charge was at once virtuously rebutted by ATLA's president who argued that if any ATLA member suggested 'we should take a position in our self interest he would be thrown out of the room'.) In a similar vein the House was told by an Illinois Democrat: 'in ten states . . . with more than half the registered cars in the country, among the 1799 legislators in 1969 were 665 attorneys and 164 insurance salesmen . . .' In Illinois attempts to pass a no-fault insurance law had been 'defeated by legislators in the insurance and legal professions'. This, again, should be judged in the light of the $1 billion (about one sixth of all legal fees) estimated to accrue to the legal profession each year for their services in handling automobile negligence cases.

In late June 1972 the Senate Commerce Committee reported the bill in a form which gave the states two years to produce a scheme and if the states failed to do so still tougher requirements enforceable by federal law would come into operation. No doubt the same interests will clash in the House Committee and in floor debate – and the final form of legislation will represent a compromise.

Here then is one profile of a very common legislative – pressure group interplay: Senatorial initiative responsive to and backed by an articulate consumer interest, supported by a section of an 'interest' that is to be regulated, opposed by others; clear but qualified Administration support for a proposal emanating from the 'opposition party': and a steady counterpoint on the theme of state responsibility for enforcing any regulation that may be agreed – the more 'conservative' elements in the structure leaning, often quite passionately, in the direction of the states.

POLLUTION AND REGULATION

The public concern with ecology and the environment – albeit one which preoccupies 'middle class' persons more than it does welfare recipients or the black 'underclass' – has had a considerable though varied impact on politics. Let me just cite two measures passed into law in 1970 which limited the 'freedom' of key industrial interests – the oil producers and automobile manufacturers. The Water Quality Improvement Act was passed after over three years of debate. The Senate and House had quarrelled over whether the owners of vessels had 'absolute liability' for oil spills or only for 'wilful and negligent discharges', the Administration and the House preferring the latter formula. Penalties of up to $14 million were set out as a deterrent against oil pollution from tankers – and $8 million in the event of oil spills from onshore or offshore installations – with a provision for unlimited liability in cases of wilful negligence or misconduct – an outcome that can hardly have been gratifying to the oil interests. 1970 also saw the revision of the Air Quality Act of 1967. This key environmental measure contained a requirement that automobile manufacturers should by 1 January 1976 meet standards which reduced engine exhaust emissions by 90 per cent of the 1970 levels – with the possibility of a one year extension for manufacturers who 'tried hard' but in good faith needed extra time. The setting of the deadline was firmly inserted by Congress and not left, as the President and auto manufacturers wanted, to be determined by the newly created Environmental Protection Agency. It may well be that this measure, unlike others that have been passed both before and since, sought to make impossible a very common way by which 'interests' (either with the connivance of Congress or because Congress has failed to notice) extract the teeth from the controls that threaten them. The power of interested groups cannot always be controlled narrowly and in detail by federal law. Very much (often too much) discretion is left to be determined by the interplay and bargaining between the groups whose interests are subject to regulation and the bureaux which have to devise and apply the regulations. Thus, a recent paper on the pollution issue by two economists[6] has argued that 'the regulation/enforcement strategy pits the power of the pollution-control authorities against the power of the polluter in an unending sequence of skirmishes and battles over licensing and the enforcement of regulations. As a consequence the enforcement process is long and drawn out and often inconclusive.' It is surely often in the interest of the interests to move the battle away from overt public dispute into what I would describe as the 'corridors of regulation' – which are always lawyer infested. The exercise of administrative discretion within these corridors is no guarantee that a many-headed problem such as that of pollution will be solved. On the contrary the multiplication of regulatory bodies, so dear to liberal reformers – and the multiplicity of regulative ploys – remove the 'problem' into an area of technicalities, escape clauses and jurisdictional detail. And if an interest cannot find its way around them it can only be for want of trying – or for lack of easily purchased legal advice.

ENVIRONMENT AND AEROSPACE

The most significant victory for the environmental lobbies came in March 1971 when the debate and controversy over the supersonic aircraft development programme was concluded. This episode is of interest for it combines an environmental theme with an aerospace theme – and the outcome suggests that the 'civil-industrial complex' is not invincible. Both Houses of Congress voted to remove $134 million of appropriations destined for the SST by the Department of Transportation. Environmental arguments were most potent in the debates and in the hard lobbying by which the debates were preceded. It was a fairly crucial confrontation between Administration spokesmen, aerospace companies, and labour interests on the one hand, and environmental anxieties on the other. The relevant House Appropriation subcommittee voted twenty-six to fifteen in favour of a continued programme – perhaps somewhat reassured by the view of the Environmental Protection Agency's Director that the issue to be determined was an *economic* one: the environmental issue would be clarified if the proposed two proto- types could be constructed and tested. But the House itself was not persuaded and the proposed funding was deleted by a 216–203 vote: a week later on 24 March the Senate too was to confirm this by 51 to 46 – despite strong appeals for SST on employment and balance of payments grounds from, *inter alios*, Senator Jackson (who represented an already stricken aerospace state), George Meany and Treasury Secretary John Connally. This was a signal defeat for the President and for the great variety of interests which had pressed for a continued funding of SST. The pro-SST campaign across the country had been spearheaded by the National Committee for the SST and its ally Industry and Labour For SST – which early in 1971 had mounted a letter writing and mass media campaign – financed by interested parties such as Boeing and the International Association of Machinists – an AFL-CIO affiliate. These bodies were confronted by the Coalition Against the SST – supported by a number of en- vironmentalist and conservationist groups, e.g. Environmental Action, the Sierra Club and the Friends of the Earth, as well as by Common Cause and a number of economists including both Milton Friedman and J. K. Galbraith. Their ploy was to link the environ- mental and economic considerations and this was done with much skill and effect by John Gardner, Common Cause's President. They were unwilling to accept assurances that the commercial SST, already deprived of permission to fly over land, would not be built if environmental hazards were demonstrated. The economic arguments upon which their otherwise miscellaneous group of economic experts were agreed were indispensable weapons in their effort to kill the project and keep it killed.

The proponents of SST were, however, not to yield so simply. On 12 May, less than two months after the apparently 'final reverse' for the SST lobby, the House, on the recommendation of its Appropriation Committee, proposed that a sum of over $85 million be allotted to Boeing and General Electric by way of termination payments – funds which could, nonetheless, be used for further work on the prototypes during what remained of the financial year. While preparing this comeback, the pro-SST lobby had in fact stopped all open campaigning. The Administration, while dismantling its SST planning staff, was quietly working, through 'normal' channels, to persuade House members to reverse their earlier positions. Much

of the credit for the switching of votes was attributed to the efforts
of the House Minority leader. The argument that he had found most
persuasive was that it would be more expensive to kill the SST than
to proceed with it. Interestingly this argument was torpedoed on the
day following the House vote by a statement from Boeing's chairman that the cost of a revived and renegotiated SST project would
be between $500 million and $1 billion. Clearly the web linking
Congress, Administration and outside interests is not exactly seam-
less – the various efforts to secure a common objective are not
completely synchronized. It is hardly surprising that the House
Minority leader observed that Boeing's estimate 'could not have
been made at a worse time'. By the time debate on this matter in the
Senate was completed (19 May) the Administration had come
round, in its turn, to admit that it would be more expensive to
continue SST than to cancel, while expressing pained concern over
the level at which Boeing had pitched the costs of renegotiation.
Amid this confusion the Senate had no hesitation now in insisting
on a genuine, though adequately funded, termination.[7]

THE MILITARY-INDUSTRIAL TANGLE

The interplay between military interests and the political system
has long been of interest – well before the post-war surge of military
appropriations. The Army Corps of Engineers with its special role
in civil engineering, and the veteran groups with their privileged
social benefits and medical care, have long enjoyed special fields of
political influence.[8] But the last twenty years have seen the growth
of a much more pervasive military-political linkage supplementing
what can, quite fairly, be called a military-industrial alliance. There
is no need to claim that this takes the form of any conspiracy – rather
at all these levels there has been a coincidence, real or supposed,
between military planners, defence contractors and members of
Congress. In the words of a recent writer, Adam Yarmolinsky, in
The Military Establishment: 'The biggest contract awards have tended
over the years to go to districts of key members of the military
committees who in turn usually vote for the Pentagon's program.'[9]
It should be recalled that over the period 1950 to 1972 defence
appropriations rose from just under $13 billion to over $70 billion –
and that until the late 1960s, with the cleavages over South East
Asian policy, Congress overall acquiesced in the shape and scale of
military expenditure rather than exerted any effective countervailing

power. Nor in the absence of criteria for measuring the relative merits of defence and non-defence expenditure did it attempt to set out an alternative set of priorities to those which moved successive Administrations. One need not convict Congress of falling victim to a 'military metaphysic' to appreciate how the network of regional interests and military programming led to this result. The evidence suggests that Congress was lobbied on military matters far more assiduously by 'governmental lobbyists' than by defence corporations themselves – and that the major hurdle for a defence contractor was overcome when a weapons system had been 'sold' to the Pentagon.[10] Over and above this pattern of 'conventional' military lobbying pressure has taken less conventional forms on the interesting, though infrequent, occasions when interservice rivalries, or service disagreements with the Secretary for Defence, have been ventilated before Congressional committees.[11]

The links between the Pentagon and its industrial-scientific suppliers may be traced back to the dependence of the services, especially but not only the USAF, upon 'outside' corporations to supply not only weaponry but also the research and development upon which new weapon-systems depend. Yarmolinsky quotes one source as suggesting that the Air Force intelligently anticipated the crop of political advantages which such an external constituency would bring – committed as such a constituency would be, at a time of great scientific and technological achievement, to expensive and, where possible, open-ended, development projects. Unique buyer and seller relationships were to emerge. While, in one sense, these relationships reduced the autonomy of the corporate supplier it is also the case that, in the short run, there were ample opportunities for economic gain. A good illustration is provided by the tangled affairs of Lockheed. In 1965 the USAF estimate for its proposed force of 120 giant jet transport C_5A's – a Lockheed Georgia project – was $3.4 billion. By mid-1971 the costs for eighty-one of these machines was estimated at $4.5 billion. There is evidence that cost overruns on this scale (especially in the aerospace industry where government agencies are the sole purchasers) reflect not just inflation but also a rate of profit far higher than that which would obtain in 'competitive' conditions and higher by far than any known computation of profit margins in industries outside the defence fields. There is evidence too of skilful recourse to the 'strategy' whereby defence suppliers offer low estimates for an initial run of a weapon or aircraft but are assured, via contracts with the Pentagon, of much higher and generous compensation by way of subsidies on later runs. With the complexities of this strategy we are not here concerned – suffice it to say that it has not yet been controlled by any known technique either of congressional scrutiny or of sophisticated PPB: and that when it backfires it produces interesting political revelations and reactions. Thus Lockheed eventually had to take a $200 million loss on its C5A venture – and this led it into its troubles on yet another of its projects – the Tristar aircraft with which the fortunes of Rolls-Royce were also so intimately involved. Their Tristar troubles led the Treasury to propose a guarantee to Lockheed of some $250 million against urgently needed bank loans by Lockheed. (This resulted in an interesting clash of interests within the aircraft industry. General Electric, as a manufacturer of jet engines, sought to oppose it – unless Tristar was to use American-made engines.) Senate opposition was spearheaded by Senator Proxmire who observed that thousands upon thousands of small businesses fail but 'lacking the political clout of Lockheed' they had not aspired to any government guarantee. On the other hand potential users of Tristar, already committed, and the inevitable subcontractors testified for the Administration's guarantee proposal. Other interests, less closely involved, praised the virtues of the threat of bankruptcy and of the market forces from which they felt Lockheed was being insulated. The idea was extended to take the form of a bill authorizing loans of up to $250 million for individual businesses in distress – an extension which Proxmire denounced as a 'Lockheed guarantee bill in disguise' and a 'big business giveaway of the worst sort' and which McGovern thought should be expanded yet further into a $2 billion guarantee for farmers and small businesses. In the end a very narrow Senate vote on 2 August 1971 passed the Lockheed guarantee by 49–48 votes – with three abstentions, including those of two Senators from Texas and Washington – both states heavily dependent on aircraft production, but not Lockheeds.

THE LIBERAL 'ELITE' AND A WORD ON POLITICAL PHILANTHROPY

Of continuing importance in the American context is the part played by the organizations which represent, to quote one of their critics,[12] the 'moderate wing' of the power elite – bodies which, with support from business, have exerted a powerful intellectual and political pressure. A good example of such a body is the Committee for Economic Development: there is certainly evidence that it can prefigure or pave the way for what later becomes Administration policy. They are indeed in a peculiarly prestigious position to influence such policy both by their personal contacts with the executive and by their role as 'a major supplier of expertise to Congress'. The CED was founded in 1942 as a business led and financed body which, in the fashion of the time, saw as a responsibility the need for 'planning' ahead to avoid post-war reconstruction and so avoid a recurrence of the very recent depression and mass unemployment. It naturally came to play a leading role in the staffing and formulation of Marshall plan policies – representing a much weaker commitment to traditional business ideology than, say, the NAM. 'Moderate' cause groups (of which CED is only one example) unsurprisingly share 'interlocking' leadership – not least through their connections with the great foundations, through informal links as well as through foundation support to quite specific and costly research projects. CED showed a considerable ability to move, as times changed, into the fields of budgetary and monetary reform as well as into foreign policy matters, such as the issues of technical assistance to developing countries in Latin America and elsewhere. In the last five years the CED has moved to a concern with the controversial and currently unsolved and untractable problem of welfare reform. Gilbert Y. Steiner in his recent account of *The State of Welfare*[13] in the United States chronicles the CED's rather gingerly and restrained approach to this problem in 1968 and 1969. This began in the period when the Nixon Administration was preparing to devise and accept a scheme (presented in 1969 and still not cleared through Congress) for a family assistance programme. Its first policy forum on welfare in May 1968 reported that

> Agreement among the participants was unanimous that the present welfare system needs a major overhaul but opinion was divided on the issue of income maintenance . . . Most felt that substantially more research and experimentation would be needed before a reasonable judgement of the problem could be made.

But Steiner himself concludes:

> the . . . statements of . . . interest in reform, coupled with failure

to offer a specific policy proposal, made it possible for the President's men to pursue welfare reform with some confidence that there would be business support for the product and that no particular business-sponsored proposal had to be taken into account in the planning process. When what became the family assistance plan was in the drafting stage the White House politely invited comment from the CED leaders. They bought family assistance . . .

CED concern with welfare did not stop at the point recorded by Steiner. In 1970 a CED spokesman (whose corporate base was Xerox) appeared before Congress to urge that welfare legislation should include establishment of a federally supported national programme of daycare centres and should provide for a phased takeover by the federal government of all state and local welfare costs within a five year period. And in June 1971 another spokesman appeared before the Senate Finance Committee to oppose the Administration's revenue sharing proposals which, he said, 'failed to meet adequately the needs of the country's principal cities for relief of their welfare load. Welfare is a national problem which calls for national relief . . . the wish to shift decision-making to the grass roots under these circumstances is a theoretical and not a valid practical argument for this proposal.' These are strong and independent words – and their tone is far different to that adopted by narrowly sectional, regional or corporation interests.

A further word, however brief, may be appropriate on the role of the foundations. It would be hard to deny their important role in elite policy-formation in international affairs and in research which has led to (and at times legitimized) policy decisions on both internal and external affairs. Though they are currently being accused of timidity it could also be argued that some of their interventions in internal domestic policy areas, in the service of what I call political philanthropy, have shown a mixture of over-confidence and rashness. The Ford Foundation[14] for example, in the 1960s, financed a number of politically controversial and often unsuccessful experiments in the area of social and community development and it was involved, especially in New York, in what became rather explosive experiments in the community control of schools. Daniel Patrick Moynihan[15] has described how in those days of ferment, which led up to such ventures as the New York scheme for Mobilization for Youth and the national Economic Opportunity Act, the spokesmen for Ford could, for example, display an interest in community action that was 'ostensibly directed exclusively to the somehow apolitical question of *process*'. Of course its consequences were drenched in politics. And small wonder – for, on Moynihan's account, 'The Ford Foundation . . . purposed nothing less than institutional change in the operation and control of American cities' – and with this was allied the ploy of letting 'the need for outside intervention . . . appear locally initiated', a posture in which Moynihan detects 'an element of deception' . . . Alas the intellectual underpinnings, especially in sociological theory, for these experiments in social engineering were to prove (and indeed appeared to many at the time) too fragile and insubstantial to bear so heavy a political and administrative load. The sometimes disorderly results, and Johnson's presidential reservations, were to bring down the curtain on these ventures.

REPRISE

There has been much speculation as to the directions in which American society is evolving – and these speculations are, of course, highly relevant to the question of the viability of American political institutions. Yet even if we accept the least extravagant of these speculations – those which argue that it has entered, not without lags and frictions, the 'post-industrial' era, it does not follow that group pressures will disappear or that the real diversities that they reflect will be resolved by some, as yet unknown, cybernetic political process. Indeed new diversities and interests will be created – and they will fight out their battles with newer and more sophisticated weapons. There will remain argument over whether, on balance, the American legacy of group pressures will make (or has made) for greater rigidities than are socially and politically acceptable. Of course Robin M. Williams is right to suggest,[16] as he does in his classic work *American Society* that 'the marked articulation of pressure groups' may be 'a rigidifying influence upon the social order': and to add 'it is so by definition to the extent that such groups are successful in gaining political privilege'. Yet it is also true that, for those willing to remain within the 'system' the interest groups will retain a representative function and form islands of free expression, however selfishly motivated, within a polity that is bureaucratically overloaded and likely to become, even under a Republican regime, more centralized and, no doubt, in a special American manner, more *dirigiste*. The survival of interest groups may be a necessary condition for greater flexibility and more effective. because more open and informed, essays in participation.

Peter Madgwick

The American City—
An Ungovernable Enterprise?

THE THESIS THAT THE AMERICAN CITY IS UNGOVERNABLE DOES NOT look difficult to sustain. American cities contain acute and chronic problems. There are the problems of the poor – unemployment, discrimination, overcrowding, crime; the middle-class – environmental problems of transportation and pollution; and the problems of race, and of law and order. These problems arise from, or are exacerbated by, the city itself, which is never simply a neutral arena for its people. Since the mid-1960s it has been fashionable to refer to an 'urban crisis': the term connotes instability, breakdown, and violence, and appears to be justified by the rioting which has occurred sporadically in the cities since 1965. While the more pessimistic prophecies for the long hot summers have not been fulfilled (even meteorologically), it is clear that violence and tension in the cities have increased; alienation, by some measures,[1] is widespread, and the drift of people away from city centres has, with variations, continued.

There is of course some exaggeration in the talk of urban crisis. Urban studies have prospered on the crisis (and perhaps the crisis has thrived on the ideas of the urbanists). But there is little agreement among academics on the nature of the crisis, and in any case general statements about American cities are notoriously difficult to validate. The media have also contributed to the idea of crisis. The extent of rioting has been magnified. The casualty rate has not been high by the standards of, say, the Homestead strike of 1892, Germany in the 1930s, or recent urban guerilla warfare. About one hundred and twenty persons were killed between 1964 and 1967, but most of the deaths occurred in three major riots (Watts, Detroit, and Newark) and were caused by the over-reaction of the forces of law and order, not by the rioters. Serious rioting has been confined to a few big cities, and the rather special case of New York figures prominently in illustration of 'the American city'. Rioting has, in any case, diminished so far in the 1970s. Few problems get worse and some improve a little. Partial solutions, erratic, haphazard and inadequate, no doubt, are attempted. Cities living on the verge of bankruptcy survive, and voters register and turn out in city elections in proportions higher than in Britain.[2] The city seems still to provide sufficient satisfactions, or at least to engender hope or aquiescence, and to hold off revolution.

The margin between survival and breakdown is, however, a fine one and the plight of the cities is critical enough to put stress on the political system. The existence of an 'urban crisis' is not in itself evidence of the failure of city government. Partly the crisis is due to migration brought about by the mechanization of agriculture and the attractiveness of the cities as providers of jobs, homes, or welfare. But whatever the cause, the classical criticisms of American city government gain significance in face of the urban crisis. According to this critique, the city lacks autonomy, failing to gain power from the state and federal governments, and losing power to commissions, boards and special districts. Executive power is similarly fragmented, and political parties are ill-adapted to the building of responsible power. This situation is to the advantage of irresponsible interest groups. The fiscal structure of American government reinforces the constitutional and political restrictions. Widespread corruption increases costs, decreases efficiency and invalidates political responsibility. Thus, it is argued, city governments cannot deal with the urgent problems now presented to them.

This classical critique of city government is at least oversimplified, though basically not mistaken. Thus, there are some customary lines of admiration to set beside the classical critique: the 'openness' of the system; the possibilities of developing executive-centred power; the potential of the political party for coalitions, for communication and for insurgency. In other ways, however, the credibility of city government is not obviously enhanced. There are several political developments which affect the capacity of city governments: changes in political ethos; the impact of major federal 'programmes', the growing influence of professionals and the insurgency of new pressure groups, the entrenchment of the suburbs. Further, there is less certainty about the nature of urban problems, and different diagnoses have different implications for politics. Finally, the salience of the cities as the arena of problems may not be matched by the political importance of cities in the total machinery available for the solution of problems.

Altogether a review of the state of American city governments in the light of the classical critique leads to conclusions which do not encourage, while not totally destroying, belief in their viability. In the face of America's urban political institutions, the optimist requires at least a modicum of faith to sustain him.

THE DISCONNECTIONS BETWEEN AREA AND AUTHORITY

The city, more than any other unit in a confused system of government, is uncertain of its jurisdiction. The territorial boundaries of the city do not fit the social patterns of living, working and communication. The powers the city wrests from the state are diffused into local districts and special boards. The federal government has provided assistance at a cost in further administrative complication. The complexity and instability of the system disguise its rigidity. Mayors have found the system time-consuming and frustrating to work. But the greatest threat to the viability of city government comes not from Washington or the state capitol, but nearer home – from the suburbs.

Federal aid for urban programmes has been welcomed by the mayors as 'federal salvation'. Federal expenditure on all civilian programmes has more than trebled in a decade. But the saving of the cities has not been without costs to them. The capacity of the cities to deliver social welfare and urban renewal has been increased, but the autonomy and directness of city government has been diminished. Federal programmes arrive with strings, and federal administrators, attached. The city may be bound by federal standards in employment practices and building standards; more important, the grant of money requires the submission of a case for federal sanction. The degree of federal power over the city is far from absolute. The city retains initiative, and the ultimate freedom not to use the programme. In between there is an indistinct area of consultation and negotiation. The loss to the city arises mainly from the diffusion and complexity of decision-making, rather than from a simple transfer of power to the national or state government. Indeed, it has been argued that the tendency of grant programmes is 'to subsidize the decentralization of American political power' – since money spent locally constitutes patronage and is a source of local political power.[3]

Still, federal aid for the cities is a bonus and is likely to grow in response to the needs. Current trends in White House thinking suggest that the federal government may eventually take over the responsibility for the major welfare provision against poverty by a simple scheme of income maintenance (artfully called a 'negative income tax' to distinguish it from other welfare 'handouts'). This would relieve the cities of the onerous and unequal burden of supporting a welfare system which in other countries is assumed without question by the national government.

While cities are the pensioners of the federal government they are the constitutional creatures of the states. The cities are contained, even controlled, by the states. The restrictions imposed on the city may be severe. Mayor Lindsay of New York has found it difficult or impossible, for example, to change the hours of police work or to establish off-course betting, against the opposition of the state legislature. 'We are subject to the will of people who neither live in the city nor, often, know anything about its problems'.[4]

Not all mayors feel as frustrated as Mayor Lindsay. In some cities 'Home Rule' has provided a degree of autonomy, and state governments may concede a wide measure of discretion to local governments as a matter of policy. Many state governments are moving to a new awareness of the problems of the cities, and some have established agencies to deal with urban affairs.[5] State governors and the newly-reapportioned legislatures are open to the pressures of the city delegations.

Federalism is an inescapable fact of American political life. An obvious simplification of the system would be for the biggest cities to become states. But such a radical change would not be acceptable to the states and indeed goes against the arguments for the consolidation of multiple and fragmented units of government. This is the local aspect of the city's problems in relating power to area. The power extracted by the city from the federal system may be diluted by or lost to other districts and units of government within the city; and the city's own jurisdiction may prove to be inadequate for the problems it must deal with. Herein lies the metropolitan problem, which confounds the complexities of the federal system.

The most serious aspect of the metropolitan problem is not the lack of co-operation or co-ordination between the larger units of government, the cities, and the states. Here modern communications have overcome some of the disadvantages of fragmentation; and consultative machinery, informal ententes, alliances and treaty organization do much more. [6] Regional organizations of a functional or a general character seem to work, where sharp necessity provides incentive and dynamic. The federal government provides rather shadowy regional links, based on very large regions. But the natural metropolitan co-ordinator in the American system is the state, which perhaps for this purpose needs to be reinvented.

City government suffers more now by the constant threat of relatively tiny units of government to the integrity of the larger. There is a strong tendency for the neighbourhoods of a metropolitan area to become municipalities. [7] The New York Metropolitan Region's notorious 1400 governments are matched for example in Fridley, Minnesota, where 15,000 citizens labour under eleven layers of government, each with the power to tax. [8] Neighbourhoods are natural social units, homogeneous in interests and outlook, available for political organization, approved by the fashion for neighbourhood government and able to exploit the constitutional encouragement give to fragmentation. Mainly the neighbourhoods are the fast growing suburbs, concerned to protect their advantages from the depredations of the central city's poor (and the mayor acting on their behalf). Co-operation with the central city, in zoning regulations for example, is difficult, and consolidation is almost out of the question. There have been only a handful of 'metropolitan consolidations'. Dade County (Miami), together with Toronto, have been described as lonely monuments to an idea whose time had not come. [9] But the central city like the suburbs may also acquire its own sense of identity and interest.

Indeed, the metropolitan problem which was once about the need to annex the neighbours, is now just as much about the need to hold on to existing jurisdictions. It is not without significance that Mayor Lindsay moves out of Manhattan from time to time to tread the stony suburban pastures of Brooklyn and Queens. The city delegation in the state legislature now has to fear the suburban neighbour as much as the up-country one. [10] The entrenchment of neighbourhood and suburban interests represents a more serious threat to the viability of city government than the vagaries and frustrations of the federal system.

The fragmentation of governments at all levels is, of course, related to inequalities in economy, services and amenities. For example, in Dayton, Ohio, the property-tax valuation per school child varies from under $6000 in one, partly black, school district to $24,000 in another, an exclusive suburb. Where British government has tended to secure equalization between areas (though this is far from total), American government has tended to protect or create inequality. The defence of differentials then provides a justification and reinforcement of fragmentation. The cities suffer twice over from the fragmented differential: by immigration from poor southern states attracted by better welfare provision, and by emigration and defection of suburban dwellers.

THE FINANCIAL WEAKNESS OF THE CITIES

Federal and metropolitan patterns of government weaken the city financially by creating a disparity between tax-base and service-load. While money is not exactly equivalent to power, the cities would function more effectively if they had unrestricted access to enlarged financial resources. Cities come to the tax trough after the federal government and the states, and there is little left. Income and corporation taxes, the propellants of modern government, are pre-empted. Further taxation of this kind, pay-roll or sales taxes, have a comparatively low yield and tend to drive business beyond the city boundaries. The property tax is left as the mainstay of the city's independent finance, but it is of course regressive and inelastic. Thus the city has an inadequate tax base on which to provide services for the poor and the commuters.

The Revenue Sharing Act of 1972 acknowledges but does not solve the problem. The Act provides for the sharing of federal revenues with states and localities – in English terminology, a block grant. A reform of this kind has been canvassed for some years, not least by the mayors of the big cities. The manner of the reform actually carried throws interesting light on the federal approach to city government. It might have been predicted that revenue sharing in the form likely to be adopted (i) would provide only for transfers from federal to state government; (ii) would incorporate some residual federal controls; (iii) would be less than adequate for meeting urgent social expenditures; and (iv) would do very little to equalize social conditions throughout the United States.

In the event the federal government has been more generous in distributing power than money. A portion of the federal revenues is to be shared freely with the localities as well as the states, just as the mayors have urged. But while the first two predictions have been invalidated, the last two have been proved true. For the six billion dollars to be allocated under the Act is partially offset by reductions in other federal grants for social services. Some cities claim that they will have smaller grants than before. The gain in local autonomy is thus a little unreal. The cities have gained some freedom to lose their battles in their own way.

The distribution of finance might be of less moment if it were plain that the USA had ample resources to meet the needs of the cities, once these needs were recognized. In that case the cities need only await the scaling-down of America's immense expenditure on national security. Earlier arguments for revenue sharing were in fact based on the assumption of a substantial surplus in the national finances. This is not, however, an immediate prospect, and it seems safer to assume a continuing overall restriction on the total funds available for all kinds of domestic expenditure. Hence, the fiscal disadvantages of the city are highly relevant to its credibility as a unit of government.

THE FRAGMENTATION OF EXECUTIVE POWER

The executive leadership of the mayor is seriously weakened by constitutional and political factors. He may have to share power with other elected leaders and often lacks control over some areas of the bureaucracy and over crucial financial decisions. Politically he is a salient figure, struggling for re-election and vulnerable in all directions. He may himself exploit the media, but is often abused by them.

Of the mayor's traditional rivals in the power game, the specialist professionals, bureaucrats, and technocrats seem to have increased their standing and influence. In a shifting scene, the specialists gain importance from their own steady commitment to professional goals. This is an old story. The more modest, clerkly traditions of British local government are absent. Bureaucracies have always tended to exploit their monopoly of skills, their established position and their relative invulnerability to public pressure. Bureaucratic perspectives tend to be narrowly professional; for example, housing policy has been dominated by specialists in mortgage insurance; transportation by those concerned for a national highway system and the regulation of carriers. Specialists tend to have an excessive faith in their own specialization.

However, a new problem in city government is not immobile self-serving bureaucracy, but rampant bureaucracy. Specialist agencies now fight their political battles openly and vigorously.

The head of a New York city agency actually led a street demonstration outside City Hall against policies in which his own department was involved. A more fundamental shift in power is signalled by strikes of municipal employees.[11] These have increased in numbers and virulence and now threaten one of the basic assumptions on which modern public services have been developed, the underpayment of public employees. The uniformed services and the teachers are not of course formally and directly involved in policy-making, but their rates of pay have policy consequences, just as the size of the welfare budget (for example) has consequences for the pay of policemen or teachers. Municipal strikers make municipal policy, and are well aware that this is the case.

Technical developments in the 'hardware' of city government have also diminished the independence of the mayor, and enhanced the influence of specialists or specialisms. The most obvious case is of long standing: the planning of American cities has been dominated by road engineering and high-rise building. New techniques in house building and mass rapid transit, for example, are likely to diminish the control of cities over their own destinies. The incursion of computers into administration may also shift the centres of local power, as it has to some extent in national government.

Corruption is a pervasive and debilitating condition of city government.[12] It provides the mayor with an extension of his rewards, but by its nature corruption cannot easily be controlled for political or other purposes. Much of it, in any case, arises in the agencies beyond the reach of the mayor. The extent of corruption is difficult to measure. No one knows whether the corruption which comes to light in the courts is the tip of a large iceberg or scum on the ocean. The citizen seems to take the iceberg view, and this plainly weakens the credibility of city government. Corruption adds to the financial costs of operating the cities, undermines the normal incentives to efficiency, and bends or breaks the lines of executive control.

While the executive branch of city government has thus tended to crumble, the possibilities of a mayoral coalition have not prospered elsewhere. The mayor has often been the spokesman of the poor and the inarticulate. But the underdogs now bark for themselves and the mayor is faced with organized challenge and hostility, rather than a dependent clientele and unquestioning support. The mayor is like a colonial governor in an age of nationalism.

For all the inadequacies of the mayor's position in city politics, the office still confers great political resources and still opens up the possibilities of executive-central power. The prominence of the office, which makes its incumbent vulnerable, also gives the mayor importance and standing. He is ultimately and crucially responsible for the maintenance of order. He is the spokesman of the city, a source and focus of communication, and the advocate of the city's case in the state capitol and in Washington. He is the ring-holder, conducting the competition, even if he can neither win himself, nor guarantee victory to others. Above all, the mayor is the promoter and broker of the shifting coalitions which constitute political power in the cities. He can ally with the interest groups against the bureaucracies, or with one against the other, or both against the rest. He can join with his fellow chief executives in other cities and in the states and even with the President. The urban system seems to demand a presence at the centre, and the mayoralty fulfils that presence. City manager schemes have attempted to change the nature of the presence, but not to dispense with it.

There are two strategies by which the mayor can build a base from which to extend and operate the personal resources of his office. Of these the political party is still the most effective and the most responsive to voters. The best known contemporary exponent of party-based power is, of course, Mayor Daley of Chicago.[13] Mayor Daley's party organization has both the virtues and vices of the classic party 'machine'. There is a tightly controlled exchange of votes and political support for services rendered by the city. The services include some 'good government', some municipal buildings, modest reform (even of the police), good relations with the unions and with the poor and the blacks. Daley has kept the city quiet, left his options open when he could, and inched forward when he had to. If political power is what the mayor needs, Mayor Daley has demonstrated how to get and use it.

But the achievement is not without cost. Machine politics, as practised in Chicago, is a politics of bargaining and rewards – but without issues or talk. Some of the bargains are unequal. The labour unions have done well: organized labour is perhaps the single biggest factor in the unique survival of the big city organization in Chicago.[14] Contractors and downtown business interests have also prospered. On the other hand, the poor and the blacks (led by white precinct captains) have had less return for their solid support of Daley at the polls.

The stability of this system may well be cracking as the poor and the blacks demand a higher price for their votes. In the logic of the system, they will get some of what they ask, for a machine mayor is necessarily responsive to pressures. Thus party organization may offer not only an effective but also a democratic source of power for the city mayor.

A second source of power for a revitalized mayoralty is the enlarged city council or 'urban legislature'. Curiously, Chicago again offers an example, for its city council, with fifty members, is unusually large. Detroit has only nine, and twelve or so is about average. Larger city councils might improve formal channels of access by the citizen to the city government, and thus moderate the tendency for the citizen to veer erratically between passivity and protest. The use of some at-large elections (and even proportional representation) would extend the representativeness of the council.[15] At the same time the responsibility and vulnerability of the mayor would be diffused. Party organization could overcome the difficulties of collective decision-taking.

Conciliar politics is not of course new in American cities; mayors have always had their councils. But separate elections and the tradition of a separate executive have perhaps unduly removed the mayor from his natural political allies. The mayor, like the president, 'needs help'; but the mayor-council system already has the potential to provide a parlour and front-porch version of the kitchen cabinet.

ARTICULATION, ACCESS AND PARTICIPATION

Political parties in the cities do not consistently function as the organizers of responsive and responsible power. There are few genuine competitive two-party systems. Single party systems and uneasy coalitions are tempered by gusts of insurgency. The Democratic Party as a conservative party of the left (and cities tend to be Democratic) seems often to function as a block on the road to reform. The system favours defensive politics and discourages innovation.

In a relatively unorganized situation interest groups are influential, and may be dominant. This is not to say that American cities are ruled by 'a power-elite', rather than by a plurality of interests. Both co-exist and the exact distribution of power depends on definitions of terms, criteria of measurement, time, place, types of issue and kinds of decision. Cities probably gain some freedom through the relative disinterest of the 'power-elite' in local politics. However, major economic interest groups tend to protect their operations against serious threats, and normally have the political power to do so. They control important elements in the city's economy; they have influence over the media; and they tend to colonize civic associations and governmental boards and commissions which have an impact on their concerns.[16]

There is, nevertheless, some capacity in urban party systems to counter interest group dominance, and offer lines of communication and access for the citizen. City government has had a quality of 'openness', which W. S. Sayre has discovered in New York City. He praises the city's 'openness, its receptivity to new participants, its deep commitment to bargaining and accommodation among a very wide range of groups, and its opportunities for leadership by a great variety and number of its citizens'.[17] This is also true within limits of other cities besides New York. Moreover, turnout in elections is comparatively high, and there is a fairly strong commitment to participation.[18] Of course, openness, like pluralism, is an imprecise and relative term. The point remains valid only if the premise is allowed that openness in a mass democracy will be rather narrow and very uneven, and does not amount to a capacity for change.

It is true, too, that for all its failings, the traditional city party organization has provided opportunities for access and limited participation. The old boss-ruled party machine was greedy and monopolistic, but it needed votes and paid for them by offering contact and services at a neighbourhood level. The machine was, writes one of its many admirers, 'the best instrumentality yet devised to give the ordinary citizen access to his government, and to provide a non-bureaucratic method by which the citizen could have his personal problems attended to'.[19] The machine offered these advantages of mediation and communication on its own terms: the assumptions included a dependent citizenry, politics without issues (or even talk), and a static society. The poor were given limited power in a context which was arguably more congenial to them, and more easily managed by them, than are the highly verbalized, talk-dominated modes of middle class issue-oriented politics.

The classic machine declined as the immigrant poor declined, and welfare services, education and the media developed. But the

tradition of political organization on ward and precinct level
survives, and with it the possibility of political services to neighbourhood and individuals.

A third virtue of the urban party system is that the looseness of
its structure has permitted bursts of insurgency by dissident groups.
The cry of reform has often rallied sufficient support to move an
entrenched majority, though not very far. Democratic political
clubs have been active in some states, though Mayor Daley in
Chicago and Mayor Wagner in New York were not concerned
to seek their support. The 'fusion' politics which brought La
Guardia and Lindsay to power in reform coalitions illustrates the
potential effectiveness of minority groups and third parties, but the
New York party system is peculiar.[20]

Thus the city political system appears to provide a shifting
pattern of limited partisan organization disturbed by the erratic
and powerful intervention of interest groups. The uneasy balance
of these forces is now upset by new pressures which seriously
challenge the ability of city government to function. New protest
groups have exerted substantial pressures and these have included
clamant demands for participation and reform. The old balance of
power has been broken, and a reassuring if unproductive stability
has been lost.

The new pressure groups include the bureaucrats, technicians,
police, teachers and so on, and also neighbourhood groups, the
poor, the blacks and the browns. These 'newcomers' lack the skills
and standing necessary for middle class politics. They are less ready
to negotiate, to accept compromise and to defer rewards. They
are inclined to use violent or quasi-violent methods of protest,
in pursuit of greatly enlarged expectations. The young are prominent
among the newcomers. Mayor Stokes is reported to have told the
President in 1969 that 'most of the turmoil in Cleveland is being
caused by 13 to 18-year-olds. What do you do – send the National
Guard into a High School?'

As a consequence of this novel militancy,
local administrators are finding themselves thrust into roles for
which they are ill-prepared, either by training or disposition.
School principals must deal with organized classroom disruptions
and the demands for student control; University presidents are
compelled to act as military commanders-in-chief; planners and
technicians are called upon to defend their expertise against the
strident militancy of neighbourhood groups and the professional

challenge of advocacy planners; public housing authorities are forced to negotiate with striking tenants; welfare personnel must adjust to a philosophy which regards the client as partner rather than recipient.[21]

The incursion of the newcomers into city (and national) politics has been encouraged and legitimized by the acceptance of neighbourhood participation as a goal for local government. 'Participation' was a favoured remedy of the 1960s for urban (and democratic) ills. The basic diagnosis is not really open to question. Political participation is not very high, and this is a pity, because it may make people feel better about what happens to them; further, and perhaps more doubtfully, it changes for the better what happens to them. There are obvious difficulties about the meaning and measurement of participation, the practical possibilities, the consequences, and the extent of the demand for participation beyond voting. Despite these problems participation was heavily sold in the 1960s.[22] The Economic Opportunity Act and the Model Cities Act included specific provision for 'maximum feasible participation'.

In the event few schemes for participation have fulfilled all these hopes. New York's neighbourhood city halls have not survived. In urban renewal, where communication and consultation with 'relocatees' seems a minimal requirement, participation has encountered a formidable difficulty – neighbourhood groups may fight against each other and against the programme. The city government may find that it is organizing its own protest movements, and the black poor may find they have been granted a legitimate instrument of political power. Thus participation tends to raise the level of agitation and conflict, but not of resolution and decision.[23]

To be fair, however, too little is known about the operation of participation for firm judgements to be made. For example, a study of participation in three cities under the Model Cities Program led to mixed, but not wholly negative, conclusions.[24] Experience in Philadelphia and elsewhere has shown the difficulties of persuading the poor to participate. School decentralization in New York City demonstrated the capacity of professionals to resist a redistribution of power.[25] No simple judgement is possible. Some kinds of participation may succeed in some circumstances. The effect is probably to complicate and even invalidate decision-making while gaining some community values which are impossible to measure. In situations of racial conflict, participation is a difficult, but conceivably also a valid strategy for reducing tension.

Mayor Lindsay offers a hopeful judgement: 'After discounting all the disputes it became clear that the potential for self-help and self-reliance was present in the poorest, most deprived neighbour-hoods of New York City to an extent undreamed of by past leaders'.[26] H. Kaufman, on the other hand, considering the record of participation in New York City, believes that the fashion will decline: 'In a relatively short while, what is now unrestricted warfare between neighbourhood spokesmen and agency bureau-cracies will resolve itself into the more familiar pattern of head-quarters-field relationships, a form of intra-bureaucratic conflict. Neighbourhoods will be better served as a consequence, yet the civil populace will not have to find time for continuous public service in addition to full-time private work.'[27]

This would still leave the existing old-fashioned institutions of participation, elections, parties, civic associations and the media, of just talking casually at the store, or on the courthouse steps. These belong to a more passive system which offers stability (or immobility) rather than purposive dynamism (or ill-directed agitation).

ETHOS AND IDEOLOGY

The climate in which city politics goes on has turned cheerless and abrasive. The contradictions and conflicts of the political ethos have sharpened. Conservatism remains strong and seems to have gained in confidence and articulateness through the resurgent Republican Party. There is room for speculation about the identity and partisan preferences of the middle American and the blue collar worker of the 'silent majority'; but there can be little doubt that welfare for the poor is a minority cause. Those Americans who have reached the security and comfort of the middle class by playing the game according to the old rules, do not rejoice to see the rules changed and prizes distributed to all. Many Americans accept Mayor Daley's 'bootstraps' theory of society[28] and lament with Archie Bunker (America's Alf Garnett) that they live in a society 'where the minorities are in a majority'.

At the same time liberalism remains influential, and radicalism is a new force in city politics. The old middle-class reformism has a firm if narrow place in the American political tradition. The city must cope with the new ecological anxieties of the middle class, pressures from commuters for cheap public transit, and old liberal pressures against poverty, discrimination, and deprivation. These pressures may come, irritatingly enough, from well-serviced suburban tax-havens, where the only blacks in sight are the maid-servants.

The old liberalism has been by-passed by the new radicalism. This amorphous movement (which had its greatest triumph at the Democratic Convention of 1972) is based on the aspirations, if not the solid support, of the young, the blacks, and the poor. It rejects the old liberalism as 'custodial', and aims at a fundamental shift of power through quotas and mass participation. It seems unlikely that the regular Democratic Party, or the candidate, Senator McGovern, fully accepted the radical implications of the position. Yet the main thrust of the new radicalism cannot be ignored: it fits the rhetoric of revolution which runs uneasily beneath American conservatism; it suits the volatility and the abrasiveness of the American political tradition. And it seems likely to have a continuing impact in the cities where the young, the blacks, and the poor can be most easily organized (not to say exploited) for political ends. In scale and accessibility the urban political system can provide a target or channel for radicalism.

Conceivably, the profound shifts in political ethos and ideology which seem to be going on will bring about new, firm, and relevant political alignments. Lively and meaningful politics may lead to the mobilization of forces for change. It seems just as likely, however, that new political conflicts will make the tasks of city government more, not less, difficult.

PROBLEMS AND EXPECTATIONS

The credibility of city government depends on its capacity to satisfy the expectations of its citizens. But expectations have risen while problems have become more difficult to solve. The processes of democracy tend naturally to raise expectations and to promise fulfilment. American democracy is especially vulnerable to claims that governments must pursue equality, happiness, and so on. Commitment to impossible goals is a birthright of all Americans, and modest expectations are part almost of the pledge of allegiance.

In city government such commitments have been increased and made more precise by radical protest and by liberal enthusiasm for major programmes. The inevitably sporadic and episodic nature of protest activity has been obscured by the media, which confer a misleading sense of spread and continuity.[29] Faith in major programmes of urban aid may equally be misplaced since the problems of the city are much less capable of solution in the short term than the programme promoters dare (or do) say.

The diagnosis of urban ills on which the major programmes have been based has recently been challenged. Banfield,[30] among others, has argued that the city's problems are due to the existence of a 'lower class', culturally prone to unemployment, crime, and social inadequacy. Thus the liberal's characteristic guilt for the past and optimism for the future are dismissed at a stroke. Forrester[31] does not share all of Banfield's pessimism but offers his own kind of determinism in a massive and intricate model of the dynamics of the city. This suggests that the only changes worth making are those changes in internal incentives which affect the basic economic processes and control the levels of migration, employment, and demand for housing. Daniel Moynihan, once a 'Great Society' man and formerly (1968–70) President Nixon's Special Assistant for Urban Affairs, has moved to a neo-liberal position, sceptical about the actual effects of the major programmes, diffident about easy solutions and advocate of 'benign neglect'.[32] These novel diagnoses of urban ills contradict the conventional wisdom and raise the possibility that even a radically modified urban political system, capable of action on behalf of the weak and the disadvantaged, might still fail to discover and pursue correct solutions. Indeed, if the laissez-faire view is correct, the drive of interventionist liberal governments to take action of any kind is itself pernicious.[33] Thus, arguably, city government has too little power and drive for positive solutions, and too much for benign neglect.

Neo-liberal (or old conservative) views of the city may or may not be right, but it is clear that the short-term solubility of urban problems cannot be assumed. Nor are technical advances – trailer homes, pollution control, new forms of rapid transit – likely to quickly transform the social inadequacies of the city. The pressures of people on resources raise intractable problems for city government. Peace in the cities, as in the world, is a process, not an event.

THE CITIES AND THE POLITICAL SYSTEM
American cities are not autonomous: they depend on the rest of the political system, and they cannot save themselves. In a sense, therefore, the future of the cities depends on diminishing their new prominence, on presenting a 'low profile', and persuading people that salvation lies elsewhere. The achievement of American

city government would thus lie unheroically in turning away the wrath of the citizenry to other more responsible and less vulnerable targets.

This seems, however, to diminish the role of the cities beyond what is necessary, feasible, or acceptable. In fact if the cities need the total federal political system, that system needs the cities – not to deliver services but to sustain the confidence which is essential in holding diverse communities together. Even the limited prescriptions of the pessimists, i.e. economic adjustments, long term, low yield social policies, still require cities to have their own governments. Indeed, the 'holding operation' required by the pessimistic diagnosis requires politicians more than administrators. The cities need education, persuasion, and political leadership. Government is a beneficient illusion (not a confidence trick) and local governments may help to maintain that illusion.[34]

There are serious impediments to the city's effective service of such a political purpose. It may be that some of the arguments of the classical critique of city government can be doubted or countered. There remain, however, fundamental weaknesses in the urban political system: the countervailing strength of suburban, neighbourhood, and professional interests, financial inadequacies, and the gap between the problems the city faces and the expectations of its citizens. Their hope may lie in a kind of minimal incrementalism, that the city government meet their needs not 'too little, too late', but 'just enough, just in time'.

A more ambitious goal – 'distant and splendid' in the words of Robert Dahl[34] – might be that cities

aim for the point at which practically everyone in the city believes with good reason that his claims ordinarily receive a fair hearing, and decisions, even when adverse to his claims, have been arrived at with understanding and sympathy. . . .

This degree of responsiveness is not excluded, nor is it encouraged by the political forms of the American city.

R. H. Pear

The US Supreme Court: from Warren to Burger

THE PRACTICE OF JUDICIAL REVIEW RARELY RUNS SMOOTHLY alongside the spirit of popular sovereignty. The Court is not easily reformed, for its own professional norms, its precedents and its (partially) collegiate character provide it with ample justification for standing aside (if it so wishes) from the surge of popular passions. But that it is credible cannot be in doubt. Were it less credible, in the sense in which 'credibility' is applied to the legislative and executive branches today, it would be a less controversial institution. Credibility in this context means, I take it, ability to make an appraisal of the important facts, the relating of these to the rules and the production of an answer which people can understand. In this the executive branch and, even more, the Congress are seen to fail. The anger which the Court arouses comes from strong disagreement with its all too clear pronouncements in sensitive areas.

In the 1930s criticism of the Court came from the propertied classes on the whole. Then it was felt that the Court was bestowing its blessing, as it was, on increasing government interference with private enterprise by broad constructions of the interstate commerce and tax powers of the Congress. Bizarre reasoning was detected by the legal professoriat who could point to decisions where the interstate character of the commerce in question was barely discernible. The Roosevelt Court was looking for results that would solve problems: the problems of the anti-labour practices of employers, of providing for widows, orphans, the aged, and the unemployed, and of ensuring a fair standard of living for the American farmer. That Court had two important guides: Mr Justice Holmes's dictum that the meaning of a constitutional term is to be gleaned from 'its origin and line of growth'[1] and the general doctrine, judicial self-restraint (also Holmes's), which accepted that legislatures, not courts, should design and elaborate (if necessary in administrative law) the policies of governments.

The Roosevelt Court greatly enlarged the areas of state and federal power. The Warren Court accepted all that it had done and proceeded to enlarge (or at least not allow to be diminished) the important areas of personal liberty. The liberal Roosevelt Court construed the constitution very broadly to achieve desirable goals. Warren's Court however arrived at many of its results by a strict construction. Mr Justice Abe Fortas (a past member of that Court) is quoted as saying 'Its greatest virtue was that it was a strict constructionist court. Particularly on due process and equal protection, the Warren Court went back to the wording and meaning of the Constitution'.[2] (Fortas went on to predict that the Burger Court would remain firm on racial matters but would backslide on criminal procedural safeguards and personal liberties.)

The opponents of the Warren Court criticized it on grounds both of strictness and looseness: it was coddling the criminal[3] and the communist[4] by too strict a view of those persons' constitutional rights against government; and for looseness to the point of irrelevance they would cite their bête noire *Brown v Bd. of Education*,[5] the great desegregation decision. Here they claimed was a flat assertion that separate education facilities for the two races are inherently unequal, along with another unproven assertion that such separation was psychologically damaging to the children involved. Totally absent from the decision was any of the legal argument so beloved of Southern segregationist lawyers.

In July 1957 Senator Jenner introduced a bill to deprive the US Supreme Court of jurisdiction in cases concerning the constitutional validity of:

(*a*) proceedings against witness before congressional Committees.[6]
(*b*) removals of government servants on security grounds.[7]
(*c*) state anti-subversion laws.[8]
(*d*) subversive activities of teachers.[9]
(*e*) admissions to practise law at state bars.[10]

Jenner's initiative failed. It would have been both disastrous and ridiculous had it succeeded for the effect would have been to deprive the Court of the right to affirm lower court decisions which the Senator might have approved.

The School desegregation decision could, it was thought, be avoided by the states. The one man – one vote decision[11] (Legislative Apportionment) which came in 1962 was equally unpopular in Congress where moves were made to have such issues removed from Supreme Court jurisdiction.

It was the Warren Court's protection of unpopular political dissenters and the black minority which put it outside the main stream of American values in the 1950s and early 1960s.

As we are being constantly reminded by Republican publicists and scholarly psephologists[12] the voting majority in the USA is not young, not black, not college-educated, not even gravely disturbed by Vietnam and it is the votes of this majority that the politicians seek.

Judicial controversy in the 1960s was about individual rights and libertarians were thankful that the courts were creative in this area, for the Congress is rarely minded to increase the freedoms of ordinary people. Freedom of speech, of religion, of assembly, searches and seizures, double jeopardy, self-incrimination, cruel and unusual punishments, citizenship, except for the last (which Congress seems more interested in depriving people of, or making peculiarly burdensome), these are areas in which federal legislation is not to be expected unless it be to restrict them. As L. Henkin writes,

> The Supreme Court is no longer defining and adjusting the frontier between the powers of governments: it is defining and re-defining prohibitions on government on behalf of the individual . . . Where the Court is obviously adopting revised meanings for the Constitution as in *Brown v Bd. of Education* and *Shelley v Kramer* it is also reflecting deep changes in today's United States and in the world of which it is a part. It is obvious that the Supreme Court is not out of this world.[13]

For academic commentators on the Warren Court a major issue was the concern for (and search for) neutral principles that should guide interpreters of the constitution. The foremost advocate in search of these was H. Wechsler of Columbia University whose Oliver Wendall Holmes Lecture at Harvard in April 1959 generated an important discussion.[14] Wechsler is not to be labelled, straight off, as a conservative because he finds difficulty in accepting some of the Warren Court decisions, for it is not the decisions that worry him, so much as the manner in which they are arrived at. One does not have to be a supporter of white supremacy to say, for example, that the law enforced by a state could uphold the validity of a testament which made it clear that the money was to go to a white not a black (to give the example popular with teachers of law).

Wechsler wants decisions to be given by the Court according to neutral principles – and if no decision can be given on such principles let the Court abstain from judgment. Wechsler and his friends believe, of course, that issues for which the law may have to provide should be looked after by legislatures and that a judgment of the Supreme Court should be 'A principled decision . . . one that rests on reasons with respect to all the issues in the case, reasons that *in their generality*[15] and their neutrality transcend any immediate result that is involved. When no sufficient reasons of this kind can be assigned for overturning value choices of the other branches of the government or of a state those choices must of course survive.'

Wechsler finds too many instances of faulty logic (or even an absence of reasoning) where precedent is piled on precedent. He cites the sequence of *Grovey v Townsend*,[16] *United States v Classic*,[17] and *Smith v Allwright*.[18] The first case established that having declared itself a wholly private organization a Democratic Party in the South could exclude Negroes from membership and hence from the primaries; to *Classic* in which election officials were prosecuted for wilfully failing to count a voter's ballot in a Democratic primary in Louisiana; to the third case in which, basing itself on *Classic*, the Court held that primaries are part of the total election and therefore Negroes cannot be excluded from them. Wechsler's question is, if this means that parties cannot be organized on racial lines where in the constitution is that principle to be found? In view of the religious freedom guaranteed by the First Amendment could religious parties be proscribed? 'I should regard this result too as one plainly to be desired but is there a constitutional analysis on which it can validly be decreed?'

On restrictive covenants (*Shelley v Kramer*)[19] the difficulty is in seeing why 'the state may properly be charged with the discrimination when it does no more than give effect to an agreement that the individual involved is, by hypothesis, entirely free to make'. Moreover in the Girard College case[20] the state of Pennsylvania acting as trustee under the will of Stephen Girard ran the college in accordance with the terms of the will (whites only). Having been found by the Supreme Court to be discriminating in a way not allowed to a *state*, as a state, Pennsylvania put in 'private' individuals as trustees who continued the testamentary discrimination. By denying further review the US Supreme Court must be seen as not disapproving this state action.

The effects of past decisions on present cases are sometimes explicit, but not always clear enough for those who want principled

decisions. If primary education must be interracial for educational
and psychological reasons does it follow legally and logically that
parks, bathing beaches and golf courses must be integrated?
Sometimes the Court affirming *per curiam* gives no reasons at all
for its affirmation.[21]

There is the danger that if one doubts the logic of decisions
which result in greater racial equality, aid and comfort will be
given to the segregationist enemy. This is indeed a political risk,
but not one which should scare the scholar off the high slopes of
constitutional exegesis (though it often does). Believing that courts
should act cautiously in advancing the law to meet new circumstances is quite consistent with believing that legislatures should be
bold and resolute.

American constitutional lawyers have a rich enough store of
materials from which to extract good legal reasons why the
progressive decisions of the Warren Court are also 'principled'.
Their disagreement with Wechsler arises from their belief that
truly neutral principles are not to be found in the US constitution,
and in their adherence to an important Holmesian slogan 'The life
of the law has not been logic; it has been experience'. E. V. Rostow
asks:

> Does Wechslerian neutrality mean that in construing the
> Constitution the Justices should never declare statutes or
> administrative action invalid unless their action satisfies a standard
> which cannot be met? Is it the doctrine of judicial self-restraint
> carried to the point of complete passivity? . . . Does it mean that
> in their essential task of discrimination – that is of deciding when
> situations should be treated differently by law – the judges should
> disregard inequalities of bargaining position or in voting power;
> that the protection of individuals and minorities against transitory
> majorities ceases to be the dominant theme of the Bill of Rights;
> that in reconciling the competing claims of different parts of
> the Constitution the Court should not be required, or allowed to
> decide, whether in a given instance in the absence of statutory
> guidance, the constitutional interest in a fair trial outweighs in
> constitutional importance the constitutional interest in a free
> press?[22]

L. H. Pollak while sympathizing with Wechsler's concern for
logic and principles has strong doubts about the notion of neutral
principles.[23] The Thirteenth, Fourteenth, and Fifteenth Amendments are not neutral; they were put into the constitution to

emancipate, in more than one sense, the formerly enslaved. They are strong unneutral principles as is the principle of freedom of speech. Would Wechsler doubt that, as Cardozo wrote in *Palko v Connecticut*,[24] freedom of speech is 'the indispensable condition of nearly every other form of freedom'?

Charles Black[25] is in forceful disagreement on the neutral principle issue with Wechsler and the title of his article makes it clear that he does not wish any one to believe that the *Brown* decision is in some way not grounded in basic constitutional law. The equal treatment of Negroes everywhere and in all respects is what the Fourteenth Amendment commands. 'First the equal protection clause of the Fourteenth Amendment should be read as saying that the Negro race, as such, is not to be significantly disadvantaged by the laws of the state. Secondly, segregation is a massive intentional disadvantaging of the Negro race as such by State law.' No subtlety is called for here. There has in his view never been any doubt as to the meaning of the equal protection clause. Nobody on the spot has ever believed that separate Negro facilities were, or were ever intended to be, equal to those used by whites; all segregationists knew that black facilities were intentionally inferior. History supports the view that segregation was the South's answer to the presence of blacks who could no longer be enslaved. For Black the question 'must segregation amount to discrimination?' may be an interesting one for sociologists, but not for the Supreme Court. Considering that segregation was introduced without the consent of the blacks the sole question for the Court is, does discrimination inhere in the actual segregation laws imposed by the Southern states in the twentieth century?

A last word on neutral principles has been uttered by M. S. McDougal of Yale. 'The reference of legal principles must be either to their internal logical arrangement or to the external consequences of their application. It remains mysterious what criteria for decision a "neutral" system could offer'.[26]

Hostility to the Warren Court was fairly widespread in Congress and in the states. Its decisions on school segregation and fair legislative apportionment hit directly at the state's right to do as it liked – with educating its own blacks and in its own state politics. The 'law and order' forces in Congress felt bitter about the *Miranda* decision and at the way in which the Supreme Court dealt with the repeated attempts of the government to ban (*de facto* not *de jure*) the Communist Party and its affiliates. In 1964 the Supreme Court could note with implied approval that the government had conceded that 'membership, or even leadership in the Communist Party is not automatically a crime'. [27] Attempts of the states to get in on the anti-subversion act were discouraged in the *Nelson* case [28] and in cases which showed up the slipshod manner in which state attorneys-general and state legislative committees pursued dissenters. [29]

The Warren Court was not however indiscriminately permissive. In the 1968 draft card burning case [30] the Chief Justice wrote 'We cannot accept the view that an apparently limitless variety of conduct can be labelled speech wherever the persons engaging in the conduct intend thereby to express an idea'. Mr Justice Douglas dissented, doubting the legality of the draft in the absence of a declaration of war by the US Congress.

In the closing days of Lyndon Johnson's Administration it was common knowledge that Chief Justice Warren wished to retire and would do so as soon as a successor was decided upon. Johnson chose Mr Justice Abe Fortas, an influential and talented Washington lawyer, well known in the political community. Fortas had added to his already not illiberal reputation by arguing and winning the important case of *Gideon v Wainwright* [31] which established the right of all to have counsel provided for their defence in criminal cases. But on appointment to the Supreme Court Fortas had not severed all his connections either with the White House or with certain financial persons whom he continued to advise for a substantial fee. The Senate refused to confirm Johnson's choice and Fortas will go down in history as the only example of a Supreme Court Justice whose nomination as Chief Justice failed to be confirmed because he had not cut his ties with his political and business associates.

Warren Earl Burger, Nixon's choice for Chief Justice, was a respected judge from a lower federal court whose confirmation presented no problems. He was thought to be soundly conservative and a strict constructionist, in Nixon's sense of the term, not Mr Justice Black's. It is not entirely unimportant who holds the Chief Justiceship, for although each Justice is entirely responsible (with the help of his learned young law clerks) for what he writes in his decision, the Chief Justice can be influential as chief administrator of the Court's business, in assigning the writing of both the marjoity and the chief dissenting judgments, and above all in framing the questions to which the Court will address itself.

Burger's first important case presented the same question that opened Warren's first term, school segregation in the South. Burger held rigidly to the *Brown* line, stating that 'Under explicit holdings of this Court the obligation of every school district is to terminate dual school systems at once and to operate now and hereafter only unitary schools.'[32] But not quite 'plus ça change . . .' for this time the US Department of Justice was arguing against speedy desegregation. In two other cases[33] the Burger Court followed what would probably have been a Warren line, helping to enforce racial equality. But in *Evans v Abrey*[34] it upheld the return of a public park to private ownership, and the consequent exclusion of blacks from enjoyment of it. P. B. Kurland[35] placed the new Chief Justice squarely in the middle bloc (with Justices Harlan and White) in that they do not use the judicial process for strenuously aiding black–white equality nor do they oppose too strongly discriminatory acts by individuals.

On apportionment a badly-divided Court upheld most unconvincingly a product of *Baker v Carr* which held that there must be re-districting of a junior college district because 60 per cent of the child population there had only 50 per cent of the adult elected trustees. . . . Redistrictio ad absurdum.

With Burger's appointment and Fortas' retirement the Court remained at eight. President Nixon's first nomination, the Southerner Haynsworth, was found unworthy of appointment by the US Senate in November 1969. Judge Carswell also from the South was the President's next choice. No strong voices were raised to sing his praises as a learned man of the law. In fact the unfortunate judge was recommended by one of his sincere supporters in the Congress as being admittedly mediocre and therefore truly representative. The judge's memory seemed none too accurate for on examination by the Senate committee before confirmation he seemed to have forgotten that he was an incorporator of a whites-only private club. By early April 1970 the Carswell nomination (supported by the slenderest credentials put forward this century) was in trouble and by the end of the month it was defeated. Judge Blackmun's nomination was then advanced. He was a friend of the Chief Justice, a fellow Minnesotan, and a federal appeals court judge. Blackmun's nomination was accepted by the Senate. In October 1971 Mr Justice Black died and Mr Justice Harlan retired. The President nominated Assistant US Attorney-General Rehnquist, a brilliant lawyer (Stanford University Law School) and a one time Goldwater booster from Arizona and Lewis F. Powell, former

president of the American Bar Association, a greatly respected
Richmond (Virginia) lawyer who did not believe in fighting for
white supremacy. Both nominations were accepted with relief.

The Nixon-Burger Court therefore consists now of five Republican
appointed Justices (Stewart was appointed by Eisenhower) and
four Democrats. No great changes in the law are yet apparent –
the exception is the abolition of capital punishment in which all
four Nixon appointees voted for retention.

It was in the area of criminal procedures that the law and order
forces hoped for change, for they felt that the *Miranda*[36] judgment
gravely hampered the work of the police. A little detail is called
for here as the name of Ernesto A. Miranda means a lot to the
American criminal lawyer. Miranda was a poor Mexican who
was found guilty of kidnapping and rape for which the sentence
was twenty to thirty years imprisonment in an Arizona gaol.
Miranda's conviction was based to an important extent on a
confession he was said to have made; evidence of police pressure
or brutality was not part of the record. The case therefore concerns
the admissibility of evidence obtained from a person in police
custody and the Supreme Court majority speaking through Chief
Justice Warren ruled that for such evidence to be admissible the
suspect must be: (1) warned that it may be used in evidence; (2) told
that he can remain silent; (3) told that he can have a lawyer present
to advise him what to say; (4) told that if he cannot pay for a lawyer
one will be provided. In Miranda's case he was not advised that
he could remain silent or that he could have a lawyer. His conviction
was not therefore upheld. From this judgement Justices Harlan,
Stewart, and White dissented and Justice Clark dissented in part.
Mr Justice Harlan's dissent pointed to the difficulty of being certain
that all four ingredients of procedural fairness were simultaneously
present – if one were missing the prisoner went free, while Mr
Justice White thought that making such procedures mandatory
would not help the innocent man who can quickly say his piece
and go home.

The Burger Court has not yet faced the same set of facts, a court
rarely does, but in *Vale v Louisiana*[37] Chief Justice Burger dissented
along with Mr Justice Black in a case where they thought the
majority opinion unduly hampered the police in their apprehension
of drug pushers. Vale, a known drug-pusher, was arrested in the
street while making what the police thought was a sale. While
holding him his house was searched (without a warrant) and

heroin seized. Vale got a stiff sentence. Was the search and seizure lawful? A majority of the Court said it was not. There was no emergency, no consent, no warrant and the police were not in hot pursuit. The case turned on an interpretation of the facts, the minority judgment taking the view that if time had been taken up in obtaining a search warrant, in that time the evidence would have been removed.

In 1971 the decisions of the Court were certainly not 'unprogressive'. In March[38] it held that a man too poor to pay fines for traffic offences should not be sent to a prison farm and that women on relief who could not find the $60 to commence proceedings for divorce should be allowed nonetheless to start proceedings. In the Gilette and Negre cases[39] with Mr Justice Douglas in dissent it held that conscientious objection must be to all wars and not just to those the objector considered unjust or illegal. In June 1971 it upheld a California statute which said a district referendum should be held before low rent housing (i.e. for blacks) was undertaken. The ruling will certainly offend blacks for no referendum is required for high rent (i.e. white) housing.[40]

In July 1971 in the *New York Times* (Pentagon Papers) case the three supposedly conservative Justices, Burger, Blackmun and Harlan all held that the US government had not made the case for the suppression of the publication of the Pentagon Papers (which were anyhow three years old). The other Justices considered that the First Amendment forbade the censorship of the *New York Times*.

In *Wisconsin v Yoder* (decided 15 May 1972) the Court upheld the Winconsin Supreme Court's view that the religious freedom provision of the First Amendment protected the right of Amish Mennonites not to send their children to school after the eighth grade (fourteen years of age). The Amish people's case was that their religion and way of life demanded the inculcation of the virtues of hard physical work on the farm and that the typical American high school course was designed for white collar or college aspirants. To public primary education for their children they had no objections, but after age fourteen Amish education was in the form of physical labour and appreciation of its rewards. The Wisconsin trial court however found them guilty of not attending school up to age 16 as the law requires and fined them $5.

The Wisconsin Supreme Court reversed the trial court on First Amendment grounds and the US Supreme Court upheld the state supreme court. The US Supreme Court decided that Wisconsin's

interest in a compulsory education system could not prevail over
the Amish people's First Amendment rights. Chief Justice Burger
wrote the opinion for the majority and in laying out the factual
background mentioned that though the Amish were dissenters
they were a notably well behaved and peaceful people possessed
of many admirable old-fashioned virtues. This observation was
commented upon somewhat harshly in the opinion of Mr Justice
Douglas the lone dissenter. Does one's First Amendment freedom
depend upon the reputation for law and order of your community?
Douglas's main reason for dissent however was his doubt as to
whether the young people's wishes had been taken into account.
The contest had been between the State of Wisconsin and the
parents.

If Burger seemed liberal in the Amish case (Powell and Rehnquist
took no part in the case) all four Nixon appointees plus Mr Justice
White moved to the less libertarian side in *Apodaca v Oregon*
(decided 22 May 1972). Here some armed burglars had been found
guilty by an Oregon court on a less than unanimous jury verdict.
According to the majority opinion the Sixth Amendment to the
constitution which guarantees jury trial does not require a jury
to be unanimous. The contrary view is that to meet the 'reasonable
doubt' requirement in trials a jury must be unanimous, and (an
additional argument in the American context) unanimity coupled
with the requirement that juries should (in appropriate circumstances) be racially mixed is a potential protection for the black
minority. Mr Justice Powell pointed out that unanimity is required
in federal courts but Oregon's '10 out of 12' law is not thereby
unconstitutional.

In July 1972 the Nixon Court abolished the death penalty
throughout the United States. A decision had been awaited by the
inhabitants of America's death rows for many years; there have
been no executions since 1967. The grounds for abolition lie
in the Eighth Amendment to the Constitution (. . . 'nor cruel and
unusual punishments inflicted') and the equal protection part of
the Fourteenth Amendment ('No state shall . . . deny to any person
within its jurisdiction the equal protection of the laws'). To reach
this result it has to be accepted that the rope or the electric chair
or the gas chamber are cruel and/or unusual forms of punishment
and that people may be unequally treated in regard to capital
punishment. For the latter proposition the support is sadly overwhelming; the poor, the ignorant and the black are far more

likely to be deprived of their lives than the rich and well defended. 'The law' bears unequally too in that those who live in one state may die for a crime that is not capital across the border.

The vote on the death penalty was five to four, the four being the Nixon appointees. All nine Justices wrote opinions, only two, Brennan and Marshall, declaring that capital punishment per se is 'cruel and unusual'. Justices Douglas, White and Stewart voted for abolition because in the cases under review the death penalty had been applied 'wantonly and freakishly' because only a tiny minority of persons in the USA convicted of murder or rape actually paid the supreme penalty. Their opinion left open the possibility that a law which called for capital punishment for a clearly defined type of crime (e.g. murder of a policeman) might be constitutional if applied uniformly. The four Nixon appointees dissented mainly on the ground that the abolition of executions is the business of legislatures not courts. The Chief Justice considered that the majority opinion gave no 'final and unambiguous answer' to the general question 'is the death penalty constitutional'.[41]

No spectacular repudiation of the Warren Court's libertarian attitudes has yet taken place and it is perhaps unrealistic to suppose that it will. In some areas of the law where the Warren Court was out of touch with popular feeling, in particular the busing controversy, Chief Justice Burger for the Court has followed the Warren line in upholding the busing arrangements made in the Charlotte and Mecklenburg districts of Virginia. Other pressures are at work here: the Nixon administration has put restrictions on the use of federal funds for busing while the more radical blacks are making the point that the (white) assumption that good education for blacks can only be obtained when in the same class rooms as whites is an insult to blacks. It is possible that, as an issue, busing could be overtaken by a new demand for separate (but superior?) facilities for blacks to make up for the years lost in slavery and subjection.

To repeat – it is not easy to reform the Court. Justices chosen by presidents last longer than their nominators and turn out, often quite soon, to have opinions not expected of them. Oliver Wendell Holmes was an immediate disappointment to Theodore Roosevelt. Black, the Alabama Klansman, became the foremost, even the fanatical defender of individual liberty. Frankfurter the dangerous radical who had worked on behalf of Sacco and Vanzetti and, even worse perhaps, had supported the Boston police strike, soon developed into the leading philosophic conservative on the Court. Earl Warren, a pretty good Republican governor of California, developed into a staunch defender of unpopular minorities against the assaults of public opinion and governments. 'Impeach Earl Warren' screamed from the billboards in the 1960s.

The United States Supreme Court will, one fondly hopes, always be enveloped in fruitful controversy with itself as part of the argument. Were the Court to become quite passive it is difficult to see where important issues of personal rights and governmental powers would be seriously discussed. In the past the Congress did pay attention to these matters but for nearly a century now it has ceased to consider constitutional issues. The US Congress may be the most representative assembly in the world in the single sense that its members are tremendously responsive to local pressures, threats and encouragements, but as a body capable of wisely assessing the needs of the United States of America and acting accordingly it is a failure. Even its claim to control the executive and the bureaucracy in large matters is hollow, for these institutions make their mutually profitable bargains with segments of the legislative branch – rarely with the legislature as a whole. One thing is clear, no legislator sees more than a small part of the game; and if a president sees very much more (as he does), his opportunities for describing what he sees and publicly recommending measures are few and all too formal. The presidential press conference no longer illuminates. Since Franklin Delano Roosevelt there has been no fruitful give and take. Presidents are in danger of getting more protection from verbal probing than European Royalty.

It is for these reasons that the Supreme Court is so necessary today. Whether or not judicial review is democratic in character, as is most eloquently urged by V. Rostow,[42] the activity of reviewing is like stopping the film to see if in fact A's rights were infringed by B. There is of course a certain unreality and artificiality about aspects of this procedure, for review in most cases takes place some years after the event: the Court may not choose to review your case and your complaint has to be one for which in principle there can be some redress. But in the end what is reviewed is real, is a live issue, and is of importance to all or to substantial numbers of people in the United States.

The Court educates even when its logic fails to measure up to Wechsler's standards. A reason is usually to be found somewhere in the judgment. Even if a reason is absent there is a result, and to know that the Court has decided and that is the law will be sufficient for most citizens going about their business.

To say that the Court is a great educator is not to say that it teaches quickly. It is even arguable that judicial opinion is not formed in courts where cases are heard on appeal but rather in the law schools where Supreme Court decisions are ruthlessly dissected by young men who will one day become judges. What alters judicial attitudes is probably the same set of changing circumstances that may alter the thinking layman's views of right and wrong,[43] the difference being that the judges may be compelled by the circumstances to come to a decision which they would like, if possible, to be supported by some public plausible reasoning. For the Supreme Court it is of great importance whether they overrule a case because of a grave constitutional defect, because of a procedural imperfection, or because they disagree with the lower court on the facts of the case (or on their significance). In these days of judicial self-restraint it is always more convenient to disagree with the lower court on the two latter grounds. For the citizen and the potential prosecutor a decision not upheld by the Court for whatever reason throws doubt on the usefulness of that law, a cause for rejoicing or otherwise.

The late Mr Justice Frankfurter never tired of saying that fundamental changes in people's attitudes toward each other cannot be brought about by court edict:[44] they are a little more likely perhaps to be changed by the actions of their own representatives in the legislature, but no legislation can make people act out beliefs they do not have. This was Frankfurter's somewhat indirect way of educating people in what they ought to believe. He was probably the Court's greatest educator.

At the conclusion of Henkin's 'Reflections' he reminds us that Holmes in *Lochner*[45] protested that the Fourteenth Amendment did not enact Herbert Spencer's *Social Statics*, but 'many of us seem prepared to assume that the Constitution did enact John Stuart Mill's "On Liberty"'.[46] A very proper observation and one likely today to be ignored by the majority of political scientists but not, fortunately, by teachers of constitutional law.

America, the Flayed Man

STUDENTS OF ANATOMY, WE ARE TOLD, HAVING MASTERED THE skeleton pass on to a more elaborate simulacrum of the human frame. This takes the form of a sectionalized replica from which, as it were, the skin has been removed so as to expose the muscles, nerves, arteries, etc., and which thus allows the workings of the organism to be studied in sophisticated detail. This latter model continental students know as the écorché: to their English colleagues it is the 'flayed man'.

It was in a somewhat comparable condition that the American body politic was exposed to analysis by some forty assorted social scientists assembled in Manchester during a weekend of November 1972. The interlocking sections of the model before them were expounded in the foregoing seven essays. Most of the participants were Britons, but a few were specialists from abroad – Raymond Aron from the Sorbonne, Gabriel Almond from Stanford, Stanley Feingold from the City University of New York, and Robert E. Lane from Yale. The theme of their investigations was 'The Credibility of American Political Institutions', and the date (be it noted) was precisely ten days after the United States elections.

There are of course more senses than one in which America has always been, and still is, the flayed man of political scientists. In so complex an organism the climician of politics can trace symptoms of whatsoever malady or malfunction he is disposed to find. Indeed, he may peel away the outer integument for the express purpose of demonstrating the pathological case, the awful warning. Almost exactly one hundred years ago Herbert Spencer was urgently pressing his American disciple, promoter and amanuensis to send him 'a supply of typical illustrations of the way in which your political machinery acts so *ill* – its failures in securing life, property and equitable relations'. 'I want to use the case of America', he explained,[1] 'to show how baseless is the notion that the *form* of political freedom will secure freedom in the full sense of the word'. After which we are scarcely surprised to note that the material Spencer received he deployed in a chapter headed 'Political Bias'. And to many another European since Spencer's day the flayed man has served as the whipping-boy for the sins of popular democracy.

Whether from this kind of bias the proceedings of the Manchester conference were entirely free, the reader must judge for himself from the report which follows. Admittedly, no single approach to contemporary American politics is wholly without questionable presuppositions. In this particular instance – and leaving aside the concept of 'credibility', which was found to have certain drawbacks – why, one might ask, was it decided to focus attention on *institutions*? Why prefer the static to the dynamic, the model artefact to the living body? The conference's choice might be defended as going along with current trends. The number of recent books, articles and anthologies on American public policy and policy-making suggests an awareness among political scientists that the behavioural revolution of the 1950s and 1960s neglected some significant variables. The importance of formal organization, within which and about which so many conflicts occur, needed reasserting. Behaviouralism may concentrate too narrowly on the microscopic phenomena of relations between persons and between small groups, treating the larger phenomena as mere aggregations of these. To redress the balance it might be felt necessary from time to time to look at the formal institutions, at the macroscopic structure within which the private and informal transactions take place.

From whatever motive, the latter model was the one the conference chose to examine, under a number of thematic heads. But it was with some general reflections that their chairman, Max Beloff, rang up the curtain. Discussion, he suggested, could usefully embrace not only American political institutions but the policies emerging from them: for policy *did* emerge despite the enormous complications of governmental machinery in the USA. There it might be found that of recent years consensus was more readily forthcoming for foreign policies than for domestic; perhaps because over foreign affairs the United States had less control or choice. But even in domestic affairs, comparing 1972 with 1968, Beloff was struck by the absence of a sense of crisis. Was this because the solutions sought four years ago had been found? Or found unsuccessful? The federal government had stemmed inflation. Was the deadweight of national prosperity now such that those who did not share in it had temporarily relinquished the struggle? Whatever the reason, Americans despite their heterogeneous group loyalties seemed now to be responding as a whole to certain nationwide impulses.

ELECTIONS AND PARTIES

A natural starting point for discussion had been provided by the elections just concluded. They had revealed, thought Beloff, an almost European stability of political allegiance on the voters' part, tempered by a greater willingness than heretofore to split the ticket. Did this suggest that Americans rather liked to see an executive/legislative deadlock embedded at the centre of things? Or would the case have been far otherwise with a different Democratic presidential candidate? These were two of the questions canvassed at this juncture by Michael Steed's analysis, which began by noting several peculiarities. The voters had broken two records. They had put Nixon among the very top scorers in terms of electoral support. And they had opened the widest gap ever known between the presidential and congressional voting tallies by party. From these circumstances Steed deduced that parties were of declining importance to the President, each successive candidate for the White House gathering around him his own peculiar combination of supporters. The consequent intra-party and cross-party realignments were likely to persist for the immediate future. The gap between presidential and congressional balloting showed, not an American preference for deadlock in Washington, but the contrast (not necessarily a time-lag) between the old alignments and the new. Variations in the pattern of this gap, and particularly that between the balloting for President and for Senators, suggested that the vote for Nixon was a vote for a temporary situation, not a lasting realignment but one easily reversible; rather as when in 1960 Nixon had scored best in those states and regions where in 1956 he and Eisenhower had done worst.

The percentage of general turnout was low: to find a lower we might have to go back as far as 1924. Regarding fractions of the electorate, Steed noted strong movements of ethnic minorities, particularly of Jews and Italians, toward the Republican ticket. But the more recent Latin minorities, such as Cubans, had remained staunchly Democrat. Not only the blacks but Spanish-speaking Americans seemed now to have emerged as an identifiable political bloc. How much, he asked parenthetically, would they influence America's foreign policy in the future as Jews had sometimes done in the past? The Republicans were still building up in the South, especially the Deep South. Statewide movements toward a genuine two-party system had everywhere continued, and there now remained very few which could still be described as single-party states. Among urban voters Steed detected a slight shift in McGovern's favour in cities of over half a million souls. As for issues, peace in Vietnam did not seem to have been a crucial one. 'Environmentalism', coupled with 'consumerism', probably was – witness the Democratic senatorial victory in Colorado. Some slight aura was observed to surround the terms 'law-and-order' and 'ethics'.

Feingold saw little that was strikingly original about the recent elections; he was more impressed by the recurrence of previous features. The usual party realignments had taken place, representing only temporary and not very significant shifts of allegiance. Between the voting for the President and for his party could be seen the customary divergence. The personalization of the presidency had proceeded apace. The important thing about a candidate for that office continued to be his symbolic identification. Once again, the winner was he who had contrived to alienate the fewest and least significant sections of his potential following. The Democratic Party remained as vital as before. In short, nothing very remarkable had happened.

This view was promptly gainsaid by Lane, to whom it was evident that a more enduring shift had indeed occurred in United States politics. For one thing, American society itself had changed. The poverty line had fallen and incomes were levelling up. More than half the country's workforce was now to be found in service industries, not on the production line, and the skilled segment of it was becoming more Republican in outlook. As in its economic, so in its cultural and religious aspects, America was becoming homogenized. Thirty-nine per cent of the Jewish vote, and 15 per cent of the Negro, had gone for Nixon. Another index of secular change was the unmistakeable signs of a massive lack of confidence in United States political institutions themselves – a rise in the number of 'independent' voters, a weakening of identification with party and the party system. So, electorally speaking, everything was becoming malleable. Again, there was a new shaping-up over issues as the old liberal/conservative dichotomy ceased to obtain. Today's liberals were no longer liberal on *everything:* welfare issues dating from the New Deal had declined in salience. Altogether a new and more fluid style of politics was emerging in the USA, in which both issues and personalities would have larger importance.

Aron asked for greater clarity. Had the critical factor in the
recent elections been the nation's social structure or had it been
the personalities of the two presidential candidates? Looking back,
Feingold could see no convincing explanation in the social structure
at any rate of why the Democrats had so consistently since 1932
remained the majority party in Congress and country. But, interjected Steed, the point was that the make-up of that Democratic
majority had been changing. The crude aggregate figures of state-
by-state balloting concealed enormous relative voting shifts between
Democrat and Republican. Democratic majorities in Congress,
Almond added, were very heterogeneous. Only at presidential level
did the polarization of outlook, which had been developing within
the Democratic Party for eight years or longer, show up clearly.
For at least as long again, he prophesied, the party's great problem
would continue to be the blacks. Ionescu suggested that the crisis
of the Democratic Party should be seen in a more general and
comparative perspective. It was the crisis of the progressive parties,
usually considered as the working-class parties, which in advanced
technological societies were feeling the effect of the political
emancipation of the workers and their organizations, which were
no longer in need of political representation and patronage.

The future of the Democrats was one of the two main points
canvassed by Fotheringham when introducing his paper on the
parties. In his view the battle for control over the platform and the
nominating process was likely to be rejoined when Democratic
delegates reassembled in 1974 for the novel expedient of a midterm
national convention. What was then decided about the machinery
for selecting future delegations would have the greatest significance
for the party's liberal wing. But whatever the outcome the Deep
South, now the most strongly pro-Nixon area of the United States,
would remain for the foreseeable future the odd man out.

The other topic Fotheringham regarded as central to debate was
the ambivalence of the electorate discernible when Americans voted
respectively for President and for Congress. Over a period, three
factors were significant here. There were the election results
themselves, where in particular the successes of Eisenhower,
Nixon and Wallace demanded explanation. There was the relative
importance of the major campaign issues – war, race, law-and-
order, etc. And there were the alleged changes in American society:
did the latest voting realignments suggest temporary swings or
long-term trends? The smallness of the swing in the 1972 congres-

sional elections led Fotheringham to guess that the former was the case. This contrasted with the steady decline his figures revealed in the number of areas, outside the South and Border states, where the Democrats could expect to win a majority of seats. To ask whether the Democrats were any longer the majority, as opposed to the plurality, party of the nation was therefore to pose a very complicated question indeed.

Their fate naturally dominated a good deal of the subsequent discussion. Noting the tendency for global figures to mask the significance of relatively small but crucial shifts, Almond pondered the changed source of party militancy. Once upon a time the Democratic drive used to come from established institutions such as the trade unions' political apparatus. Now its source seemed to be a small nexus of party workers, mostly young and many of them students. Was this change a transient phenomenon or durable? Fotheringham felt there had been some fortuitous element in the way these new militants had achieved prominence: McGovern was more to their liking than Muskie, and it was he who had come best out of the primaries. But the aftermath of 1972 might reduce the importance of these new activists. On the other hand, if they could stay organized and press as strongly again, they would be assured of some say in choosing delegates to the projected 1974 Democratic convention. But Steed, said Ionescu, had talked about the decline of the parties, and did not that imply something more considerable than shifts in their sources of drive? True, agreed Fotheringham, the magnetic field of the party label had weakened, especially in presidential contests. This was because of the new primacy of issues, which had come to determine the attitudes of presidential candidates, the orientation of their campaigns, and even (in 1972) the character of the actual candidate chosen. Samplings showed that in 1972 the number of professedly independent voters had continued to soar as the number of confessed Democrats had dropped. Nevertheless it would be premature to announce the demise of the Democratic Party in particular. Senator Edward Kennedy had good contacts with all sections of it, at least outside the South, and if he could pull it together again at the national level its survival and even revival seemed assured. In what shape it would be remodelled – how far the city machines would reassert themselves and how firm a foothold the former McGovernites would manage to retain – the near future would show. Ionescu, asked whether the party was not faced with a radical transformation?

Would it not have to yield the South to the Republicans or lose its trade union support? Fotheringham thought the first eventuality possible, the second unlikely, particularly as the present rift with organized labour was partly attributable to the personal revulsion of the aged George Meany, president of the AFL-CIO, from McGovern. Vale mentioned that some twenty AFL-CIO unions, in addition to the Teamsters and United Automobile Workers, had jointly and publicly announced that they were raising voluntary contributions from their memberships on McGovern's behalf; though of course they would not have had at their disposal the fund-raising facilities of their parent federation's Committee on Political Education (COPE).

Finer raised the matter of mutual realignment between the two major American parties. From an Anglocentric viewpoint it had always been wishfully thought that, slowly but surely, the Democrat/Republican relationship was more and more coming to resemble the mutual posture of Labour and Conservative in the United Kingdom. Did the shooting of George Wallace now bring this prospect nearer realization, by leaving the South to be drawn irrevocably into the Republican camp? Had he remained in the race, Wallace would have blurred the dichotomy by carrying that region again into an independent third-party position. Steed agreed there was now solid evidence that party realignment had moved closer. But what impressed him more was the transformed role of the parties' national conventions. There had been no open convention since 1932; thereafter the victorious nominee had emerged clearly on the first ballot. Only in form was the quadrennial gathering still the engine for evolving the candidate: in actuality it was the pre-selected group who would form the presidential party of that year in support of the already emergent leader. Wallace stressed the importance of incumbency to the successful candidate, an importance that could be critical when the popular vote was close. Since 1936 every incumbent who ran again had been elected, and where no incumbent had competed the prize had been won (save in the exceptional case of Eisenhower) by a margin of one per cent or less.

The equivocal attitude of George Wallace did not go unremarked. Would he have stuck to his original intention to work through the Democratic Party this time, rather than lead his followers into an independent third? He had been holding his cards, thought Nicholas, very close to his chest. If the opening for a third party had looked good in terms of primary results, he would surely have left himself free to seize it. He had been careful to endorse no candidate, but had given a very cordial interview to Spiro Agnew. Finer would dearly have loved to see how Congress would have resolved a choice thrown into its lap by a combination of Wallace and the constitution.

Nicholas was fascinated by the prospect of this extraordinary midterm national convention promised by the Democrats for 1974. Normally after a presidential struggle a party needed four years of quiet to put itself in order. Instead the Democrats proposed to put themselves publicly on the spot. In so doing they might be laying an extra rod to their back. Still close (as they were) to recent defeat, still lacking for the future a father figure, it might be said of the Democratic Convention that they had lost a party and not yet found a role. But in looking at that small part of the Democratic organization which chose its presidential champion, Feingold warned, we should be careful not to equate it with the party structure across the nation. This latter had suffered no breakdown, had not been much infiltrated by the McGovernites, and possessed continuing resilience. Recent reforms might increase the hazard of polarizing the party in national convention: they would not touch the wellsprings of its organization in the states. This distinction was not altogether clear to other disputants present. Fotheringham pointed out that it was upon his having gained the biggest number of committed *state* delegations that McGovern had based his claim. The recent opening-up of their national convention might prove very important indeed for the Democratic Party as a whole if fairly equally matched rivals for the nomination presented themselves next time. And what did Feingold mean, demanded Nicholas, by saying that the party's formal structure remained unimpaired? Was this structure one simply of form, or of real power? A containing mould into which one poured the source that captured the party label? Or a structure which existed in the literal sense that it could uphold its standard bearers? Feingold in reply insisted that the Democratic structure in the states remained, despite the events of 1972, no more accessible to insurgents than before, and that the rules of the party game played there had survived largely unchanged.

THE US SUPREME COURT
The US Supreme Court could not so easily be linked with the main lines of discussion, remaining as it does somewhat *hors série*

of governmental institutions. Yet it can be shown to bear at least some negative correlationship with the American political party. Historically it has always been the latter's function to sponsor, as it were, and induct each successive new section of the American populace (the immigrant, the urban poor) into the political arena – in exchange, of course, for their votes. Somewhere during the present century, however, parties seem to have abdicated, or simply failed to discharge, this politicizing function. The blacks have been brought into the system not by the party but by the Supreme Court, and Congress has felt bound to follow where the latter has led.

Its voiding of all discrimination and segregation on racial grounds as unconstitutional is only one reason for conservatives' discontent with the Supreme Court of the 1950s and 1960s. On other grounds also the high bench incurred throughout those decades the charge of being excessively liberal, or of moving too far ahead of public opinion, or of trespassing in the 'political' field. Such criticism has been unexpectedly strengthened by the misgivings of academics who have argued that the Court has of late been leaning too far toward a 'purposive' or 'policy-making' jurisprudence. It is many decades now since the American judiciary, under the influence of Roscoe Pound and others, began its move away from a 'strict constructionist' to a 'teleological' concept of its duty. In abandoning a purely mechanistic reading (if indeed it had ever held one) of constitution and statute, has it of late been showing an inordinate affection for social policy-making as an end in itself?

Pear offered his paper as a background to such current controversy. Since this latter tended to shape itself also along a supposed liberal/conservative dichotomy on the bench, it was useful to begin by studying the present composition of the Burger Court, heir to sixteen years of Earl Warren's liberalism. It comprised, beside the Chief Justice, one associate justice (William Douglas) left over from Rooseveltian days; two Eisenhower appointees (William Brennan and Potter Stewart); one nominee of Kennedy and one of Johnson (Byron White and Thurgood Marshall respectively). Add to these Nixon's new choices, Blackmun, Powell and Rehnquist, and then, with White as a pivot, it became clear that the incumbent President could hope to enjoy the prospect (if their attitudes fulfilled his expectations) of a five to four majority congenial to his own conservative way of thinking.

What indications were there that this swing to the right had already occurred? While eschewing the phrase 'law and order', Nixon had boasted of his nominations that they would 'strengthen the forces of peace against the criminal forces in America'. And indeed recent rulings pointed to a Court less sympathetic, though only marginally so, to the criminal. Thus, additionally to cases cited in Pear's paper, the Court in *Harris v New York* (February 1971) allowed the statement of a drug peddler, not informed at the outset of his constitutional right to silence and counsel, to be used in order to destroy his own credibility. And, generally speaking, the Burger Court had been construing 'the equal protection of the laws' less broadly than its predecessor. However, Pear was at pains to point out other aspects of the many-sided concept of liberalism where the high bench had stood fast. It had upheld, for instance, the right of Students for a Democratic Society to form chapters freely, and the right of the state of Massachusetts to distribute contraceptives. It had overturned an Idaho law which gave preference to men over women in the administration of estates. The meeting was invited to consider the implication of such decisions as possibly constituting a trend, or to turn to other aspects of today's Supreme Court they might deem more significant.

Almond went straight to the question of the predilections of individual justices. Could one here speak of a 'legal culture' in the USA, or at least posit the influence of the bar and the legal profession upon judicial attitudes? Pear, while pointing out that one could not observe a Chief Justice at work, suggested that, if attempting to predict the line taken by justices, we should look at the law schools of which they were the products. We might then better understand how the Warren Court's liberal thinking ran ahead of the country's as a whole. Aron believed in the existence of a kind of minimum common opinion in the United States, setting limits to the Court's freedom to slip back from its present position on, e.g., segregation. Did this common opinion express itself at the polls, and thereby confirm Mr Dooley's aphorism that 'the Supreme Court follows the election returns'? Walles argued that it certainly ought not to; and Pear was unshaken in believing that in the law schools, rather than Dr Gallup, lay the root of judicial behaviour.

Certainly, emphasized Feingold, one could not attribute the liberalism of senior justices infallibly to presidents, whose appointees in the past had proved unpredictable in their attitudes on the bench. That the mood of the nation at large and of the Congress was less liberal than that of the Supreme Court, Feingold had no doubt, or that the latter must therefore be expected to swing back a little toward the dominant consensus of opinion. It had received conspicuously little support from Congress over liberty of the person and even less from the public over the 'protection' of criminals. Save in the matter of Negro voting, no real substantive legislation had followed in the wake of its civil rights rulings. Harking back to Aron's point, Ionescu stressed that the judiciary's credibility was inevitably linked to its popular esteem. If a normative relationship existed between Supreme Court and public, one must always ask how much the latter trusted the former? Would not the conservative trend of the present Court have the effect of bringing the two closer together again?

The prospect of non-alignment did not in any case greatly worry Hayward: indeed it ought to be regarded as one of the salutary checks and balances of the American system. Nor did it follow that the older the judge, the likelier he was to be out of step with public opinion. In this matter of age Finer saw a possible point of comparison to Congress, with whose committee chairmen Supreme Court justices might be considered coeval. The significant difference would then reside in the respective intellectual origins of their opinions, the justices having imbibed theirs from the law schools. But unlike the Supreme Court, objected Pear, Congress does not opine as a whole. Indeed it has often, as over Vietnam, deliberately abstained from expressing a collective opinion for as long as possible. And as for the views of individual Congressmen, evidence existed to show that they were as likely to obtain them from their favourite columnists as from anywhere else.

What worried Maidment about the new jurisprudence in certain notable judgements of recent years, *Brown v Board of Education* was an example, was the absence of the kind of legal or constitutional arguments one normally looked to the federal bench for. The Court's seeming, and regrettable, preoccupation with policy results had too often been leading it into positions which were theoretically unsustainable. That was especially so in the matter of legislative apportionment – instance *Colegrove v Green* and *Baker v Carr*. But these, protested Feingold, were rulings where the justices were badly split, and therefore not good bases to argue from. Nevertheless, Maidment insisted, judicial opinion must base itself upon some reputable ground. The current desire to make law 'relevant to society' alarmed him: the older and more conservative judicial approach had drawn great intellectual sustenance from the constitution. But was the constitution, countered Nicholas, really neutral in the Wechslerian sense? Surely in the past an un-neutral constitution had been at the disposal of a conservative jurisprudence, and one so intellectually disreputable that it could not possibly sustain a significant reversal of the Court's opinion today? If so, Aron need not fear that the Court would be moved by changes of fashion to unmake what it had made, so as to revert from non-discrimination to discrimination.

But if the law itself came to be thought of as merely an instrument of current policy, for how long, Beloff speculated, would the mystique of constitutional law survive? In point of esteem, as Lane reminded the meeting, one must never underrate the occupational prestige of a Supreme Court justice. When American citizens were polled on a particular issue they showed a much greater deference to something denominated 'public law' than to 'public policy'. Nor was it true to say that in the matter of desegregation the Court's stand lacked reinforcement. The withholding of money by the Department of Health, Education and Welfare was no less sharp a coercive weapon against non-compliant areas. Through grants-in-aid, too, the federal government leaned heavily against communities and institutions reluctant to liberalize themselves. Such administrative controls over state action provided a means of implementing the court's rulings that one must not overlook: though, as Pear reminded the meeting, they had the disadvantage of being vulnerable to small shifts in legislative policy.

Other points raised *en passant* included the query: what is a political question? An acceptable answer might be, one which can be resolved by another branch of government than the judiciary. The Supreme Court had been compelled into the 'political' field of legislative apportionment because neither Congress nor the state assemblies would tackle it and existing state referendal procedure was itself tainted with malapportionment. In other areas too, Feingold pointed out, judicial policy-making had been required to fill a need. Thus, the entire legal notion of privacy in the United States had been a judicial construct, beginning with Brandeis's celebrated article of eighty years ago.[2] If the conference regarded, as some of those present plainly did, this judicial activism as a menace, the moral would seem to be, 'Don't live in a country with a written constitution'. But – a final alarming reflection – would not Britian be in just such a predicament within the EEC from January 1973 onward?

THE CONGRESS

John Lees introduced his paper as an attempt to set in juxtaposition
a number of significant changes which had been going forward
in Congress for some recent years, and one which laid special
emphasis on mutations occurring in certain features of its internal
organization. His survey, based in part on a series of personal
interviews with a great number of Congressmen and Senators
during 1971, showed that, on the one hand, some influences
operated nowadays upon Congress with diminished impact.
Inter-party competition was one such: the Republicans now
accepted their minority status, and their recent self-remodelling
on Capitol Hill posited this continuing condition. But corres-
pondingly, other and new forces were working to modify both
House and Senate, though sometimes in different ways. Relations
between Congress and party were changing, and in particular
new intra-party organizations were growing.

These burgeoning trends had certainly not been stultified by
the elections of November 1972. Many constituencies had been
redistricted to meet apportionment criteria. Several committee
chairmen had fallen at the primary hurdle and, though Congressional
longevity was still an electoral asset, one must expect redoubled
attacks on the seniority system to be mounted through the party
caucuses. Committee membership had undergone a great turnover:
one might say that increasingly the whole committee structure
was being opened up. A black caucus was now an established fact.
And there had been a remarkable influx to both parties of new and
young legislators.

Did this influx of youth, Roberts wanted to know, presage a
change of legislative climate? Numerically, observed another
questioner, the new intake was almost as large as that of 1964,
and this time they had not been swept in on presidential coat-tails
but were there, so to speak, in their own right. What was known
of their ideological commitment? Lees saw no evidence that the
newcomers were in outlook a whit less liberal, or at least issue-
oriented, than those they had displaced. Certainly they were not so
'machine-minded' in the sense that they were less preoccupied with
old-style constituency politics or with building up their own
security of tenure. There was irony in the consequence that a liberal
president would probably have had easier sledding with the new
Congress. Lees had, however, to confess to Gould that the number
of committee chairmen from the South had not dwindled. What, it

was asked, of the black caucus? Almost all the Negroes in the House saw themselves as representing a national black constituency, and perhaps as a consequence were generally liberal in their posture. Adding all these factors together, inquired Maidment, could one venture to predict the emergence of a moderate centre in Congress? Lees allowed that there might still on occasion be found a conservative coalition – a concept, however, very complicated to analyse and sometimes verging on the mythical. Its obstructive potential declining with its numbers, it could no longer pose a serious threat if, as appeared to be the case, congressional parties by their own internal actions were opening up fresh routes of access to the centres of power. Henceforward there would remain fewer obstacles in the path of any Democratic majority that could be found for sustaining more progressive attitudes.

Discussion then narrowed its focus on to the individual legislator. To assess Congress's performance, Moyser argued, one should be looking not only at the structural relationship between its members but at their individual capacities. Every Senator was known to be greatly beholden to his personal staff. Ought we not then to examine the quality of the latter, more particularly as determining the quality of communications to legislators? Lees agreed that one must not overlook the legislator's assistants: but having talked with many such, he would stress their diversity of type and function. Their duties ranged considerably, from the merely parochial to representative employment on their master's behalf so wide as to provide virtually an extension of his personality. Some in due course stepped into their employers' shoes. At least one such in Mississippi recently had read the signs and crossed over to the other party. Beloff wondered whether their influence was comparable with that of the justice's clerks upon the justice, and whether this influence was entirely above suspicion? The meeting shuddered with him at the recollection of Messrs Cohn and Schine's mission to Europe on behalf of the late Senator Joe McCarthy.

It then moved on to consider Congress's public image. Why, asked Ionescu, had Lees begun by describing the federal legislature as the least credible of American institutions? Where did this scepticism spring from – was it from Congress's failure to make visible in the first two years its general attitudes on such a great national issue as the Vietnam war? Lane answered by reference to the findings of the Michigan Research Survey Centre, which had been polling the American public about their impressions. Did people think the Congress likely to do what was right? Did it serve the general interest or a few private ones? Was corruption commonplace on Capitol Hill? etc., etc. The scale of responses, he was sorry to have to report, revealed a marked falling-off in the public's esteem for its lawmakers, accompanied by a notable secular rise in cynicism. When questions were put specifically about Congressmen – do you think yours more likely to help you? – responses over the years 1960 to 1964 had shown an affirmative rise. But now there was a dramatic decline in the esteem American citizens were prepared to show their representatives. This was the case with white and black respondents alike, and was not confined to the right-wingers' view of the Democrats or the left-wingers' of the Republicans. Both sides thought both parties inadequate to the national occasion. Neither party was felt to be addressing itself to the country's needs. This draining away of public confidence in Congress's political efficacy, in strong contrast to the popular approbation of the 1950s, had been going on for too long now to be treated as just a passing spasm of discontent.

Throughout the remainder of the session various participants strove manfully to lighten the gloom. As to public opinion polls, Roberts pointed out that the halving, between 1966 and 1972, of the number of respondents willing to affirm confidence in their machinery of government had regard to American political institutions in general. On that showing, peculiar disapprobation had not been reserved for Congress alone. Almond warned that pollsters' material was very volatile stuff which should be handled with care. Every time Johnson or Nixon took action on the Vietnam war there was a sharp positive response in the polls, and in the intervals when the war went badly, a sharp decline. It could be used to show of any major organ, from the President downward, that every time it took a positive step it lost *some* section of its supporters. Even its youngest critics, said Ionescu (and even the blacks, Almond would add), were still concerned to improve Congress, not to abolish it. The fact, Lane suggested, that more young Americans than ever before had registered to vote in 1972 did not suggest disillusionment. And a proximate general election, observed Aron with the Paris of May 1968 in mind, could always be relied on to defuse a revolutionary situation. Madgwick was consoled by reflecting upon the vast pilgrimages to Capitol Hill to do reverence to a national monument. Finally, if public attitudes towards the

Congress were ambiguous, this circumstance, said Lees, would be
borne very heavily in mind by the newcomers gathering there in
January 1973.

INTERESTS AND PRESSURES

Any study of American pressure groups, said Julius Gould at the
outset, and any evaluation of their performance, must begin by
recognizing certain features of the context within which they
operate. One such feature in the USA was the absence, probably
for the indefinite future, of a strong 'non-confused' party system
such as the conference had already desiderated. Another was the
repeated failure of legal attempts to control American lobbies or
even to limit the size of their campaign expenditures: here political
realism shaded into cynicism. A third circumstance was the limit
of American consensus about public policy, though one should
note that even those groups who expressed violent dissent might
still be appealing implicitly to historical, constitutional sanctions.
A fourth was the diversity within the pressure-group camp, which
experienced its own internal tensions. For it housed a heterogeneous
company – the professional societies, self-administering and powerful; environmental and welfare groups, from whom much would
still be heard for their objectives were by no means attained;
the military-industrial alliance, which was not just a form of words.
And parallel with these one must consider the extraordinarily
important role played by the big foundations, educational agencies,
and scientific and research establishments.

Even this catalogue Almond did not find exhaustive. Gould
had not mentioned the political organizations generated by newly-
politicized populations, whether of Chicanos, American Indians or
students. These were novel phenomena, inasmuch as they combined
the old lobbying methods with an anti-system attitude. All of
them, as Gould agreed, appeared at times to be rejecting orthodox
rules and values. But how far did they believe themselves to be
affirming, or take for granted, the traditional American dispensation?
Far enough, Almond thought, to give one grounds for doubting
whether a general revolution was imminent in the American way
of life. What the blacks usually wanted was simply what the whites
had already got. Campus protest had been contained, and students,
a group with high turnover of membership, could not maintain a
head of steam indefinitely. Of all current claims, perhaps that of
women for equal treatment with men had most substance and

durability.

At this point, however, the meeting immersed itself in definition. Had Almond not moved too far, asked Beloff, from the classic definition of the pressure group as a tightly-knit corps of producers who used their organizational capacity to wrest something out of the political process? How could one meaningfully apply the term to twelve million blacks; or to women, half the United States' adult population; or to students, a transient category possessing no productive bargaining power? Either one must narrow one's definition to comprehend, in each specific instance, those people active on behalf of a quasi-group, or else be content to compare Women's Lib politically with, say, Garrison's anti-slavery movement. But Almond protested that this concept was too static. Many American political movements had begun as pressure groups (ethnic, in the case of immigrant peoples) which became assimilated in due course into whatever party proved most responsive to their demands and voting potential. Would not an appropriate British example be the Chartists, who represented the politically deprived majority of a country's adult male population? But the Chartists, retorted Beloff, were pressing for the franchise which today's feminists already had.

Finer now clarified the issue: customarily, he suspected, one accepted a typology embracing both 'status' and 'cause' groups, of which the one strove for its own material interests, the other for certain alleged communal goods. Suffragettes were best regarded as a group of the latter kind, purporting to act as the vanguard of the female constituency at large; similarly with racial pressures. The National Association for the Advancement of Coloured Peoples was the structured group: their clientèle, the blacks at large, might be described as the *mouvance*. If American pressure groups were more conspicuous than their European counterparts, that was simply because in the USA the whole process of government had a greater visibility.

One delegate was particularly sceptical about the credentials of many who publicly claimed to 'represent' a movement. In order to make such a claim effectually one used formerly to have to be one of its accredited officers. But nowadays, it seemed, any 'personality' could through the mass media appear as the self-appointed spokesman of an alleged movement. 'Ralph Nader and his raiders' did not wait to acquire a following.

Ionescu raised the question of interest groups participating in matters of national concern in the interdependent industrial society. Fighting inflation, for example, was a *dirigiste* experience, where numerous groups might be called upon to co-operate with the government. Such co-operation, Finer observed, was likely to be much more readily forthcoming from economic groups in the USA than in Britain, in which latter country the trade unions could manifestly thwart governmental proposals for reform by simply refusing to budge. American unions were likely to respond much more consensually. A union leader's request to his followers, Gould observed in passing, was likely to carry much greater weight if made in the name of the President than on behalf of a Prime Minister.

Here, continued Gould, was a good illustration of his point about the value of countervailing forces in a society, so as to allow the striking of a fair balance between (in this instance) the consequences of inflation and the evil of unemployment. The strength of an interest group provided a kind of guarantee that even under conditions of great *dirigisme* society would remain stronger than the state. More generally, if in any country relatively deprived classes of people were to be enabled to reach out for various kinds of equality, such as those implicit in the fact of American citizenship, they needed a legitimized means of organizing themselves in support of their claims. Interest groups, inasmuch as they provided these means, were vital to a free society.

THE AMERICAN CITY

Madgwick presented his paper as a calculatedly moderate view of the cities' predicament, neither complacent nor alarmist. He might have underestimated the degree of urban discontent and its connexion with colour. On the other hand he held no brief for Caraley's 'black tinderbox' view. He had also been deliberately cautious in his estimate of what might be the practicable or desirable rate of urban reform, and of 'citizen participation' as a means thereto. He would be content to dwell chiefly on practical matters – what cities did, how well they performed, and the essentially political task of holding them together. Limits of space compelled him to generalize: but he was well aware how considerations of size, location, etc., of cities affected their respective problems.

The discussion went straight to specific examples, namely Chicago and New York. Madgwick agreed with Gould that Chicago was well governed because Mayor Daley's administration performed

well; but it did so because the system permitted Daley to exert
political power centrally and compactly. New York, by comparison,
was sprawling, decentralized in structure, and saddled with a
massive racial problem. Its wage rates too, Pear noticed, were
lower than the Lake City's. But, as Lane pointed out, this question
of 'governability' was of a kind to demand output analysis. Urban
protest movements might be product or process. 'Chaos' might
signify no more than a strike of garbage collectors. In terms of
water-supply Chicago might be doing better than New York: in
health, education and welfare the reverse could hold.

Almond was anxious not to play down the law-and-order problem,
of which the city was the locus. Projections showed that negritude,
with all its attendant worries, would continue to increase at the
city core. The suburbs needed the central city, but access to it
was becoming increasingly problematic. A constructive approach
was of course needed, and this would entail careful costing. But if
New York's forward planning to fill its potholes were a typical
example, commented Nicholas, the cost analysts were chasing an
ever-receding target. The crisis, Feingold agreed, was becoming
costlier every year, and the re-election of Nixon, who had made
plain his disinclination to grasp the urban nettle, was a dismal
portent. One problem was that of class. The United States was the
one country in the world where suburbanites fled the city. Whereas
in Britain public transport was used by all social classes, the
American middle class 'will not be caught dead in New York's
subway for fear they may be'. This possibility Madgwick had
regularly braved, yet could not avoid the sense of the American
suburban home as a kind of garrison, open to the outside world
only through the air-conditioning vent.

But what, asked Aron (one of whose colleagues had been mugged
hard by the Columbia campus), could Nixon effectively promise to
do? One tended to forget that insecurity in big cities was a historic
problem – instance 19th-century London or Paris. No very
persuasive solutions were forthcoming. Madgwick had observed
at first hand how certain city problems – law and order, school
bussing and racial quotas – had been electorally crucial ones in
1972, but these issues were unconstructive. Studies like Banfield's
struck him as pessimistic determinism, calling to mind those British
local authorities of the 1920s who had deprecated council house
construction on the ground that tenants would only keep their coal
in the bath. Feingold was convinced that the federal government

could and should assume more responsibility: yet not on the lines of the past forty years, when its efforts to encourage greater house-buying by means of subsidy through the Veterans or Federal Housing Administrations had had the effect of inducing greater class segregation. The whites always moved on and out. For political reasons there was not the remotest possibility that the problem could be solved piecemeal and locally by (e.g.) the creation of a 'Greater New York' through administrative absorption of adjacent areas. If London had done better, this was because its metropolitan authority had long possessed jurisdiction over the suburbs. Ever since the creation of the London County Council, as Beloff observed, the capital city had benefited from very large building enterprises backed by state money, a phenomenon un-paralleled in the USA. So a massive programme of public housing such as we had known here was seemingly not the answer over there. Even if politically feasible in the States, it would induce breakdown of the community by taking the stable element outside the city and leaving the worst behind. Public housing schemes, with their low social connotation in the USA, might even be locally resisted, said Madgwick, citing the attempt to introduce one into New York's Forest Hills district. The British analogy would not hold. Housing projects over here could safely posit a genuine sense of community. But how, demanded Nicholas, could one talk about putting governmental institutions into an urban jungle?

In a quantitative sense, said Lane, there was no housing 'crisis' in the United States anyway. One should be careful to look at each element of the American city's predicament individually, as Coleman had recently done.[3] This had reported that over a test period where blacks and whites were given roughly similar quality of schooling, blacks were behind whites about one-and-a-half years at the sixth grade, two-and-a-half years at the ninth, and three at the twelfth. Controlled experiments with bussing did not indicate any great difference of achievement between groups transported to schools out of the city centre and those remaining behind for their education. And to take blacks and immerse them in a white setting was a ticklish business calling for great discretion. The Headstart Programme had been disappointing. On the other hand, small and expensive research devices had shown that low IQ's once raised would often persist at the higher level. If the drop-out rate of blacks from the courses of New York's Open University was quite considerable, so too was the persistence rate, and that without jeopardy to the better students.

At the end of the day the conference groped for firm ground. Must we really conclude, asked the Chairman, that no constitutional, legal or administrative arrangements make any significant difference to the problems of American cities? Lane deprecated pessimism. Much present discontent was subjective in that it implied higher standards than formerly. Objectively a longer perspective showed New York's homicide rate to be slightly lower than in the 1930s, its drug addiction markedly less than in the 1920s. Overall, America's rate of crime increase was dropping as the average age of her citizens rose. And there were encouraging signs that some attempt was at last to be made, by application of 'negative income' assessment to the South, to dry up black immigration to the nation's cities at its source. Since the black birthrate was now falling to approximately the white, the racial problem was at least no longer self-generating. All in all, Lane would describe the urban plight as 'nearly desperate but not totally desperate', and still soluble if help were, as Madgwick put it, 'just enough, just in time'.

THE PRESIDENCY AND THE
FEDERAL ADMINISTRATION

Since there was some fortuitous overlap between them, and some degree of complementary approach, it was decided to take the papers of H. G. Nicholas and V. Vale jointly at the same session.

As to the insulation of the President, Nicholas expressed a prophet's pardonable pride in the way the circumstances of the election had borne him out. How strongly, two examples would suffice to illustrate. First, Mr Klein, grandly denominated Director of Communications to the White House, had gone on record at a very early stage of the campaign as announcing (according to the *New York Times*) that President Nixon would not risk losing the Democratic support that had given him a commanding lead, by pressing for a Republican majority in Congress also. He did not intend, said the spokesman, to shift the emphasis from his own success. The number one consideration was the presidential race, on which he would be concentrating the limited amount of campaigning he undertook (though Nixon did in the event intervene later in a congressional contest in North Carolina). And after 7 November had come and gone, the Republican National Chairman could only express a pious hope that the President would work with his own party for the next two years. Could anything, commented Nicholas, more firmly underline the point his paper made about presidential detachment from his party, in Congress and outside?

A second development illustrated the point he had made later in his paper about the modern President's strength *vis-à-vis* Congress. Nixon had proposed to the latter that it accept his budgetary total of one quarter of a billion dollars and remit him withal the authority himself to cut appropriations to any programme which brought aggregate expenditure above this figure. Only the Senate's refusal to go along saved the House from the consequences of its compliance. Despite this rejection, George Schulz, Secretary of the Treasury, gave it as his view that the President would nevertheless exercise 'his constitutional right' to withhold any funds voted in excess of the desired limit. What incident could more clearly emphasize the impotence of Congress to control the chief executive?

Discussion at first seized upon personalities rather than processes. Almond felt that insufficient attention had been paid to the varying impacts of presidential styles, in particular to the contrast between active and passive approaches to governing. But Nicholas was impressed by how little difference, other than of intensity, these variations nowadays made, over-ridden as they were by the factors making for increased centralization of the high executive's power. Gould, too, felt that presidential achievements were better attributed to accidental circumstances than to personal character. It might be true to say, however, that over the last twenty years presidents had become much more sensitive reflectors of public opinion and had reacted more swiftly and flexibly to changing public situations and moods. Nicholas doubted even this. A president on his lonely eminence tended to lack means for sounding out and keeping in touch with either. Nixon's reactions to the Far East debacle had been slow: even though convinced of the political necessity to wind down the Vietnam war, he had taken four years to reach the present, still inconclusive, situation. How far did the contemporary President identify himself with his party? Whenever, Maidment suggested, it appeared to him to be in his own interest to do so. That would not be, said Beloff, when his party was, like the Republican, in the minority. But Nicholas remained unshakeable in his belief that a president today, even when a Democrat, was reluctant to go on wearing a party label. He no longer proclaimed himself 'proud to be a Republican/Democrat because . . .', but increasingly pressed his claim to represent the whole nation.

It was with pessimism that Roberts viewed the pluralism of the

American federal system. The presidency was separated from the rest; only two Presidents of this century had served a full eight years; and the national parties were discontinuous phenomena. In such circumstances as these it was a wonder government worked at all; *a fortiori* long-term planning to a twenty-year horizon was extremely difficult if not impossible. Whereas the national capacity for making decisions was improving at an arithmetical rate, the demands of American society upon it, for education, transport, the environment, etc., were increasing in geometrical proportion. The proportion of gross national product being consumed by government was rising annually – to the pride of McGovern but the despair of economists like Friedman. Techniques such as programme budgeting were evidently no great success. Those to whom the task of planning fell lacked social indicators, data, and skilled staff. And even if all these were made available there would remain one serious obstacle in the planners' path, namely the fact that the executive's planning functions could be exercised continuously only by non-elected officers.

But did American policy-making, queried Beloff, really suffer such unique disabilities because of inadequate planning machinery? True, there was a turnover of top civil servants with each presidential change. But discontinuity in the legislature was neither so marked nor so important; and the President himself enjoyed the prospect of a longer run in office than most European heads save in the Fifth French Republic. Roberts's reply was to point out that under the United States' separation of powers the executive had no roots in the legislature, and the cabinet was therefore devoid of legislative experience.

What Pear wanted to know was, whom did the American bureaucracy serve? It was powerful, but its loyalty (unlike the British case) was divided, part of it being permanently owed to congressional committee chairmen. This again made coherent planning difficult. There could not be, added Hayward, anything comparable to the 'One parliament, one government, one plan' proclaimed in unitary France at a recent juncture, where people were aware that planning was taking place *outside* the democratic process. When dealing with bureaucracy there was always conflict between the vertical and the horizontal approaches. What American planning stood in need of was a strong lead from the executive. But could a president carry through a movement to reform Congress without loss of democratic legitimacy? Hayward doubted that any occupant of the White House could so entirely control the techno-bureaucratic process as to bring about really *comprehensive* reform.

Lane proposed a different line of approach. It was possible, though not very profitable, to categorize forms and systems, compare the centralized with the decentralized, calculate the degree of inertia, count the number of typewriters, and so forth. But he would prefer to see systems evaluated in terms of outputs. It was practicable to apply a set of criteria of institutional response to each social policy domain. Thus, social security policy-making was very slow to respond to demand, was incremental in process, yet had not fallen off in performance. Policy-making in education faced the very difficult task of bringing all schools up to the same preconceived standard. Other yardsticks were applicable when judging the effect of manpower policy, inflationary-deflationary policies, and so on down the list. What was unprofitable was to study process independently of criteria. Rather, one should aim to answer the general question – do the presidency and the administration respond to social need soon enough and in adequate measure?

It was Almond who now drew together the two threads of planning and presidential character by drawing attention to a recent set of case-studies in the formation of policy.[4] This concluded that there was a demonstrable difference in the way decisions were reached in, for example, the Bay of Pigs invasion and the Cuba missiles crisis. Its findings not only provided the White House and bureaucracy with the opportunity to weigh and reflect on all the different procedural alternatives but showed that presidential typology *did* significantly influence the choice between them. Aron, incredulous that the federal bureaucracy managed to work at all, demurred that in those two particular cases the decisive factors might have been the quality of the intelligence reaching the President and the newness of his favoured advisers to their job. The best of processes could not insure against poor performance: hence the costly failure of the F111 aircraft. But Almond's objection to Lane's approach was that it took no account of the less tangible results of a President's own predilections. A sympathetic leader might provide at the very least symbolic support in a particular area of policy: Nixon's creation of a Cure for Cancer Agency was a narrow example. A wider one was of course the early New Deal itself. The outcome, though not strictly quantifiable, was far from insignificant in human terms. One should never overlook the nonmaterial influence of this 'presidential resonance'. Madgwick preferred the concept of a 'presidential penumbra', within which lesser institutions felt it congenial to plan and act. Thus, the circumstance that it was Nixon who occupied the White House gave the Republicans of New York confidently to believe that social programmes in that state, though not to be dismantled, might be susceptible to cutting down.

Relationship of process to performance drew the fire of other questioners too. Could one say that the United States now presented the best example of a crash programme in social reform? Seeing that the mobilization of support was so colossal, the expectations so enormous, must not any degree of resultant administrative change inevitably appear disappointing? How easy was it to assess, quantitatively or qualitatively, whether in any field the kind of programme selected was yielding the results desired? Could one conclude beyond reasonable doubt that simply by pouring more and more money into a welfare programme one could ultimately solve the problem of poverty in America? Lane conceded that the crash poverty programme had proved a glaring example of the 'maximum feasible misunderstanding' type of enterprise. Yet in the course of extracting workable schemes from a seemingly chaotic mess one *could* learn what to avoid; and the present, relatively successful, manpower programme was the outcome of this kind of trial and error. Something was learned even from programmes that were dropped. At state level, both New York and New Jersey had undertaken studies which showed that results *are* susceptible to strict criteria of evaluation, and can guide the administrator in deciding how much was needed early, how much later, or how and where the work-incentive curve would impinge on 'negative income' schemes.

Ionescu could contemplate without surprise the existence of conflict within the federal bureaucracy itself, agencies, bureaux and departments in competition, but wondered to what extent one could distinguish the levels of quality and efficiency of types of American bureaucracy: federal, state and private? Though unable to illuminate the mutual attitudes of federal and state civil servants, Vale pointed out that Washington could choose from a wide spectrum of relationships with the bureaucracy of private industry, several of which his paper specifically mentioned. More inimical (in his view) to good planning was that formidable 'triple alliance' between federal bureaucrat, congressional committee chairman, and clientèle group, which so heavily pervaded the executive-legislative relationship in the United States.

Finer was anxious to take a deeper, yet at the same time more comparative, view of the difficulties encountered in a Western democracy where no real machinery existed for public planning. If one desired to know whether planning was more or less difficult in America one must look well beyond the President into the process at all levels. European presidents and cabinets do not plan. Parties when facing the electorate compete for the middle ground. So neither president nor cabinet nor public do anything more than set targets and invite responses. We must look at the relationship internally. With whom and at what level does a plan begin? To what extent can the initiator overpersuade his superior or overbear the institutional checks and balances imposed by the system? It was notorious that in the USA the bureaucratic corps was much more sectionalized than in Europe, and that the American civil servant was subject to a two-way stretch of responsibility, to his bureaucratic chief and to the parallel Congressional committee. All this rendered policy-making more incremental and less consistent. Reverting to technique, Hayward noted the suspicion, not entirely unfounded, 'of American politicians that PPBS was a way of smuggling policy and even ideology in through the back door. Congressmen, lobbyists and others, recognizing the threat it posed to the old bargaining methods of policy-making, naturally opposed the novelty. Vale commented on PPBS's limitations, now made visible to British eyes also by the Department of Education and Science's recent flirtation with 'Output Budgeting'. The policy outcome, he remarked, would always be determined by what the Department accepted *a priori* as its criteria of success, whether these were better examination results, or more children going on to higher education, or reduced juvenile delinquency. To a great extent your answer lay embedded in your premises.

In summing up, Nicholas felt that the two papers emphasized two different aspects of the chief executive. Vale was worried about presidential inefficiency: he himself about presidential irresponsibility. Not unnaturally it followed that the two papers gave pride of place respectively to policy areas domestic and foreign. While he derived some shred of comfort from Vale's points about the interdependence of president and administration, they were not sufficiently discrepant with his own to allay his misgivings.

INSTITUTIONS AND FOREIGN POLICY

Limitations of space having compelled the paper-readers virtually to omit American foreign policy making from their purview, the conference welcomed the chance of devoting its final session to this institutional area. Discussion was opened by Raymond Aron.

Fundamentally there was no question, in Aron's opinion, of either expecting change or demanding improvement in the institutions and processes available to the President when dealing with foreign affairs. The existing organization, more elaborate than that of any other country, was potentially adequate. The President, elected monarch that he was, could command a wide range of services from the State Department, National Security Council, numerous intelligence agencies, and other special groups in times of crisis. What was important was whether and how he used them, and here the decision was his alone. This discretion, greater than any one man in Britain or the USSR possessed, was terrifying in its implications but not newly so. What was novel since 1945 was the way the President could use his freedom to involve the USA in military activities without Congress's declaring war. This circumstance arose, not from the American situation peculiarly, even in France and Britain it was possible for the government to bring the country into an unexpected and unwanted conflict, but from the general external circumstances of today when warfare was not infrequently waged in the name of peace.

To what extent was a president exposed to pressures from Congress and public opinion? Superficially, more so than was, for example, a British foreign secretary. It had been taking Nixon all of his first four years to wind down the war in Vietnam to its present level: but from the moment of his inauguration he had had to start to think about meeting popular demand to bring the boys home. On two recent occasions, over the 1963 test-ban treaty with Russia and in 1972 over the anti-ballistic-missile system, Congress had been notably suspicious and critical. In 1954 Congress's resistance, after legislators had met their constituents during the Easter recess, had been one factor in the President's decision not to intervene to save Dien Bien Phu. On the other hand Lyndon Johnson had been able to extract the Tonkin Gulf resolution, with all its subsequent implications, by giving the Senate information which if not wrong was decidedly partial. In the short term, Aron concluded, the President's freedom to take important decisions of foreign policy was very great and beyond reach of the Senate to deny him. To put it another way, his *marginal* scope for independent action in foreign affairs was greater at the moment than in the past. Yet he must always be acutely sensitive to their interaction with domestic response, as signified by demonstrations like that at Kent State University. Over a longer time-span the mood of the country would again come to be seen as the most important factor.

This last consideration did not, however, allay Nicholas's fears. Agreed, he said, the President could be the object of public harassment, as over Vietnam. And an extra-governmental explosion like the Kent incident – an obvious British parallel was the Suez affair – could blow an errant leader back on course. But what struck the foreign observer was the distance at which he could, if so minded, hold criticism away. Nixon did not have to read columnists he did not like, was not obliged to confront his critics publicly, and rarely chose to face searching questions at press conferences. Under the White House roof he had established his own kind of mini-State Department. All this indicated a less responsible system than the British parliamentary encounter of government with opposition, across the floor of a public forum under procedural rules. The basis of the American situation, being constitutional, was permanently there. But recent changes of quantity Nicholas saw as having induced a change of quality in American foreign policy decision-making. Judged either by process or results, this removal of so much beyond the reach of healthy debate was inherently dangerous. What price, he asked, was the country paying for the supersession of its State Department by 'master-minds in the White House'? No previous Secretaries of State had so wholly acquiesced in this transference of power.

Certainly, allowed Aron, the current style of 'the Nixon-Rogers-Kissinger cabal' combined all the elements which enhance the insulation of the presidency from other governmental organs. He doubted, however, whether this condition would or could persist indefinitely, even through Nixon's second term. ('Henry Kissinger knows nothing about the Common Market'). But how, interjected the Chairman, could it be suggested that such methods had been vindicated by success when the reverse was so patently true? All Kissinger could do now was to disguise for as long as possible the harsh fact that the USA had just suffered the first defeat in war it had ever known as an independent nation. Surely Americans when they came to recognize this failure would react against the policy-making methods responsible for it? And would

they not then, and rightly, blame the military elements in particular?
The problem of Vietnam had throughout been much more accurately
assessed by the civilian agencies of the federal government. Aron
disagreed. On the contrary, de Gaulle's disengagement from Algeria
was successfully presented as a great triumph of statesmanship,
though France lost everything there. Nixon *inherited* defeat from
his predecessors, and the progressive decline of the USA's position
in East Asia could not have been stemmed anyway. The manner
in which he disengaged from Vietnam might in the public mind
rebound to his credit. The 'great trick' of Nixon and Kissinger
had been to insert local withdrawal within the context of a modified
conception of the role of the United States in the world. As for the
military's responsibility, Aron had studied the Pentagon and found
its approach sometimes more responsible and sceptical than that
of certain civilian advisers who had become military-minded.
Perhaps the fault lay with institutes like RAND who taught civilians
to think in military terms: W. W. Rostow, for example, was always
trying to sell the President new devices for 'counter-insurgency'.

Finer's doubt was whether a country which conducted its policy
through an established Foreign Office and an official opposition
really did so more successfully? In Britain the opposition usually
failed to elicit any additional information and the Foreign Office
was hermetically sealed against pressures, so that the Common
Market had been the only foreign issue much debated here publicly
in recent years. The sole difference he saw was that anxiety in
Britain could make itself felt at Westminster more rapidly than
grass-roots concern in America could rise up into Congress. But in
Britain, objected Feingold, 'divisive' issues do not usually in fact
divide parliament. And in the States opposition to foreign policies
tends to take extra-parliamentary, non-party, channels. So the
American electorate in 1964, and perhaps in 1972, *believed* they were
expressing an informed opinion.

Would failure in Vietnam lead to a change, if not of institutions,
at least of attitudes in the USA? Just possibly the latter, thought
Beloff. What impressed him was the extraordinary tolerance
Americans showed towards the activities of persons like Kissinger
who enjoyed no constitutional status whatsoever. Even a temporary
representative of the British government, like Lord Goodman in
Rhodesia, would not be allowed to operate for long in such a
capacity without undercurrents of suspicion, so great was the
importance attached to the susceptibilities of parliament. What had

caused dissension over here had been comparatively small and isolated affairs – Suez, Rhodesia – whereas the great and dramatic changes implicit in Britain's decline as a world power had transpired with relatively little repercussion upon her political institutions. But that, commented Gould, was only because the trauma of loss of empire had deliberately been kept below the surface. Upon that matter the British élite had agreed, in a conspiracy of silence, not to engage in public controversy.

Attention shifted back across the Atlantic when Roger Williams proposed to distinguish between three types of presidential problem. There were, first of all, crisis situations where the President is limited more by his personal abilities, and those of his assistants, than by constitutional circumstances. The Bay of Pigs and the Cuban missile episode would do duty as illustrations of this first category. Second, there were chronic situations, with which the President's freedom to cope was limited as much by his institutional position and the operation of constitutional checks, as by anything else. But we should recognize under that head his possible constraint by informal checks also – bureaucratic division or inertia, vested group interests, and public opinion. Thirdly, there were the long-term problems, requiring of the President vision rather than a penchant for quick judgement. Problems of strategic defence in the 1960s were of this order: environmental problems, on the contrary, were not yet treated as long-term but only tactically. Occasionally a president managed to enlist readier help in tackling a chronic problem by representing it as a crisis situation. Thus, Kennedy led Congress into a space programme by persuading it to commit itself, with virtually no discussion thanks to the rivalry of the USSR, to 'get to the moon' first. Johnson maintained the Vietnam war for a long period on the strength of the Tonkin Gulf 'emergency' resolution. A president was not, of course, *compelled* to seize such chance for action as was opened to him by a crisis situation. But he neglected at his peril any opportunity thus offered for intelligent long-term anticipation.

Taking all these considerations together, Williams would define presidential 'style' in foreign affairs as an amalgam of three quite different capabilities. It comprised ability to cope with, and perhaps capitalize on, crisis situations; skill in inducing others to give him help and form, as it were, institutional alliances with him; and persistence in a sound, steady, long-term view. The President's dilemma, perhaps the predicament of America as a whole, lay in the fact that the problems whose gravity seemed to be increasing most quickly were of the chronic kind, and these he was least well equipped to handle.

The conference chose to use the last half-hour of its time in broader considerations of institutional responsiveness as a whole. Whatever the presidential reaction might be, observed Feingold, the American public itself did not see national crises like Vietnam primarily as *institutional* crises. Therefore institutional change such as would reduce the President's discretion in foreign policy-making was not generally regarded as a priority. Had Vietnam, however, affected America's *domestic* institutions? Not so greatly as her urban problems, thought Almond, which were the likeliest to produce changes of process ('revenue-sharing' for instance) and performance over the next twenty years. What most impressed Finer was the sheer difficulty in getting institutional change of any sort in the USA. Since this required piecemeal capture of party organizations on a nation-wide scale, no wonder so much was left to the discretion of the President as a fail-safe emergency system. And no wonder radicals such as Students for a Democratic Society were inclined to rationalize the use of direct action. One criterion of the 'credibility' of an institutional system was its degree of responsiveness to the dissatisfied – high in Great Britain but low in the United States. If you were reduced to lying down in the path of a bulldozer, your system was not responsive enough.

Lane concurred in thinking this question of responsiveness a very crucial one, but insisted that it must be surveyed and compared within the respective contexts of national policies. Thus, in the last decade the federal government had suddenly and swiftly responded to the demand for better schools and colleges for blacks: for their voting rights, by contrast, they had had to wait a century. Washington had addressed itself promptly to the problems of inflation, poverty, and manpower training. There was no housing crisis. But a bill on water pollution had been vetoed by the President, and Congress had got bogged down in 'negative income'. On roads and transport the government's response had been little or nil; and though the USA spent more *per capita* on health than any other nation, the poor results indicated that the nature of the response was dysfunctional. So our terms were too blunt. We ought to be asking, not is the American institutional system *in toto* responsive or unresponsive? but why does it respond well in some cases and not in others? Much would then be found to depend on private attitudes within the interstices of the system.

A system's responsiveness, Almond reminded the meeting, was directly related to its load; and that laid upon American institutions in recent years had been enormous. The last two decades had seen large-scale politicization of minority groups, a mobilization of students and intelligentsia, and a coming to terms with the swift advances of science and technology. Ecological and environmental issues had broken up old political and social alliances. When to these one added the Vietnam experience, it was small wonder that the American system had not tackled everything with success. Yet some radical action had borne fruit, and certain institutions and processes had recently made a step-level change.

Other participants asked for distinctions to be made. Beloff looked for differences between those institutional changes which were truly innovatory and those that might prove merely transient. Feingold was for differentiating between institutional responsiveness to public awareness of a problem and direct responsiveness to the problem itself. And Lane pointed out the large number of meve-ments, immigration was one, taking place quite outside the governmental sphere. Society was not synonymous with the state, and many pressures, such as those generated by trade unions, were better regarded as cultural than political phenomena.

It remained for the meeting, looking back over the conference's six long sessions, to decide what in retrospect appeared the most seminal property of American political institutions. Was it their credibility or, as Ionescu felt, their responsiveness? Or should one, as Madgwick advised, speak merely of process and perfor-mance? Participants were still debating choices with enthusiasm when the Chairman's concluding remarks brought two days of zestful, but by no means exhausted, controversy to an end.

* * * * * *

So much for the symposium of November 1972. By way of postlude it is irresistibly tempting to speculate as to which aspects of American institutional politics would chiefly engross the same international gathering were it now, some eighteen months later, to be reconvened? Meeting under the cloud of the Watergate affair, less than a man's hand at the time of the last general elections, could such an assembly be persuaded to divert its gaze, even for a single session, away from the White House? One would hope so, for there remain many parts of the American political anatomy – our flayed man – where the metabolic process has proceeded almost entirely immune from whatever cancer has temporarily afflicted the Presidential organ.

Let us leave that fascinating malignancy until the last, and instead begin by examining the least affected areas, of which the Supreme Court remains one of the most obvious. Here, surely, Professor Pear's prognosis is confirmed. The final session of the Court's term has witnessed no abrupt deflection from the innovative course charted during its sixteen years under Warren. The justices, old or new, are still in fruitful colloquy among themselves. The main focus of attention continues to be the rights of the individual American. In its cautious but unremitting redefinition of these the high bench has been attracting less popular criticism than heretofore and at the same time showing rather more consideration toward state legislatures and the lower courts.

Particular areas of the executive the justices have continued to regard as off limits: notably so when on 4 August 1973 they refused to order an immediate cessation of bombing in Cambodia. Certain familiar issues, however, have continued to crop up. Legislative reapportionment for one, when the Court lately but for the first time invalidated multi-member districting in a state where it thought 'the totality of the circumstances' indicated an intention thereby to dilute the voting power of minority groups. Unanimously it has voided a redistribution of seats in Texas which would have entailed a disparity of 4.1 per cent between that state's most and least populous Congressional districts. Another such recurrent topic is, predictably, 'free speech': one recent judgment held that neither the First Amendment guarantee nor the Federal Communication Commission's 'fairness' doctrine should bind television or radio stations unconditionally to sell time to individuals or groups simply desirous of airing their views on public issues. As for the free speech of federal employees in political matters, the Court has recently declined to widen existing limitations imposed upon that category by the Hatch Act and by congruent state laws. Its continuing care for the consumer it has displayed both through a readiness to protect his terms of purchase on long-term credit and by a refusal to limit the scope of federal aid to him in the form of food-stamps.

Over public schools, the advocates of complete desegregation and perfect racial proportions have been left to balance gain against loss. On the one hand about half the justices have declared themselves unwilling to pursue exact racial mixtures across administrative boundaries. A lower federal court had ordered that city schools of Richmond, Va., be merged with those of two adjacent counties so as to create a better balance of black and white. This directive had been reversed on appeal; and now the Supreme Court by splitting four to four has in effect upheld the reversal. On the other hand it has uttered a clear warning to school systems outside the South that segregation *within* their respective boundaries renders them no less vulnerable to legal penalties than heretofore. Overall, then, the Court appears still to be maintaining the principle of desegregation *de jure* while distinguishing particular instances of apartheid *de facto*. Within the same pedagogic field the Court on its final 'Decision Monday' of the session struck down four different kinds of state aid to non-public schools – a rebuff to Nixon, whose budgeting for 1974 had included a tax credit to parents who pay to send their children to such institutions.

Its continued independence of the executive, indeed, the highest bench has made unmistakably clear. To be sure, a five-to-four majority did seem to acquiesce in a Presidential desire that obscenity be redefined in a stricter sense. But it was a Nixon nominee who wrote the school fees opinion aforementioned, and another such who for the majority of his colleagues voided an Administration measure that would have made abortion a federal crime. And already, in April 1973, the Court had rejected the government's request to review and remove a lower court's ban on construction of the oil pipeline across Alaska. If on that issue Congress has had the last word, it is thanks only to the intense pressure of a national fuel crisis. For increasingly and ineluctably the justices are being drawn into the American's novel concern with 'environmental quality'. By recent judgements against the Pennsylvania Industrial Chemical Corporation and the Lockheed Air Terminal they have underlined Washington's responsibility to protect respectively the nation's water from pollution and its airspace from noise. In particular, and by another four-to-four deadlock, they affirmed an inferior court's directive to the new Environmental Protection Agency (EPA) that any state plan must be disallowed which would permit further deterioration of America's atmosphere. Indeed, in the course of enlarging the citizen's right to challenge actions likely to entail such detriment the Court has felt obliged to uphold state laws which exceed federal statutes in stringency.

As for 'coddling the criminal' – another aspersion Professor Pear's paper took note of – if the Burger court still refuses to expand the protective implications of certain Warren decisions, it has nevertheless made few concessions to 'law-and-order' pressures from the Congress or public. By one recent ruling it has slightly narrowed the state prisoner's avenue of access to a federal court for the purpose of complaining about the terms and conditions of his incarceration. By another it has restricted the latitude of a criminal defendant, once he has pleaded guilty, to raise retrospective claims of having been deprived of some constitutional right at an earlier stage of the process. And a pair of cases in which a plea of 'unreasonable search' was disallowed have exemplified the continuing diminution of the impact of *Miranda*. Now the high bench will scarcely be able to avoid ruling upon the admissibility of evidence obtained through governmental wiretapping authorized by someone other than the US Attorney-General or by no one at all. But hitherto the ripples of executive misconduct have hardly begun to lap the steps of the Marble Palace itself.

Nor, despite the intense preoccupation of particular Senate and House committees with White House scandal, has Watergate yet become the main issue between President and Congress as a whole. Rather, the most persistent executive-legislative clashes have continued to be over war abroad and social services at home. Already adumbrated in Dr Lees's paper, both these confrontations now merit further attention.

In April 1973 the last American troops were being flown out of Vietnam. Yet the lustre of successful withdrawal was already somewhat clouded by the resumption early in the preceding month of bombing raids over Cambodia. Officially just a foray to 'wind up' a 'corner' of the Asian war, its effect nevertheless has been to allow the initiative to pass to Congress. On the last day of May, and by the strongest attempt heretofore made to disentangle the United States from that area, the Senate voted by a wide margin to cut off all further supply for operations in Cambodia or Laos. In late June a conference committee of the two Houses insisted on tying the cessation of Cambodian bombing to an extension of the federal debt ceiling sought by the Administration. More importantly, in mid-July Congress passed legislation restricting the President's war powers to a quite unprecedented degree. This would strictly delimit the emergency in which a President could in future commit American troops to hostilities without a declaration of war. So far as the current Cambodian hostilities went, it set 15 August as the deadline for American disengagement. Nixon, complaining that only thirty days' grace would be afforded him as Commander-in-Chief for protecting the country by arms without the affirmative consent of Congress, answered the latter that he would comply 'reluctantly'. As for his principal peacemaker, one may parenthetically note that Dr Kissinger's addition of the Secretaryship of State to his previous function of special adviser to the President has elicited mixed reactions from individual members of Congress. Some affect to see it as obliterating the last trace of independence in the Secretaryship: others *per contra*, contemplating Nixon's present vulnerability, prophesy a swift return to the earlier Eisenhower–Dulles imbalance.

Domestically, the outstanding disagreement between President and Congress last session was over the appropriate levels of expenditure on social services. At the outset of 1973 Nixon broke with precedent by outlining his fiscal proposals as far ahead as to July 1975. From which the Democratic majority leader, Senator Mansfield, inferred that many of Johnson's Great Society programmes were to be dismantled, and predicted a battle royal to restore them. It was soon joined. Already at the end of the previous session Nixon had pocketed a bill which would have appropriated more than $2½m. for vocational rehabilitation. Early in 1973 both Houses unanimously passed an almost identical measure which encountered a further Presidential veto on 27 March. Nixon's objection has been that his landslide victory constitutes a clear mandate from the American people to hold down taxes by reducing federal spending; whereas Great Society measures 'carry extravagant price tags' and 'mask bad legislation beneath alluring labels'. On the same grounds the President has since also vetoed (successfully) a measure to restore the rural water and sewer grant programme which his Administration had terminated on the last day of 1972, and (unsuccessfully) a bill to keep open certain public health hospitals he had wanted to close. The Administration has also thrown its weight against Congressional attempts to preserve the Office of Economic Opportunity (OEO), to extend a dozen federal health programmes due to expire, to increase farm subsidies and to lift the minimum hourly wage. Where his opposition has not prevailed however – and here is the contentious point – Nixon has simply refused to spend all the money Congress had appropriated. Such 'impoundment' of the unspent revenue the Democratic leader of the House, Mr Carl Albert, has declared to be an 'unwarranted invasion' of Congressional powers which is 'making a monkey

out of the legislative process'. Nixon has retorted by calling the
93rd Congress 'irresponsible on money', contrasting its approach
with his own preference for revenue sharing, whereby a flow of
power from local levels upward is to ensure 'programmes that
produce 100 cents' worth of human benefits for every tax dollar
spent'.

The President's right to impound is already being challenged
by one state (Missouri) in a federal court of appeal. On Capitol
Hill retaliation is taking a variety of forms. No little animus is
perceptible in the House's refusal to vote a further $1.5m. requested
for the White House's 'special projects' and in its eagerness to
scrutinize the amount of taxpayers' money already laid out on the
Presidential homes in California and Florida. House and Senate
have already passed legislation which could give them a veto
on any future impoundments, and are pressing for a voice in
choosing any future director of the Office of Management and
Budget (OMB). For the longer term, a Joint Study Committee on
Budget Control has been looking for ways to overhaul Congress's
creaking appropriations machinery so as to impose a tighter
discipline throughout its own section of the budgetary process.
Their main proposal is that each chamber create its own permanent
budget committee, whose membership would be drawn one-third
from Appropriations, one-third from Ways and Means (in the
Senate, from Finance), and the remaining third from the legislative
committees. In these two new super-bodies would then be vested
authority to set and enforce ceilings of appropriation and expenditure
and to establish Congress's own scale of priorities within them.
No longer would its scrutiny be diffused as heretofore among more
than a dozen discrete appropriations bills per session.

This last proposal has, for reasons which we shall see, been
running into opposition from liberals both inside and outside
of Congress. And to do Nixon justice one must mention also his
recent schemes for halving the number of full-time staff in the
Executive Office of the President to below 2000, and for merging
certain other planning functions in a new Economic Policy Council
under the chairmanship of his Secretary of the Treasury. Those
who note, however, that expenditure on the Executive Office rose
during his first Administration from $31m. to $71m. may view all
such estimates of net saving with distrust. On the national economy
Congress has agreed to renew Nixon's Phase III controls for a
further twelve months (albeit with some reservations about their

adequacy), but has eyed very warily his requests for broader negotiating authority in international trade. Watergate, it seems, may have superseded Vietnam as ground for doubting that the President is any longer the best informed man in Washington, let alone the world.

Naturally, Congress has remained the principal scene of operations by the miscellaneous interest groups. Less predictably, the highest lobbying spender of 1972 has turned out to be Common Cause, whose reported payments have exceeded even those of the national AFL-CIO. The National Rifle Association is still blocking measures for effective control over sale of firearms. Environmental lobbies, as we have noticed, can draw some comfort from recent Supreme Court decisions. But the twenty-year-old debate – with which Professor Gould's paper is no less concerned – over the future shape of America's strategic missile forces has broken out again on Capitol Hill. Last session it raged around a proposed acceleration of the Trident submarine programme, where the Pentagon's request for the appropriation of $1.7b. in 1974 was strenuously opposed by Members of the Congress For Peace Through Law.

For the connoisseur of institutional interplay, however, the most academically interesting wrangle may prove to be that over the reorganization of Amtrak – the National Railroad Passenger Corporation set up by Congress in October 1970 as a non-profit body to operate certain passenger lines for the ensuing three years. Amtrak's status is unenviable. Upon the one side it is dependent on negotiating good contracts with private railroad companies as against whom it possesses inferior bargaining power. Having managed to unload upon the corporation some of their least profitable passenger services, the companies would rather let them wither away than take them back. On the other side, although a quasi-public body, Amtrak is beholden to the Department of Transportation for budgetary approval; and for policy content – permission, for instance, to shed in turn its most unprofitable routes – it is greatly dependent on the Interstate Commerce Commission. Policy-makers in the Administration favour cutbacks in both routes and subsidies, as do Greyhound Bus Lines, Inc., who have viewed with some bitterness the federally-subsidized competition of Amtrak hitherto. Congress, which wants to loosen the Transportation Department's control over the corporation, exercises its surveillance through the Senate Commerce Committee and the House Interstate and Foreign Commerce Commission.

Both are cockpits for consumer lobbyists, environmentalists and mass transit advocates. The outcome is certain to provide yet another case study for those who share Professor Gould's approach to politics.

To move from pressure-group to party within Congress is to witness during 1973–4 a further development of several trends already forecast by Dr Lees. Notably the Democratic Study Group (DSG) – now numbering some 170 liberal and moderate members of the party, or more than two-thirds of its strength in the House – has been gratified to see adopted almost all the procedural reforms it proposed when the 93rd Congress opened, and has thereafter worked hand-in-glove with the majority leader and with the newly-formed Steering and Policy Committee of twenty-three representatives under the Speaker's chairmanship. Of these reforms even the most controversial appears to have been working smoothly. This has required that every committee chairman subject himself to the caucus's confirmation in a recorded vote taken at the start of each Congress. All twenty-one committee chairmen have success-fully run this gauntlet, most with 80 per cent approval or higher; and it now remains to be seen whether they have in consequence proved more responsive to their rank-and-file colleagues. One of the recommendations currently before Representative Bollings' committee, which discusses change in standing committee jurisdic-tions, is that in future the party should hold its caucus in the December following each election, rather than wait till January.

Not all forces for change, however, pull in the same direction along the progressive-conservative continuum. The move to create new Congressional committees on the budget has drawn heavy fire from liberals, in whose eyes the proposed composition of these super-bodies makes it all too likely they would contain an unduly high proportion of seniors. If so, there is a serious risk that they might (in the words of one DSG pessimist) 'lock the Congressional budgetary process into a conservative mould for generations to come'. Their reports would certainly be hard to amend on the floor – the proper place, so liberals insist, for what are fundamentally political issues. So here again Congress faces the perennial dilemma of its proper function. Desire to play a more efficiently autonomous role *vis-à-vis* the executive runs counter to the majority's desire for greater representativeness. Budgetary reform may yet prove to be the rock on which the DSG comes to grief.

Outside Congress too, as well as within, Democrats remain

subject to internal strain. Preoccupation with their projected national conference of 1974, for which few guidelines were set when the 1972 convention dispersed, continues to have divisive effect. Shall it be a big, morale-boosting rally, as the McGovernites wish, assembling with maximum publicity on the eve of the midterm elections? Or, as the conservatives would prefer, a gathering limited to about one thousand, held in either April or December so that the party's campaigning is not debilitated by its public differences? Again, although the last national convention determined how the 1974 conference should be made up – not more than one-third delegates *ex officio*, the remainder to come from Congressional districts around the nation – it offered little guidance, within overall quotas, as to how the latter two-thirds should be chosen. In the interim the party's charter-writing commission is still morally mandated to entertain the notion of a national dues-paying membership, organized upon seven regional bases, as a means of promoting a stronger ideological identity to counter the centripetal pull of future Democratic Presidents.

Meanwhile their leader in the House, interviewed in mid-May 1973, has offered his appraisal of party cohesion there.[5] Representative Thomas P. O'Neill rated some 175 Democrats as 'dependable', flanked on left and right by about three dozen at each extreme. What of the 'conservative coalition'? He had indeed noticed many of his Southerners voting with Republicans on certain procedural questions, such as the provision of more staffing for the minority party. But the relationship between them was not formalized in the way it had been during the 1950s. And the typical young Southern Democrat entering the House today he would describe as 'extremely erudite, . . . bright, . . . talented and speaks his mind, . . . tends to be a progressive', etc. This estimate may look a little sanguine. Yet it takes some account of the impact of Watergate in temporarily detaching many Republicans and Southerners from the President's side, to a point where what O'Neill referred to as 'the usual White House arm-twisting among conservatives' was of little avail. He is not alone in hoping to prise more and more Republican votes away from the Administration's position on key legislative issues.

And so, with this threatened desertion of the President by his own party, we come face-to-face with that condition of affairs within the high executive against which Professor Nicholas so presciently warned. It is bad enough (his paper concluded) if the

President deceives the people, but far worse if he deceives himself. More clearly than by any other of its consequences, Watergate has transformed that two-edged threat into reality. It is no longer possible to say with certainty whether Presidential evasiveness in such matters is the symptom of complicity or of ignorance. Suffice it that long after the dangers of continued insularity had become apparent to others concerned in that affair, Nixon continued to block the speaking-tube. By June 1973 exasperation among the press corps in Washington had boiled over in a collective complaint to the board of the National Press Club. The regime, they alleged, was persistently trying to restrict the proper flow of information to the public. The Office of Telecommunications Policy was behaving like a censor, the newly-styled Director of Communication like a 'propaganda ministry' which has 'no place in our society'. In particular they deplored the 'totally programmed' demeanour of the White House press secretary, Mr Ronald Ziegler, who ought to be fired. The Press Club itself in releasing this report lamented the 'deep estrangement' between the press and what it called 'the most closed administration in recent decades'. Yet still by mid-August Nixon himself had met the press only three times in 1973, making a total of just 34 such occasions during his four-and-a-half years in office. His annual average of $7\frac{1}{2}$ press conferences was looking thin beside Kennedy's 21, Eisenhower's 24 and Johnson's 25; let alone Truman's annual average of forty.

Upon this performance the early Watergate disclosures did not persuade Nixon to improve. Instead he invoked very freely that unwritten doctrine of executive privilege in whose name American Presidents have been wont to withold testimony or documents from investigatory agencies and particularly from Congressional committees. It is a doctrine grounded both in the principle of separated powers and in the practical need of the chief executive to guard the privacy of certain of his operations from public scrutiny. To the demands of Judge Sirica's federal court and of the special Watergate prosecutor, Nixon therefore at first replied that records of official transactions between heads of government departments and their subordinates, and of meetings and telephone conversations in which the President had participated, were privileged communications insofar as their disclosure would be incompatible with either the public interest or with the constitutional position of the Presidency. He also instructed his subordinates to withold testimony -- as Eisenhower had once done in reply to similar demands from Senator Joseph McCarthy's investigating committee. Against this stand, however, Judge Sirica argued that when criminal charges were involved the mere Presidential *ipse dixit* would not suffice. It was for his court to determine, after examination of the material, which communications were protected by privilege and which were not. Ingenious compromises were proposed. Meanwhile at least one Congressman was charging Nixon with having established 'a new one-term record in government by secrecy'. The Library of Congress was drawn upon for evidence purporting to show that already by March 1973, on his own behalf or of his subordinates, Nixon had claimed executive privilege more often than any previous chief in recorded American history.

As in the courthouse and in the old Senate Office building the Watergate investigation has proceeded, however, the President has step by step been compelled to abandon this position. He has waived the claim to privileged non-disclosure by subordinates, has agreed to surrender materials (whether or not in their pristine condition) to the courts, and has himself issued public statements of seemingly mounting frankness; until his current posture of full self-exposure to audiences of all kinds around the nation – the travelling rebuttal show, as cynics call it – proclaims a deliberate and complete *volte-face*. The effect of this reversal has been somewhat to displace anxieties about the Presidential office by doubts about its occupant. The long series of advances and retreats, dismissals and reinstatements, brooding withdrawal and hectic volubility, have disposed many critics to analyze the Watergate imbroglio in terms of Nixon's personal psychology. When he recently announced to a surprised Cabinet that he intended henceforward to have 'a direct line of communication' with them all, was this or was it not an implicit admission that he had hitherto been hedged around by a palace guard? And what is to be inferred from his recent 'let's get acquainted' sessions with those who have been his fellow-politicians for five years?

But it is after all with institutions, not personalities, that this book is concerned; and here the complex ramifications of national scandal provide subject-matter enough. Within the Administration it has laid its finger on the Department of Justice, the FBI and the CIA, the Securities and Exchange Commission, and even (to. investigate the finances of CREEP) the General Accounting Office Within Congress it has been absorbing the attention of six other Committees or subcommittees as well as Senator Ervin's special investigation in the marble caucus-room. As for the judicial branch, while the special prosecutor appears before Judge Sirica in Washington, other federal courts busy themselves in Los Angeles, Florida, Houston and New York with (respectively) the Pentagon papers, with the expenditures and the 'dirty tricks' incidental to Nixon's 1972 campaign, and with the indictment of his former law partner, Attorney-General, committee chairman and campaign manager, Mr John Mitchell.

Out of this compendious bagwash it is too soon to predict what lasting institutional changes will emerge. At the time of writing the question of resignation still overhangs the President himself, if only as the preferable alternative to suffering what Madison called 'the awful discretion which a court of impeachments must necessarily have to doom to honour or to infamy'. But clearly in either event the White House staff will never again be permitted to wield the authority they have enjoyed of late, and thereby a potentially useful co-ordinating device will be denied future Presidents. More broadly considered, the categories of public servant to emerge with most discredit have been of the appointed kind – permanent career officers as well as the White House's temporary recruits. Very few elected politicians have been scathed: a notable exception being the only Vice-President in the nation's history to resign office as a consequence of criminal charges. To fill his room the Twenty-Fifth Amendment has been used for the first time. It is significant that the choice has fallen upon a politician whose chief if not sole qualities are that he inspires personal trust and has not yet developed a lust after power.

For that power, not material greed, was the main motive force behind Watergate is the circumstance Americans probably deprecate most of all. To them, for the time being, the flayed man has again become the flagellated man. When the national conscience is once more clear, foreign commentators too will be better enabled to purge their judgements of prejudice.

Notes

H. G. Nicholas THE INSULATION OF THE PRESIDENCY

1. The way for this had already been prepared by Johnson, when he appointed Sargent Shriver as a White House assistant to be in charge of co-ordinating the work of existing agencies in this field – Agriculture, Labour, HEW.

2. In June 1970 George Romney was reported as saying 'The key question that the President is going to have to answer is whether he is to have the White House staff basically responsible in policy areas and playing leadership roles, or whether the Cabinet officers are going to do it.' He soon had his answer.

Vivian Vale THE COLLABORATIVE CHAOS

1. For the mature, if slightly jaundiced, reflections of an ex-bureaucrat, see Harold Seidman: *Politics, Position and Power*, New York, 1970, Chapters 3, 6 and 9.

2. See Richard E. Neustadt: 'Presidency and Legislation: the Growth of Central Clearance', in *American Political Science Review*, 18 September 1954, pp. 641–71.

3. Robert S. Gilmour: 'Central Legislative Clearance, a Revised Perspective', in *Public Administration Review*, XXI, 1971, pp. 150–8.

4. US Congress: Joint Economic Committee: *The Planning-Programming Budgeting System: Progress and Potentials*. Hearings before Sub-Committee on Economy in Government. 90 Congress, 1st session, September 1967. U.S. Senate Committee on Governmental Operations: *Planning-Programming-Budgeting*. *Interim Observations*, study submitted by the Sub-Committee on National Security and International Operations, 90 Congress, 2nd session, 1968. For an outside assessment of the new system's impact after three years see Francis E. Rourke: *Bureaucracy, Politics and Public Policy*, New York, 1969.

5. See, e.g., *Output Budgeting*, a feasibility study undertaken by the Department of Education and Science, HMSO, London, 1969.

6. By Rexford G. Tugwell, in Harvey S. Perloff (ed.): *The Future of United States Government: towards the year 2000*, New York, 1972, p. 320.

John D. Lees REORGANIZATION AND REFORM

1. See George B. Galloway, *Congress at the Crossroads*, Crowell, New York, 1946, and James M. Burns, *Congress on Trial*, Harper & Row, New York, 1949.

2. See Joseph S. Clark, *Congress: The Sapless Branch*, Harper & Row, New York, 1964, and Richard Bolling, *House Out of Order*, Dutton, New York, 1965.

3. See Roger H. Davidson *et al.*, *Congress in Crisis: Politics and Congressional Reform*, Wadsworth Publishing Co., Belmont, California, 1966.

4. See David B. Truman (ed.), *The Congress and America's Future*, Prentice-Hall, Englewood Cliffs, N.J., 1965.

5. For detailed comment of studies on Congress since the 1940s, see Ralph K. Huitt and Robert L. Peabody, *Congress: Two Decades of Analysis*, Harper & Row, New York, 1969. Note in particular the American Political Science Association's Study of Congress project begun in 1964.

6. See John S. Saloma III, *Congress and the New Politics*, Little, Brown, Boston, 1969, especially Chapter 1. On the public image of Congress, see Davidson *et al.*, *op. cit.*, pp. 47–66.

7. See, for example, James M. Burns, *The Deadlock of Democracy*, Prentice-Hall, Englewood Cliffs, N.J., 1963.

8. For discussion and explanation of these models, see Saloma, *op cit.*, Chapter 2, also Davidson *et al.*, *op. cit.*, pp. 15–37 and G. Goodwin, Jr., *The Little Legislatures*, University of Massachusetts Press, Amherst, 1970. For an example of the congressional supremacy approach, see A. De Grazia (ed.), *Congress: The First Branch of Government*, American Enterprise Institute, Washington D.C., 1966.

9. Truman (ed.), *op. cit.*, p. 4.

10. Stephen K. Bailey, *Congress in the Seventies*, St. Martin's Press, New York, 1970, p. vii.

11. Duane Lockard, *The Perverted Priorities of American Politics*, Macmillan, New York, 1971, p. 123.

12. The following analysis was greatly helped by the opportunity, in the spring of 1971, to interview a representative sample of some 100 members of Congress. Thanks are due to the SSRC for financial support.

13. Samuel P. Huntington, 'Congressional Responses to the Twentieth Century' in D. B. Truman (ed.), *op. cit.*, p. 6.

14. See, for example, Barbara Hinckley, *The Seniority System in Congress*, Indiana University Press, Bloomington, 1971.

15. Randall B. Ripley, *Power in the Senate*, St. Martin's Press, New York, 1969, p. 53.

16. Nelson W. Polsby, 'Goodbye to the Inner Club', in Nelson W. Polsby (ed.), *Congressional Behaviour*, Random House, New York, 1971, p. 105.

17. *Ibid.*, p. 8.

18. Nelson W. Polsby and A. Wildavsky, *Presidential Elections*, 3rd ed., Scribners, New York, 1971, p. 89.

19. See, for example, the personal testimony of Donald Riegle, *O Congress*, Doubleday, New York, 1972.

20. For a study outlining the influence of this committee, see James A. Robinson, *The House Rules Committee*, Bobbs-Merrill, Indianapolis, 1963.

21. See, for example, Mary McInnis (ed.), *We Propose: A Modern Congress*, McGraw-Hill, New York, 1966.

22. Bailey, *op. cit.*, p. 45.

23. For additional detail see *Congressional Quarterly, Weekly Report*, 25 September 1971.

24. See Michael W. Kirst, *Government Without Passing Laws*, University of North Carolina Press, Chapel Hill, 1969.

25. Saloma, *op. cit.*, Chapter 7.

26. Douglas M. Orr, Jr., *Congressional Redistricting: The North Carolina*

Experience, University of North Carolina, Studies in Geography No. 2, p. 121.
27. See Roger Hilsman, *The Politics of Policy Making in Defence and Foreign Affairs*, Harper & Row, New York, 1971.
28. Francis O. Wilcox, *Congress, the Executive and Foreign Policy*, Harper & Row, New York, 1971, p. 166.
29. For a similar recommendation, see F. C. Thayer, 'Presidential Policy Processes and "New Administration": A Search for Revised Paradigms,' *Public Administration Review*, September–October 1971, pp. 552–61.
30. See A. Schlesinger, Jr., 'Congress and the Making of American Foreign Policy', *Foreign Affairs*, October 1972, pp. 78–113.
31. See, for example, John F. Manley, 'The Rise of Congress in Foreign Policy-Making', *The Annals*, September 1971, pp. 60–70, and Theodore Lowi, *The Politics of Disorder*, Basic Books, New York, 1971, Chapter 4.
32. R. C. Moe and S. F. Teel, 'Congress as Policy-Maker: A Necessary Reappraisal,' *Political Science Quarterly*, September 1970, pp. 443–70.
33. See H. B. Westerfield, 'Congress and Closed Politics in National Security Affairs,' in D. T. Fox (ed.), *The Politics of U.S. Foreign Policy Making*, Goodyear Publishing Co., Pacific Palisades, 1971, pp. 161–74.
34. Edward V. Schneier, Jr., *Party and Constituency: Pressures on Congress*, Johns Hopkins University Press, Baltimore, 1970, p. xi.
35. For discussion of these functions, see Roger H. Davidson, 'Congress in the American Political System', in Allan Kornberg and Lloyd D. Musolf, *Legislatures in Developmental Perspective*, Duke University Press, Durham, N.C., 1970, pp. 129–78.
36. See John F. Manley, *The Politics of Finance*, Little, Brown, Boston, 1970, and L. C. Pierce, *The Politics of Fiscal Policy Formation*, Goodyear Publishing Co., Pacific Palisades, 1971.

Peter Fotheringham CHANGES IN THE AMERICAN PARTY SYSTEM
1. The author gratefully acknowledges a grant from the Nuffield Foundation which enabled him to study the American political scene in Washington in the summer of 1972.
2. See S. Lubell, *The Hidden Crisis in American Politics*, Norton, New York, 1971, for a respected journalist's view of 'crisis' in contemporary American politics.
3. J. M. Burns, *The Deadlock of Democracy*, Prentice-Hall, Englewood Cliffs, N.J., 1963, p. 7.
4. T. Lowi, 'Party, Policy and Constitution in America' in W. N. Chambers and W. D. Burnham (eds.), *The American Party Systems*, Oxford University Press, New York, 1967, p. 241. A favourable view of American parties is also offered by L. D. Epstein in his comparative study, *Political Parties in Western Democracies*, Praeger, New York, 1967.
5. G. Pomper, 'Toward a More Responsible Party System? What, Again?' in *The Journal of Politics*, Vol. 33, 1971.
6. W. D. Burnham, *Critical Elections and the Mainsprings of American Politics*, Norton, New York, 1970, pp. 132–3.
7. F. J. Sorauf, 'Political Parties and Political Analysis' in W. N. Chambers and W. D. Burnham, *op. cit.*, p. 55. See also F. J. Sorauf, *Party Politics in America*, 2nd ed., Little, Brown, Boston, 1972.

8. K. Phillips, *The Emerging Republican Majority*, Anchor Books, New York, 1970.

9. R. F. Hamilton, *Class and Politics in the United States*, J. Wiley, New York, 1972.

10. For amplification of this point see Epstein, *op. cit.*, Chapter V.

11. See the section which follows below on 'Party Reform', and R. Wolfinger, 'Why Political Machines Have Not Withered Away and Other Revisionist Thoughts', *Journal of Politics*, May 1972.

12. Donald E. Nicoll, 'How to Open Up the Democratic Party', *The New Republic*, 5 and 12 August, 1972.

13. See T. Wicker, *JFK and LBJ*, Part I, Penguin, Baltimore, 1970, for an account of the difficulties facing an active president in Congress.

14. See J. Turner and E. V. Schneier, Jr., *Party and Constituency: Pressures on Congress*, rev. ed., The John Hopkins Press, Baltimore, 1970 and W. W. Shannon, *Party, Constituency and Congressional Voting*, Louisiana State University Press, Baton Rouge, 1968.

15. Turner and Schneier, *ibid.*, p. 239.

16. See Lowi, in Chambers and Burnham, *op. cit.*, Chapter IX, especially pp. 238–41 and pp. 274–6.

17. *The US News and World Report's* 'Guide to the '72 Elections' published in 1972, but presumably written in late 1971, listed four 'Top Democrats', including Senators Kennedy and Jackson but not Senator McGovern.

18. S. C. Brightman, 'The Democrats Open the Door', *The Nation*, 3 May 1971.

19. *Congressional Quarterly Weekly Report*, Vol. XXX, No. 28, p. 1661.

20. R. Axelrod, 'Where the Votes Come From: An Analysis of Electoral Coalitions, 1952–1968', *American Political Science Review*, Vol. LXVI, No. 1, pp. 14–15.

21. *Congressional Quarterly Weekly Report*, Vol. XXX, No. 32, p. 1918.

22. The regions referred to in this article are defined as follows:
South: (i) Deep South – Alabama, Georgia, Louisiana, Mississippi and South Carolina
     (ii) Outer South – Arkansas, Florida, North Carolina, Tennessee, Texas and Virginia
Border: Kentucky, Missouri, Oklahoma and West Virginia
North-East: (i) New England – Connecticut, Maine, Massachusetts, New Hampshire, Rhode Island and Vermont
     (ii) Mid-Atlantic – Delaware, Maryland, New Jersey, New York and Pennsylvania
Mid-West: Illinois, Indiana, Michigan, Ohio and Wisconsin
Farm Belt: Iowa, Kansas, Minnesota, Nebraska, North Dakota and South Dakota
Mountain: Arizona, Colorado, Idaho, Montana, Nevada, New Mexico, Utah and Wyoming
Pacific: Alaska, California, Hawaii, Oregon and Washington

23. W. De Vries and V. L. Torrance, *The Ticket-Splitter: A New Force in American Politics*, Eerdmans, Grand Rapids, 1972, p. 31.

24. In 1972 Nixon won his biggest share of the popular vote in three Deep South states: Mississippi (79 per cent), Alabama (73 per cent), and Georgia (75 per cent).

25. G. Pomper, *op. cit.*, p. 294.
26. The Democratic majority is calculated against Republican Representatives only; the few 'other' parties represented in the House until 1952 are not considered.
27. W. W. Shannon, *op. cit.*, p. 116.
28. See De Vries and Torrance, *op. cit.*, p. 143.
29. A. Campbell *et al.*, *The American Voter*, J. Wiley, New York, 1964, pp. 90–2.
30. R. N. Boyd, 'Popular Control of Public Policy: A Normal Vote Analysis of the 1968 Election', *American Political Science Review*, Vol. LXVI, No. 2, p. 434.
31. Burnham, *op. cit.*, p. 10.

Julius Gould INTERESTS AND PRESSURES

1. S. P. Huntington, *Political Order in Changing Societies*, Yale University Press, New Haven, 1968, p. 130. Also S. M. Lipset, *The First New Nation*, Heinemann, London, 1964.
2. M. J. C. Vile, *Politics in the U.S.A.*, Allen Lane, The Penguin Press, London, 1970, p. 125. See also S. E. Finer, *Comparative Government*, London, 1970, pp. 245–6.
3. G. Y. Steiner, *The State of Welfare*, The Brookings Institution, Washington, D.C., 1971, p. 337.
4. Vile, *op. cit.*, p. 138.
5. Common Cause is an active 'citizens lobby' set up in 1970 and led by a former Secretary of Health, Education and Welfare: it has over 50,000 members. It has espoused a number of reform causes, e.g., limits on campaign finance (in which its fire was directed at both the parties) and Nixon's welfare reform plan. It also campaigned for a date to be fixed for withdrawal from Vietnam and (see below) against the SST. It is one of the 'cause groups' that has taken to filing suits of complaint on issues which concern it – a tactic that, of course, civil rights groups (and anti-civil rights groups too) had used with some success. Thus Common Cause, like the more narrowly focused consumer and ecology groups, has a following among young lawyers of a radical disposition.
6. A. M. Freeman III and R. H. Hareman, 'Clean Rhetoric, Dirty Water', *The Public Interest*, No. 28, p. 57.
7. A piquant footnote to these events was the release on 20 August of a two years old report on the SST, hitherto classified as 'privileged', from a presidential panel which had recommended cancellation largely though not solely on economic and commercial considerations.
8. There is also the less well-known item of educational appropriations for federal 'impact aid' to school districts where the children of military personnel are deemed to place special strains on local facilities. Congress generously alloted $612 million for this item for 1972 – over $100 million more than the Administration had asked.
9. A. Yarmolinsky, *The Military Establishment*, Harper & Row, New York, 1971, Chapter 4.
10. The debate over the Anti-Ballistic Missile in 1969 (which ended, by a very narrow Congressional margin, in acceptance of an appropriation of

$759 million) is of interest in this respect. There was a most vigorous national and grassroots campaign of opposition – with some (probably scaled-down) propaganda for the Army. The 'defence corporations' who stood to gain from ABM seem to have refrained from direct lobbying of Congress – though some of them helped to finance the media and mailing campaign that was channelled through the adroitly named American Security Council.

11. Yarmolinsky, *op. cit.*, p. 42.
12. See G. W. Domhoff, *The Higher Circles*, Vintage Books, New York, 1970.
13. Steiner, *op. cit.*, p. 103 and p. 105.
14. There are a number of sizeable though minor foundations with causes to press. Though independent they often are financed by the largest and more prestigious foundations, and led by members of the 'moderate wing' of the elite. Thus the Conservation Foundation lists among its donors the Ford Foundation and among its trustees Eugene Black. Another active group is the Center for Law and Social Policy which, since its foundation in 1968 has received large grants from the Meyer and Stern Foundations, as well as the Rockefeller Brothers Fund. This Center has as Board Chairman Arthur Goldberg. Goldberg's firm is actively involved in conservation and environmental campaigns – a recent example of its activity is its intervention in the currently unsettled Alaska oil issue. The Center, has interlocking trustee relationships with two other environmental 'consultancy' agencies that have been set up in recent years.
15. D. P. Moynihan, *Maximum Feasible Misunderstanding*, Free Press, New York, 1969, especially pp. 40, 42, 72–3.
16. Robin M. Williams, *American Society*, 2nd ed., Knopf, New York, 1960, p. 272.

Peter Madgwick THE AMERICAN CITY
1. See, for example A. W. Finifter, 'Dimensions of Political Alienation', *American Political Science Review*, Vol. LXIV, No. 3, 1970, pp. 389–410.
2. See F. Smallwood, 'Metropolitan Political Systems and the Administrative Process', in S. R. Miles (ed.), *Metropolitan Problems: International Perspectives: a Search for Comprehensive Solutions*, Methuen, Toronto, 1970, pp. 222–3. Comparative figures for turnout of registered electors are much affected by differences in methods of registration, and American turnout appears to be higher for this reason.
3. D. Lockard, *The Perverted Priorities of American Politics*, New York, 1971, p. 115.
4. J. V. Lindsay, *The City*, London, 1970, pp. 190–1; see also pp. 169–70 and 183–9. The states have been inclined in the past to regard cities as wealthy sources of funds for the states, not as the recipients of state aid.
5. S. R. Miles, 'Governing the Metropolis: A Commentary on World Opinion', in S. R. Miles (ed.), *op. cit.*, p. 477. My own interviews in Philadelphia and Harrisburg in 1970 confirm the liberality of the Pennsylvania state government in its dealings with the cities.
6. For the parallels between international and metropolitan politics, see M. Holden, 'The Governance of the Metropolis as a Problem in Diplomacy', *Journal of Politics*, Vol. 26, No. 3, 1964, pp. 627–47.
7. See J. S. Dupre, 'Intergovernmental Relations and the Metropolitan Area', in S. R. Miles (ed.), *op. cit.*, pp. 357–8; also Lyle C. Fitch, 'The People',

in *Public Administration Review*, Vol. XXX, No. 5, especially p. 486. R. C. Wood, 'The Contributions of Political Science to Urban Form', in W. Hirsch (ed.), *Urban Life and Form*, Holt, Rinehart and Winston, New York, 1963, p. 114, refers to 'the creation of new power centers across the metropolitan terrain faster than the merger or, regularizing of relations among old ones'.

8. R. Dahl, *After the Revolution? Authority in a Good Society*, New Haven, 1970, pp. 54–5.

9. Allen Schick, 'Five Theories in Search of an Urban Crisis', *Public Administration Review*, Vol. XXXII, 1972, p. 547.

10. For example, in New York, state aid to the suburbs was recently 18 per cent higher than to the cities; Fitch, *op. cit.*, p. 486.

11. See H. Kaufman, 'Bureaucrats and Organized Civil Servants', *Governing the City: Challenges and Options for New York; Proceedings of the Academy of Political Science*, Vol. XXIX, No. 4, pp. 43–7.

12. See, for example, hearings on Defaults on FHA-insured mortgages, House Committee on Government Operations, February and May 1972, pp. 262ff. M. Royko, *Boss*, 1972 gives some illustrations (but no precise measurement) of corruption in Chicago, e.g. pp. 54, 71, 76, 106 and 118. On the other hand, J. G. March, 'Politics and the City', in K. J. Arrow, *et al.*, *Urban Processes as viewed by the Social Sciences*, Urban Institute, Washington, 1970(?), p. 33, argues that 'the elimination of graft has reduced the incentives for creative political leadership in the cities'.

13. See Royko, *op. cit.*, for a good but unsympathetic account of Mayor Daley. For a more favourable account see, for example, A. L. George, 'Political Leadership and Social Change in American Cities', in M. Meyerson (ed.), *The Conscience of the City*, George Braziller, New York, 1970, especially p. 115; E. C. Banfield, *Political Influence*, Free Press of Glencoe, New York, 1961 and, with M. Meyerson, *Politics, Planning and the Public Interest: the Case of Public Housing in Chicago*, Free Press, Glencoe, Illinois, 1955; also James Q. Wilson, *Negro Politics: the Search for Leadership*, Free Press, Glencoe, Illinois, 1960. The capacity of the machine to 'get things done' is emphasized by H. Cohen, 'The Constraints', *Public Administration Review*, Vol. XXX, No. 5, p. 492: 'Since the machine in one manner or another took a cut, the premium was a high volume turnover. The more that was done, the greater the profit'.

14. Royko, *op. cit.*, p. 69.

15. These points are argued by Cohen, *op. cit.*, p. 496.

16. For a brief discussion of these points see G. W. Domhoff, *Who Rules America?*, Prentice-Hall, Englewood Cliffs, 1967, Chapter 6.

17. W. S. Sayre, 'City Hall Leadership', *Governing the City: Challenges and Options for New York; Proceedings of the Academy of Political Science*, Vol. XXIX, No. 4, p. 34.

18. See F. Smallwood, *op. cit.*, pp. 322–4 and 328–9.

19. C. R. Adrian, 'The Politics', *Public Administration Review*, Vol. XXX, No. 5, p. 502.

20. See James Q. Wilson, *The Amateur Democrat: Club Politics in Three Cities*, University of Chicago Press, Chicago, 1962, and R. C. Wood, *Suburbia: its People and their Politics*, Houghton, Boston, 1958.

21. H. J. Schmandt, 'Metropolitan America: A Mixed Bag of Problems', *Public Administration Review*, Vol. XXX, p. 188. The quotation from Mayor

Stokes is reported by N. E. Long, 'Reflections on Presidential Power', *Public Administration Review*, Vol. XXIX, No. 5, p. 449.

22. See, for example, the testimony of Senator Robert Kennedy in Federal Role in Urban Affairs, hearings of Senate Committee on Government Operations 1966–7, pp. 28 and 37; also Mayor Lindsay, *ibid.*, p. 559.

23. See, for example, Scott A. Greer, *Urban Renewal and American Cities, the Dilemma of Democratic Intervention*, Bobbs-Merrill, Indianapolis, 1955, p. 42; also J. V. Lindsay, *op. cit.*, Chapter 6.

24. Marshall Kaplan, Gans and Kahn, *The Model Cities Program: the Planning Process in Atlanta, Seattle, and Dayton*, New York, 1970.

25. For Philadelphia see E. C. Banfield, *The Unheavenly City: The Nature and Future of our Urban Crisis*, Boston, 1970, p. 130. For New York see M. Gittell, 'Education: the Decentralization-Community Control Controversy', in J. Bellush and S. M. David (eds.), *Race and Politics in New York City: Five Studies in Policy Making*, New York, 1971.

26. J. V. Lindsay, *op. cit.*, p. 124. Lindsay gives a less hopeful example at p. 129. See also A. Altschuler, *Community Control: the Black Demand for Participation in Large American Cities*, New York, 1970.

27. H. Kaufman, *op. cit.*, p. 53. See also Kaufman, 'Administrative Decentralization and political Power', *Public Administration Review*, Vol. XXIX, No. 1, p. 12.

28. Royko, *op. cit.*, pp. 132 and 182.

29. Cf. the 'black tinder box' theory of American cities advanced by D. Caraley, 'Is the Large City Becoming Ungovernable?', *Governing the City: Challenges and Options for New York; Proceedings of the Academy of Political Science*, Vol. XXIX, No. 4, pp. 209–13.

30. E. C. Banfield, *The Unheavenly City: The Nature and Future of our Urban Crisis*.

31. Jay Forrester, *Urban Dynamics*, Cambridge, Mass., 1969. See also H. A. Garn and R. H. Wilson, *A Critical Look at Urban Dynamics*, Urban Institute Paper, 1970.

32. See, for example, Patrick Moynihan's testimony in Federal Role in Urban Affairs, pp. 2639–93; and his *Maximum Feasible Misunderstanding: Community Action in the War on Poverty*, New York, 1969.

33. Banfield, *op. cit.*, p. 261; also see M. Meyerson, 'National Urban Policy Appropriate to the American Pattern', in B. Berry and J. Meltzer (eds.), *Goals for Urban America*, Prentice-Hall, Englewood Cliffs, 1967, p. 76.

34. R. Dahl, 'The City in the future of Democracy', *American Political Science Review*, Vol. LXI, 1967, pp. 969–70. See also R. Dahl's, *op. cit.*, pp. 159–66.

R. H. Pear THE US SUPREME COURT

1. Gompers v United States, Vol. 233 US, 1914, pp. 604 and 610.

2. *Time*, 21 June 1971.

3. Particularly Miranda v Arizona, Vol. 384 US, 1966, p. 436.

4. Pennsylvania v Nelson, Vol. 350 US, 1953, p. 497. Slochower v Board of Ed. of N.Y., Vol. 350 US, 1956, p. 551.

5. Vol. 347 US, 1954, p. 483.

6. See Watkins v United States, Vol. 354 US, 1957, p. 178.

7. Cole v Young, Vol. 351 US, 1956, p. 536.

8. Nelson case *supra*.
9. Slochower case *supra*.
10. Konigsberg v California, Vol. 353 US, 1957, p. 252.
11. Baker v Carr, Vol. 369 US, 1962, p. 533.
12. R. M. Scammon and B. J. Wattenberg, *The Real Majority*, Coward-McCann, 1970.
13. L. Henkin, 'Some Reflections on Current Constitutional Controversy', *University of Pennsylvania Law Review*, Vol. 109, No. 5, March 1961, p. 637.
14. H. Wechsler, 'Toward Neutral Principles of Constitutional Law', in H. Wechsler, *Principles, Politics and Fundamental Law: Selected Essays*, Harvard University Press, Cambridge, Mass., 1961.
15. Author's italics.
16. Vol. 295 US, 1935, p. 45.
17. Vol. 313 US, 1941, p. 299.
18. Vol. 321 US, 1944, p. 649.
19. Vol. 334 US, 1948, p. 1.
20. The Supreme Court considered it on two occasions: Vol. 353 US, 1957, p. 230, and Vol. 357 US, 1958, p. 570.
21. For example Mayor City Council v Dawson, Vol. 350 US, 1955, p. 877.
22. E. V. Rostow, *The Sovereign Prerogative: the Supreme Court and the Quest for Law*, Yale University Press, New Haven, 1962, pp. 38–9.
23. L. H. Pollak, 'Racial Discrimination and Judicial Integrity: A Reply to Professor Wechsler', *University of Pennsylvania Law Review*, Vol. 108, No. 1, November 1959, pp. 1–34.
24. Palko v Connecticut, Vol. 302 US, 1937, p. 319.
25. Charles L. Black, Jr., 'The Lawfulness of the Segregation Decisions', *Yale Law Journal*, Vol. 69, No. 3, 1960, p. 421.
26. M. S. McDougal, 'Perspective for an International Law of Human Dignity', *American Society of International Law: Proceedings*, 30 April–2 May 1959, p. 121.
27. M. R. Konvitz, *Expanding Liberties: Freedom's Gains in Postwar America*, Viking Press, New York, 1966, p. 167. See cases of Yates v United States, Vol. 354 US, 1957, p. 298, and Noto v United States, Vol. 367 US, 1961, p. 290.
28. See note 4 *supra*.
29. See Sweezy v New Hampshire, Vol. 354 US, 1957, p. 234; Uphams v Wyman, Vol. 360 US, 1959, p. 72; Vol. 364 US, 1960, p. 388; DeGregory v New Hampshire, Vol. 383 US, 1966, p. 825; Gibson v Florida, Vol. 372 US, 1963, p. 539.
30. United States v O'Brien, Vol. 391 US, 1968, p. 367.
31. Vol. 372 US, 1963, p. 335.
32. Alexander v Board of Ed., Vol. 396 US, 1969, p. 19.
33. Adickes v S. H. Kress & Co., Vol. 398 US, 1970, p. 144, and Sullivan v Little Hunting Park, Vol. 396 US, 1969, p. 299.
34. Vol. 396 US, 1970, p. 435.
35. Phillip B. Kurland, 'Enter the Burger Court: The Constitutional Business of the Supreme Court, O.T. 1969', *Supreme Court Review*, University of Chicago Press, London, 1970, pp. 1–92.
36. See note 3 *supra*.
37. Vol. 399 US, 1970, p. 30.

38. *Time*, 15 March 1971.
39. *Time*, 22 March 1971.
40. *Time*, 21 June 1971.
41. *Time*, 10 July 1972.
42. E. V. Rostow, *op. cit.*, pp. 147–70.
43. It is widely held that Anthony Lewis's article 'Legislative Apportionment and the Federal Courts', *Harvard Law Review*, Vol. 71, No. 6, April 1958, pp. 1057–98, was influential in persuading the Supreme Court to reach its decision in Baker v Carr. Lewis is a distinguished journalist not a practising lawyer.
44. See First and Second Flag Salute cases: Minersville School District v Gobits, Vol. 310 US, 1940, p. 586, and West Virginia Board of Ed. v Barnette, Vol. 319 US, 1943, p. 624.
45. Lochner v New York, Vol. 198 US, 1905, p. 45.
46. L. Henkin, *loc. cit.*, pp. 658–9.

Vivian Vale AMERICA, THE FLAYED MAN
1. To Edward Livingston Youmans, quoted in David Duncan (ed.), *The Life and Letters of Herbert Spencer*, London, 1911, p. 160.
2. Samuel D. Warren and Louis D. Brandeis, 'The Right to Privacy' in *Harvard Law Review*, Vol. 4, No. 5, 1890–1, pp. 193–220.
3. Cf. James S. Coleman, *The Adolescent Society: the Social Life of the Teenager and its Impact on Education*, Free Press of Glencoe, New York, 1961, and *Resources for Social Change; Race in the United States*, New York, 1971.
4. Graham T. Allison, *Essence of Decision*, Boston, 1971.
5. *Congressional Quarterly*, Weekly Report of 19 May 1973, pp. 1210ff.